A Passion to Believe

A Passion to Believe

*Autism and the
Facilitated Communication
Phenomenon*

Diane Twachtman-Cullen

WestviewPress
A Division of HarperCollinsPublishers

Essays in Developmental Science

Copyright © 1997 by Diane Twachtman-Cullen

Published in 1997 in the United States of America by Westview Press, 5500 Central Avenue, Boulder, Colorado 80301-2877, and in the United Kingdom by Westview Press, 12 Hid's Copse Road, Cumnor Hill, Oxford OX2 9JJ

Library of Congress Cataloging-in-Publication Data
Twachtman-Cullen, Diane
  A passion to believe : autism and the facilitated communication
phenomenon / Diane Twachtman-Cullen.
    p. cm. — (Essays in developmental science)
  Includes bibliographical references and index.
  ISBN 0-8133-9098-2
  1. Facilitated communication. I. Title. II. Series.
RC429.T87 1997
616.89'8206—dc21   97-21567
                                                                          CIP

The paper used in this publication meets the requirements of the American National Standard for Permanence of Paper for Printed Library Materials Z39.48-1984.

10   9   8   7   6   5   4   3   2   1

For Jennifer and Erich

In loving memory of my parents,
Olga M. DeMaio
and
Peter DeMaio,
*who taught me that integrity
without courage cannot truly exist*

Facts are stubborn things; and whatever may be our wishes, our inclinations, or the dictates of our passions, they cannot alter the state of facts and evidence.

—John Adams

Contents

Foreword

It is a privilege to open this intriguing book. Diane Twachtman-Cullen is an experienced professional who has made important contributions over the years by analyzing the professional literature and identifying the most relevant information for her audiences. The analytic skill, judgment, high ethical standards, and solid scholarship that have been evident in all of her work also characterize this book's approach to one of the more difficult issues the field of autism has addressed in the past fifty years, facilitated communication (FC).

In this volume Dr. Twachtman-Cullen presents an in-depth analysis of FC in the context of the larger movement it represents. Understanding the essence of the controversies, Dr. Twachtman-Cullen continually reminds the reader of the most central issues. Her penetrating analysis of FC is reasonable, logical, and compelling.

Although this book's careful analysis of FC should be more than enough justification to read it, it is much more than a chronicle of the FC movement. In its short history the field of autism has had more than its share of small groups vehemently advocating extreme positions. FC followers are among the most influential of those groups, and they have exacted a substantial toll from the parents and professionals involved with the problems of autism. Dr. Twachtman-Cullen writes with unique insight and courage about the FC phenomenon. A careful reading of this book provides an understanding of why movements such as FC spring up in the field of autism and what forces help to maintain them. During the time when FC was having its greatest impact, I had numerous discussions with Dr. Twachtman-Cullen, and I remember how helpful I found her thoughtfulness, objectivity, and curious skepticism. She remained open to the possibility that FC represented a new breakthrough but determined to require adequate corroboration. This book reminds me of those refreshing discussions, full of openness and expectations but maintaining a solid commitment to reason and substance.

This book will be one of the major works in the field, serving to remind us of the FC phenomenon and its short but explosive history. It also has appeal because of its thorough and systematic analysis and verification of FC—a model of penetrating thinking and evaluation. For the field of autism, Twachtman-Cullen's greatest contribution might be her explanation of how a small group can mislead the field, cautioning all as to the importance of maintaining a collective objectivity and perspective in the face of similar attacks. There will undoubtedly be other assaults to sound practice in the years ahead, and perhaps books of this kind will help us to meet those challenges more effectively.

Gary B. Mesibov
Division TEACCH
University of North Carolina at Chapel Hill

Preface

If the story of facilitated communication (FC) could be reduced to a single descriptor—one that would be agreed upon by proponent and detractor alike—undoubtedly the term of choice would be *controversial*. A technique for facilitating expressive language in individuals who are nonverbal or who are limited in their ability to use expressive language (Kliewer and Currin 1992), FC has been enmeshed in controversy since its formidable entry onto the disability scene in the United States. From its spectacular claims of success to the stark realities of the harm it causes, FC has been dramatized in courtroom after courtroom throughout this country and beyond. Described by some as a miracle and by others as a hoax, facilitated communication has captured the attention of the American public with unparalleled vehemence. It has been courted by both the popular press and the broadcast media alike, and with that attention has come the corresponding demand for answers, the most basic of which surround the question of whether the technique has validity.

The importance of establishing the validity of any new theory or hypothesis *prior* to heralding its success would seem to be an issue upon which reasonable and responsible men and women would not differ. Yet it is on that very issue that the controversy surrounding facilitated communication swirls most fervidly. Detractors have squared off against proponents, the former calling for scientific scrutiny of the method's validity and the latter claiming that such scrutiny would seriously undermine trust between facilitator and client, which is essential to the conduct of the technique.

From the earliest days, those courageous few who did attempt to experimentally validate FC were criticized for their "lack of faith" in persons with disabilities. This kill-the-messenger mind-set extended even to those who merely raised questions or called for further study of the technique. Long considered a valuable, even essential, yardstick to measure the merits of a particular methodology or treatment technique, scientific experimentation is viewed as insulting when applied to facilitated communication, a characterization that, according to FC enthusiasts, renders it impotent as a means of validation. Consequently, as facilitated communication was gaining momentum, scientific objectivity was becoming mired in an atmosphere of subjectivity and suspicion where parents and professionals were pitted one against the other. In this emotionally charged climate, polarization reigned supreme. One was either for FC or against it. There simply was no middle ground. Dedicated professionals, unwilling to embroil themselves in the controversy, either went underground with their concerns or disassociated themselves from the subject of facilitated communication altogether.

In no quarter has the dispute over the validity of facilitated communication been more vitriolic than in the field of autism, where acceptance of the technique's validity requires a concomitant complete reconceptualization of the disorder. Thus proscriptions by proponents of FC against the type of validity testing that has come to be associated with scientific inquiry have not only fanned the flames of discontent but have actually fueled the apprehensions of those whose understanding of autism causes them to raise legitimate questions with respect to the suitability of facilitated communication for that population.

Where the arena for discussion has been confined to academia or to society at large, the results have been "merely" vituperative. Charges of sexual abuse rendered through facilitated messages moved the debate into the courtroom. There the consequences took on dire proportions, and the need to determine validity took on a new urgency. The American system of justice was not about to deprive individuals of their freedom based on facilitated messages alleging sexual or physical abuse without first determining the validity of the method by which the charges were rendered. Consequently, like it or not, once the facilitated communication controversy entered the courtroom arena, testing for validity was no longer a matter of choice but a matter of necessity.

The courts having passed judgment on the issue of whether to validate, the spotlight now focused on the methods to be used in validation procedures. Here again, one saw polarization. Those who believed in facilitated communication sanctioned only qualitative assessment, dismissing traditional experimental (i.e., quantitative) research as intrusive at best and disrespectful at worst. Like a snowball rolling down a hill, the controversy surrounding facilitated communication seemed to be taking on new parties to the conflict. Not only was the technique itself on trial but it was becoming increasingly apparent that the efficacy of *quantitative* versus *qualitative* research was fast becoming party to the action. In some quarters, science itself seemed to be on trial.

My interest in the topic of facilitated communication goes back to January 1991—just a few months after the publication of Douglas Biklen's widely read qualitative study entitled *Communication Unbound* (1990) jump-started the facilitated communication bandwagon in the United States. At that time I had the opportunity to observe two of Syracuse University's most accomplished facilitators, Marilyn Chadwick and Annegret Schubert (both of whom eventually became leading authorities on the subject), as they lectured on FC and demonstrated the technique with child after child at a school for children with autism where I served as a communication consultant. My appetite whetted by that experience and bolstered by a background in speech-language pathology and autism, I saw facilitated communication as a natural subject for my doctoral dissertation[1] and one that would undoubtedly hold my interest and attention.

This book represents the culmination of that project. It is based on the in-depth *qualitative* examination of facilitated communication as it was conceptualized and experienced by three staunch proponents of the technique with three of their adult clients. I have attempted to tease out the intricacies involved in the complex phenomenon of facilitated communication as it occurred in the context of the clients' and facilitators' daily lives. The study's qualitative nature presented a corresponding opportunity for participant observation and focuses on the backgrounds of clients and the perspectives and knowledge bases of facilitators. It was designed to ensure that FC was examined not as an abstract, isolated concept but rather as a dynamic process inextricably intertwined with the context in which it was embedded. Given the negative stance of FC proponents toward quantitative research, I felt the choice of a qualitative research paradigm was not only respectful of the basic tenets of facilitated communication but also respectful of proponents' concerns regarding the controversial issue of scientific scrutiny. Finally, the choice of a qualitative research design very much reflects my own research style and my overall commitment to context.

Whereas this study focuses on a number of aspects of facilitated communication, its findings delineate most poignantly a portrait of the facilitator—that individual in whose hand, heart, and mind the key to facilitated communication may quite literally be found. What emerged from this study was both unexpected and well beyond the modest expectations inherent in a purely descriptive endeavor. The findings of this study bring to light information heretofore unknown. In some cases these findings also directly contradict many of the claims made by proponents of facilitated communication. As such, they challenge some of the basic tenets of FC and compel me to delve more deeply into possible reasons for the discordance.

A few words about the inherent limitations of this type of qualitative investigation are in order. As noted, I undertook this study as a descriptive endeavor, a portrait as it were, of the multidimensional events and factors that relate to the phenomenon of facilitated communication as it occurs in a particular setting with particular people. Consequently, one must proceed with caution with respect to drawing sweeping conclusions about the overall nature and validity of facilitated communication as an independent construct. However, whereas the subjectivity of this qualitative study may limit the nature and type of conclusions that may be drawn, the concentrated and rigorous focus on facilitated communication in context did bring important information to light and allowed valuable insights to develop—two outcomes considered vital to qualitative research.

Finally, although my main purpose is to report on my research, ultimately this book is about more than facilitated communication. It is about what I have come to call the FC culture—that sociopolitical phenomenon in which unanimity of thought and philosophy has created a class of believers whose "sacred" mission it is not only to advance the cause of facilitated communication but also to disparage the opposition. It is also about the far-reaching effects that occur when common practice disassociates itself from common sense and when ethics and responsibility fall victim to a passion to believe.

Diane Twachtman-Cullen

Notes

1. For that qualitative study, I received the Harris Kahn Dissertation Award in 1995 "for completing a doctoral dissertation of particular distinction" in the Department of Educational Psychology at the University of Connecticut. The award was based on excellence in writing, relevance to issues of practical significance, methodological sophistication, and overall contribution to the field.

Acknowledgments

In some ways writing a book is a little bit like being the lead performer in an intricate high wire act. It can be at once scary and intimidating; it does indeed require a fair amount of delicate balancing; and although the spotlight shines more brightly on the one who's front and center, the performance would not have been possible at all without the ensemble support of those whose efforts and encouragement provided the scaffolding.

I am most grateful to Bob Fantasia and the Boston Higashi School for inviting me to a demonstration of facilitated communication (FC) so early in the FC story that scarcely anyone had heard of the technique. Once sparked, my interest never waned.

I am also indebted to Merriam Cherkus-Julkowski and Orv Karan for their valuable input prior to the defense of my dissertation and for their professionalism and encouragement. To Steve Greenspan, my major adviser on this project and my close friend, I offer my sincere thanks for providing me with the perfect blend of discipline, encouragement, and much-appreciated humor to inspire me to reach past obstacles to the goals beyond. His belief in me inspired me to believe in myself throughout the long journey from fledgling study to completed manuscript.

Many thanks also to Victor Fontana for his invaluable contribution to this undertaking. How fortunate for me that his input came at exactly the right time, and that I was in exactly the right place to make maximal use of it.

I thank my peer reviewers and debriefers for expending their time and effort on my behalf for "quality assurance." Their judgments and insights enabled me to view facilitated communication from many different and important perspectives.

I am also most appreciative of Charlie Hart's help in guiding me through the world of publishing. I benefited from both his good counsel and his keen sense of humor. Many thanks also to Bernie Rimland and Dan Wegner for reading the manuscript and offering sound and beneficial advice as well as warm words of encouragement. I am grateful also to Gary Mesibov for his generous contribution to this work in the form of his exquisite Foreword.

I extend my heartfelt thanks to the wonderful staff of Westview Press—especially Marcus Boggs for believing in the project, Cathy Pusateri for guiding me through the early stages, Shena Redmond for overseeing the "end game," and Diane Hess for her respectful, if not humbling, editing of the manuscript. All of their efforts and professionalism are so very much appreciated as to pale in the telling.

And what a pleasure it is for me to bestow well-deserved accolades on my daughter Jennifer Twachtman-Reilly. A speech-language pathologist specializing in autism and related disorders, Jennifer brought her substantial knowledge to bear in so many aspects of this endeavor—from helping to design the coding categories for the semantic-pragmatic analysis to being a willing listener and valuable sounding board for my alternative explanations and insights. No mom could be more blessed, nor have had more fitting counsel.

I am most grateful to my husband, Jim, for his significant contributions to this endeavor. He gave me the precious gift of time by making countless trips between home and office so that I could work free from interruptions. I thank him also for providing the encouragement that sparked my work and the grounding that kept it from overtaking me.

I am deeply indebted to Jerome Kagan for the time and effort he expended in reading the manuscript in its earliest stages, for his helpful comments and invaluable advice and assistance, and most of all for believing in the project enough to include it in his series, Essays in Developmental Science. I am both deeply honored and most grateful to him for all of his substantial efforts on my behalf.

To Beverly Kolouch, my administrative assistant and close friend, I extend my deepest gratitude. If the truth be known, we did it the old-fashioned way with Beverly typing draft after draft—often on her own time—so that I could meet the timelines I had set for myself. In every sense of the word she was the glue that held it all together—the manuscript, the office, and at times even me! She has left an indelible mark on this book and, over the many years, on my life as well.

Finally, it is with a profound sense of humility that I respectfully acknowledge the people who infused this work with substance: the facilitators and clients who allowed me to participate in their lives. May the knowledge and insights gained through them illuminate the way for others.

D. T.-C.

PART ONE

The Prologue: Setting the Stage

Few treatment techniques have had as meteoric or as turbulent a ride to the fore of the disability field as facilitated communication (FC). This is particularly true with respect to its application to individuals with autism. From real-life dramas in the courtroom to emotionally charged docudramas on television, facilitated communication has been brutalized, idealized, and sensationalized as perhaps the most important (infamous?) treatment breakthrough of our times for people who are nonverbal. In some cases it has changed lives for the better. In other cases it has torn lives apart. For some families it has brought hope. For others it has delivered despair. FC has brought instant celebrity to some professionals while discrediting the work of others. And most astounding, facilitated communication has engendered all of this turmoil with no clear-cut proof of its validity and in the face of study after study questioning its validity. Just what is it about this technique that has the power to inspire some and disillusion others? Before we delve into the hows and whys of facilitated communication, it is important to determine what FC is and the context in which it made its debut both in the United States and in its country of origin.

The technique known as facilitated communication was developed by Rosemary Crossley in Australia. FC typically employs a manual or electronic letter display by which the nonverbal, or expressively limited, person spells out messages, often after being presented with the initial stimuli of objects and pictures (Biklen et al. 1991). In the initial stages of FC a person known as the facilitator provides hand-over-hand support to the client, ostensibly to *facilitate* message generation. According to proponents, this support enables the client to isolate his or her index finger for letter selection, helps to slow down the pace of the activity, and provides a level of comfort (i.e., trust) that allows the client to execute the movement patterns involved in the selection of specific letters (Kliewer and Currin 1992). Although decreasing the amount of physical support over time is advocated, claims of successful, independent communication by individuals have nonetheless been reported even when the level of manual support has been intense (e.g., hand-over-hand) (Biklen 1990; Biklen et al. 1992; Biklen and Schubert 1991; Crossley and Remington-Gurney 1992).

The technique has been used most widely in the United States with individuals who have autism, but its application with a thirteen-year-old girl with athetoid cerebral palsy in Melbourne, Australia, inaugurated the FC movement. The year was 1979. The child was Annie MacDonald, institutionalized since age three in what may be characterized as a warehouse for the intellectually disabled, so appalling were the conditions. The facilitator was Rosemary Crossley, architect of this new technique. The result—unprecedented at the time—would years later become a commonplace occurrence with facilitated communication. Basically, in a style and time frame that renders Annie Sullivan's work with Helen Keller anemic by comparison, Rosemary Crossley, through the medium of facilitated communication, was able to demonstrate a level of literacy and academic proficiency in the environmentally and educationally deprived Annie that quite literally boggles the mind.

Perhaps it is this very aspect of FC—its ability to astound its audience—that causes the polarization of opinions that inevitably accompanies it. With such spectacular results, it is difficult to remain neutral on the subject. One is either dazzled or dubious. FC is either a breakthrough, even a miracle, or inexplicable, perhaps a hoax. Whatever the case, in addition to the polarization and controversy, the other accoutrements of FC were also present from the very beginning of Crossley's inaugural work with Annie MacDonald: the allegedly normal mind trapped in a body that didn't work; the disdain with respect to testing for competence; and the close ties to the deinstitutionalization movement, which was fast becoming the cause célèbre of disability advocates everywhere. Forebodingly, one other feature of facilitated communication was also present from the beginning: the signature allegation, rendered through the medium of FC, of mistreatment at the hands of the caregiver. In Annie's case, the charge was that one of her nurses had tried to kill her by placing a pillow over her mouth. With that charge came another emblem of the FC movement—the ensuing courtroom drama. Thus from its earliest beginnings, facilitated communication was a force—albeit a controversial one—to be reckoned with in the disability community.

Despite publication of the book *Annie's Coming Out*, in which Crossley and MacDonald chronicle their experience, and a movie by the same name, it was not until the early 1990s that Americans discovered facilitated communication. Both the technique and its specific application to those with autism were introduced to the United States by Douglas Biklen (1990) in a widely read qualitative report published in the *Harvard Educational Review*. Since that time, application of the methodology in the United States to individuals with autism has spread at an unprecedentedly rapid rate, fueled by very extensive coverage in the national print and television news media. That facilitated communication had the capacity to capture the attention, if not the imagination, of the general public should have come as no surprise. After all, FC has all the qualities of which good copy is made: human interest, triumph over adversity, and the proverbial Hollywood ending. The latter may be summed up in one word—*vindication*. For those with disabilities this vindication took the form of recognition of their competence and respect for their rights after the years of being misjudged. For their families and advocates it meant recognition of their efforts to raise the public consciousness to the plight and the personhood of the disabled. What was overlooked was that questions of scientific validity of a technique had somehow become enmeshed with sociopolitical issues concerning the rights of the disabled. Notwithstanding, once piqued, the public's interest in facilitated communication spread with surprising rapidity throughout the country.

Two key ingredients may have interacted to create the bandwagon appeal of FC in the United States. The first is the persona of Douglas Biklen, who is widely respected in the field of special education as a tireless advocate for those with disabilities. His stature undoubtedly lent an air of immediate credibility to observations that might have been viewed with greater skepticism if rendered by a lesser spokesperson. Likewise, his preeminence in the area of qualitative research may have weighted the review of his findings in his favor in much the same fashion that championship matches are weighted in favor of defending titleholders.

The second factor that may have fueled the interest (and the eventual controversy) in facilitated communication in the United States is its specific application to autism, since in the words of one professional, FC "violate[s] conventional knowledge about [autism's] severity, chronicity, and symptomatology" (Silliman 1992, p. 63). In reality, far more than conventional knowledge was at stake in the application of FC to those with autism. An entire body of scientific research into the nature and symptomatology of autism was dismissed as mere "traditional assumptions" by Biklen and his followers. Quite simply, one could not buy into FC for people with autism and still hold to the prevailing view of the disorder. Biklen's answer was simple, albeit chilling. Acknowledging that his point of view regarding the nature of the autistic disorder contradicted much of the autism research literature, Biklen summarily called for a redefinition of autism (Biklen 1993). It should be noted, however, that Biklen's view of autism—his knowledge base, as it were—was largely derived from what he observed through facilitated communication. The circularity of his argument went unchallenged, if not unrecognized, at least in the beginning. Thus the seeds of discontent were planted, soon to be fertilized by the hype and circumstances of the rapidly growing FC culture.

This book is divided into three parts. Part 1 lays the foundation for the qualitative investigation into facilitated communication. Chapter 1 addresses the context in which that study was undertaken by first providing background information with respect to relevant literature across several fields and then providing more specific information regarding the methods and procedures used in the study. Chapters 2 and 3 present portraits of the facilitators and clients, respectively.

Part 2 addresses the contextual world of facilitated communication. Chapters 4, 5, and 6 are each devoted to a different facilitator-client dyad. Chapter 7 focuses on important aspects of the facilitated messages themselves.

Part 3 examines some of FC's most controversial issues. Chapter 8 addresses the numerous disparities that surround facilitated communication. Chapters 9 and 10 deal with the contentious issue of facilitator influence before summarizing the findings of this investigation. Finally, Chapter 11 takes a penetrating look at the FC culture and the forces that shape it.

1

Getting Down to Basics

We shall not cease from exploration
And the end of all our exploring
Will be to arrive where we started
And know the place for the first time.

—T. S. Eliot

It is not possible to fully appreciate the implausibility of the union between facilitated communication and autism without knowing the essential elements that make up the autistic disorder. This is necessary because many of the claims made by facilitated communication (FC) proponents directly contradict what is known about autism. The unidimensional view of autism as essentially a movement disorder (Attwood 1993; Hill and Leary 1993) stands in stark contrast to research findings.

Unfortunately, teasing out the essential components of this complex, enigmatic disorder is easier said than done. Our understanding of the nature of autism has undergone a number of major paradigm shifts since Leo Kanner's seminal work in the 1940s.

From Checkered Past to Coherent Present

For the most part, the early history of autism was shrouded in subjectivity and speculation. Despite Kanner's initial biological perspective and his seminal 1943 paper describing autism as an affective disorder, the 1940s and 1950s were dominated by the psychodynamic/psychogenic view of autism, which held that autistic symptomatology was largely the result of emotional impoverishment caused by poor childrearing practices. This view not only gave birth to the concept of "refrigerator mothers" but was carried to its "logical" extreme in Bettelheim's call for a "radical parentectomy" to "excise" the source of the problem (Bettelheim 1967). Although this theory of autism was based on pure conjecture without the slightest bit of empirical evidence to support it, it dominated the public's view of autism and colored our thinking and treatment of individuals with this disorder for many years. Even today, vestiges of the psychodynamic theory and its guilt-provoking sequelae bear witness to the ravages of speculation and subjectivity.

The pioneering work of Bernard Rimland in the 1960s both ushered in the dismantling of the psychodynamic theory of autism and made a strong case for viewing it as a biological disorder (Rimland 1964). Since that time, research across several fields has not only supported the biological view of autism but has extended it to include the more expansive concept of it as a neurobiological/neurophysiological disorder (Arin, Bauman, and Kemper 1991; Courchesne 1991; Courchesne et al. 1988; Dawson and Lewy 1989; Fein et al. 1985, 1989).

The most dramatic statements regarding the nature of autism have come out of the National Institutes of Health (NIH). The July 1995 *Preliminary Report of the Autism Working Group to the National Institutes of Health* documents "clear evidence of functional and structural abnormalities in several brain regions in persons with autism" (p. 14). Relating those findings to specific behavioral manifestations, that report goes on to state,

> Thus, within and across methods and centers, functional studies have been consistent in documenting deficits in late information processing and complex cognitive abilities and in association cortex and/or neurocortical systems. These results suggest that involvement is probably at the neural systems level of brain organization subserving adaptive behavior and function within society. *Where a substantial body of data have been accrued in autism, there is now remarkable consistency across centers and methodologies.* (italics added; pp. 14–15)

In many respects, in the fifty-four years since Kanner's seminal work on autism, the field has come full circle. Medical research on autism has not only implicated specific brain structures and systems but has also begun to relate these abnormalities to the overt behavioral symptomatology that occurs in the disorder (NIH 1995). The significance of these findings cannot be overemphasized, for they make a strong case for viewing autism as a multifaceted disorder in which underlying brain dysfunction results in complex, interrelated symptomatology. This view is astonishingly at odds with the simplistic FC view of autism as neuromotor in nature.

Research findings from other fields have also contributed to our understanding of autism. These too have implications for the concept of facilitated communication, since many of the claims made by FC proponents run counter to the data across several different fields.

For example, advances in the study of infant behavior, particularly with respect to the domains of language and social development, not only have led to a resurgence of interest in what Kanner termed affective contact but have also paved the way for understanding autism as, essentially, a disorder of social relatedness (Dawson and Galpert 1986; Fein et al. 1986; Hobson 1989; Mundy and Sigman 1989; Sigman 1989).

According to Dawson (1989), "The core symptoms of autism (aberrations in social relationships, verbal and nonverbal communication, and symbolic thinking) have one important feature in common: These areas of functioning normally develop in the context of social interaction between a young infant and its caretaker" (p. xvi). Dawson goes on to speculate that there exists a "basic abnormality" within the social-affective domain that not only underlies the difficulty that individuals with autism have with symbolic activities such as language, verbal and nonverbal communication, and imagination/play but also exerts an impact upon cognitive development. Furthermore, it would be difficult to imagine that such deficits would not have implications for FC, since message generation is by definition a symbolic activity.

Ornitz (1985) approaches the social impairment issue from the point of view of sensation. He argues that the social deficits in autism are secondary to disturbances in sensory modulation (i.e., the ability to regulate incoming information from the senses). Hobson (1989) posits a social-affective theory of autism in which disturbances in what he terms *personal relatedness* underlie the deficits in cognitive and symbolic functioning. Other researchers focus on the mechanisms of arousal and attention to explain the core symptoms of autism. For example, Dawson and Lewy (1989) discuss the socioemotional impairments found in the disorder within this context. They argue for the primacy of disturbances in arousal modulation (i.e., the ability to regulate states of alertness) as the mechanism that compromises the individual's ability to both attend to and process social-affective information.

Courchesne (1991) presents compelling evidence linking the social deficits in autism to problems in the area of shifting attention. Drawing a connection between experimental evidence and clinical observation, he hypothesizes that due to damage at the level of the cerebellum, individuals with autism are unable to make the rapid and flexible shifts in attention required to understand and follow the temporally contiguous pattern of the social world. As a result, according to Courchesne, individuals with autism miss the subtle social cues that regulate sociocommunicative interactions and/or, because of problems in shifting attentional focus, experience them apart from their original contexts. He concludes that under such circumstances, understanding and sensemaking are severely compromised.

Mundy and colleagues (1986) lend support to Courchesne's theory; at the same time they establish a connection between social behavior and the development of language and communication. They hypothesize that children with autism have difficulty with triadic attentional deployment, that is, with coordinating attention among oneself, another person, and some other object or event. These researchers note that this problem is reflected in the individual's difficulty with nonverbal indicating behaviors, that is, with the establishment of joint attention to a common referent (an item of interest to both parties). According to Sigman (1989), the ability to establish joint attention is an important precursor to the development of language and intentional communication and is the first indication of the child's awareness that other people may have points of view different from his or her own. In discussing this research, Sigman (1989) adopts a cognitive-affective stance, concluding that the "central disorder in autism is in the area of [shared] social understanding."

Although researchers have taken a number of different paths in their pursuit of the nature of autism, they share a common focus—the social deficits that are central to the disorder. Their research has implications not only for understanding autism but also for what behavior we may reasonably expect from those who manifest it.

Baron-Cohen (1995) approaches the subject of attention somewhat differently, postulating that human beings have a built-in shared attention mechanism (SAM) by which to handle triadic relationships. He states, "All the available evidence points to a massive impairment in the functioning of SAM in most children with autism" (pp. 64, 66).

Dunn's (1994) position regarding attentional mechanisms is similar to Courchesne's. Although she acknowledges the deficits in both sustained and selective attention in autism, she argues that they may not be specific to the disorder. She is much more definitive on the subject of modulation of attention, however. She states, "The ability to shift attention is impaired even in the highest-functioning autistic adults. This may be one of the deficits in autism that is most resistant to remediation" (p. 58).

Research into the phenomenon of theory of mind (i.e., the ability to attribute mental states to others) provides additional insight and a somewhat different interpretation of the factors involved in understanding that other people may view the world from different reference points. Baron-Cohen (1993, 1995) found that individuals with autism were impaired in their ability to attribute mental knowledge to others. The oft-cited problems in perspective-taking reflected in the sociocommunicative behavior of individuals with autism are thought to be manifestations of this difficulty. Frith (1993), a colleague of Baron-Cohen, attributes the lack of a theory of mind in children with autism to the "failure of a single cognitive mechanism" (p. 113), which she feels is responsible for the triad of impairments found in the disorder (i.e., problems in communication, socialization, and imagination).

The field of infant research has provided fertile ground for understanding the ways in which children with autism differ from their normally developing peers, particularly with respect to sociocommunicative development and symbolic play. Piaget (1962) assigned a prominent role to play behavior in the developing child, noting that there is an interplay among play, cognition, socialization, and language development. With respect to the latter, Piaget (1967) asserted that a common semiotic (i.e., symbolic) function governs the child's play and language behavior and that growth in the ability to symbolize in one area will be simultaneously reflected in the other. Nicholich (1977) also discussed the pivotal relationship between language development and play, noting that there is a correspondence between the ability to represent objects, actions, and feelings in play and the ability to represent them in language.

Research into the play behavior of children with autism has revealed a *qualitative difference* in their functional play when compared with both typical children and children with mental retardation, matched for mental age (Sigman et al. 1987). This qualitative difference appears to relate primarily to the area of symbolization; that is, observation of the spontaneous play of children with autism reveals decreased use of symbolic acts (Sigman et al. 1987) and less sophistication in the use of symbols in general (Bartak, Rutter, and Cox 1975). Wing (1981) relates the impoverishment in both play and imagination in children with autism to the deficits in their language.

From the point of view of sociocommunicative development, successful sociocommunicative interactions require synchrony (i.e., attunement) between children and their caregivers (Brazelton and Cramer 1990; Kaye 1982; Schaffer 1977; Stern 1977). Some researchers have postulated that adult caregivers are "wired" to behave in specific ways in order to attract and maintain the infant's attention (Brazelton and Cramer 1990; Kaye 1982; Schaffer 1977). Likewise, infants appear to be biologically preadapted to interact in specific ways with their caregivers (Brazelton and Cramer 1990; Kaye 1982; Schaffer 1977).

The predominant theme of research into infant-caregiver interaction patterns is a recurrent one, centering about the importance of synchrony between the child and the caregiver vis-à-vis both the development of language and communication and the internalization of the social world. Thus the well-recognized lack of synchrony that characterizes interaction patterns between children with autism and their caregivers is felt to place the child at risk not only with regard to the development of sociocommunicative skills but also with respect to understanding and internalizing the social world.

In addressing the topic of asynchrony, Cairns (1986) raised the issue of reciprocity, suggesting that "the child's relative lack of responsiveness may itself promote further distance in relationships and an unhappy cycle of increasing disengagement" (p. 27). In the specific case of sociocommunicative dysfunction, Watson (1987) suggested that the child with autism may "come into the world biologically ill-equipped to participate in early social interactions which form the basis for later communication development" (p. 92). Asynchronous interactions particularly compromise the "games of infancy" (e.g., peek-a-boo, pat-a-cake) that form the building blocks from which conversational exchanges arise (Cairns 1986; Sachs 1984). Tanguay (1990) adopts a socioemotional perspective with regard to these games, noting their role in teaching the child the importance of prosody, gesture, and facial expression in communication, areas of well-known difficulty in autism. He delineates a number of important component skills that make up the process of human communication; however, he focuses on the social communication deficits (i.e., the pragmatic elements) as the defining feature distinguishing "retarded autistic persons from nonautistic retarded persons, or normal-IQ autistic persons from normal persons in general" (p. 201).

Whereas many aspects of speech and language behavior have been studied in children with autism (e.g., semantics, phonology, syntax), there appears to be unanimity of opinion on only one of them—the area of pragmatics. The latter refers to the social use of language, in context, for the purpose of communicating specific intent. Frith (1989) cites difficulty in this domain as a "universal feature of autism" (p. 120). Paul (1987) specifies both the range of pragmatic functions (e.g., requests, comments) and the forms used to express them as *deviant*, rather than merely delayed, in autism. Further, she notes that even in more able children with autistic disorder who do develop language, impairment in nonverbal communication (i.e., a pragmatic component) can nevertheless be found. In addressing symbolic behavior in children with autism, Ricks and Wing (1975) found an absence of such pragmatic features as head nods and other meaning-carrying gestures that generally enhance and support communicative exchanges. Their absence is reflective of problems in social understanding and expression.

Taken together, studies of the speech, language, and communicative behavior in children with autism suggest that the greatest area of deficit is in the pragmatic dimensions of communication; that is, in the *use* of language for social communication purposes. This view is consistent with the notion of autism as essentially a disorder involving disturbances in social behavior and social relatedness. Conversely, it is not consistent with the unilateral view of FC enthusiasts that autism is a movement disorder.

A relatively recent line of research into the neuropsychological mechanism of executive function (EF) has yielded some interesting results. Defined by Rogers (1992) as "the ability to maintain an appropriate problem-solving set for the attainment of a future goal," executive function is believed to oversee the following aspects of mental functioning: impulse control, flexibility of thought and action, mental planning, inhibition of interfering behaviors, and the ability to keep one's plans and goals in mind (Rogers 1992). Problems that have been attributed to deficits in executive function read like a checklist of behaviors manifested by individuals with autism: impulsivity, inflexibility and perseveration in thoughts and actions, lack of future orientation (e.g., difficulty with transitions), and difficulty in self-monitoring (Rogers 1992). According to Rogers (1992), EF deficits have been found in a wide range of children and adults with autism. She goes on to state that not only is this a consistent finding, it is one that occurs across age and functioning levels. Researchers have even speculated on the possibility that problems in executive function may be a core deficit in autism (Ozonoff 1995; Rogers 1992). Neuropsychological deficits have not been taken into account in facilitated communication.

To summarize, despite disparate research interests and the diversity of opinion among investigators relative to the specific nature of autism—that is, whether it is primarily an affective, social-affective, socioemotional, or cognitive disorder—areas of general agreement regarding symptomatology do exist. For example, there is widespread agreement regarding the problems in social relatedness, language and communication, imaginative behavior and play, and responses to sensation. Investigators part company, however, on the issue of the nature of the underlying mechanism or mechanisms responsible for the particular constellation of symptoms associated with the disorder. However, some commonality may be found here as well. Specifically, even those investigators who postulate the primacy of lower-level impairment (e.g., disturbances in cerebellar functioning) nonetheless recognize that impairment in lower-level brain function will undoubtedly exert an adverse effect on cognitive development (i.e., higher-level functioning). That is, regardless of the specific "site" of impairment, the weight of evidence in the autism research literature, supported by research findings across the fields of infant behavior, language and communication, and play, suggests that the difficulty persons with autism have with socialization and symbol use will have "cognitive ramifications throughout the lifespan" (Dawson 1989, p. xvi). Clearly, the *Preliminary Report of the Autism Working Group of the National Institutes of Health* supports this contention.

A Dissenting Voice

Remarkably, despite the substantial research literature that consistently characterizes autism as a disorder affecting social-emotional, affective, cognitive, and communicative functioning, proponents of facilitated communication discount the role of all of these factors in autism (Biklen 1993; Biklen et al. 1992; Biklen 1990; Crossley and Remington-Gurney 1992). Simply stated, FC theory doesn't square with the research findings in autism. If that alone does not give the reader pause, the rationale for their position should. Proponents of facilitated communication treat the theory as fact and discard *all* experimental evidence that doesn't support the theory. A few examples are in order.

With respect to the domains of language and communication, Biklen (1993) cites the "natural language" produced by individuals through facilitated communication as challenging commonly held beliefs regarding intellectual impairment, language-processing difficulty, and receptive language problems (i.e., comprehension difficulty). As justification for his position he argues that the communication and language impairment found in autism is neuromotor in origin, the result of "a neurologically based problem of expression," and that "difficulty with communication appears to be one of praxis rather than cognition" (p. 17). Citing Crossley's *hypothesis* that individuals with autism manifest a "global apraxia," Biklen (1993) goes on to define apraxia as a problem affecting all voluntary movement—hence the difficulty in verbal expression. Further, again ignoring the substantial literature to the contrary, he not only argues against the existence of receptive and language-processing difficulties but also asserts that the "absence of usable spoken language does not justify an assumption of intellectual deficit, noninterest in social contact, absence of normal emotionals, or lack of other typical affective and intellectual abilities" (p. 42).

Through such statements Biklen seeks to dismantle the prevailing, research-based view of autism (and manages to do so in the eyes of the true believers). His lack of respect for the research literature is clearly seen in his demeaning characterization of it as the purveyor of mere "traditional assumptions." Citing *only* instances of successful facilitation as proof that these "assumptions" (i.e., well-documented research findings) are erroneous, Biklen carries his views to their "logical" conclusion—hence his call for a redefinition of autism (Biklen 1993).

Biklen's sweeping indictment of the autism research literature—and by implication, its collective body of researchers—is all the more remarkable for its audacity. For one thing, he pays no heed whatsoever to the growing body of evidence that demonstrates concordance among findings in the field of autism. Neither does he acknowledge supporting research across related fields. Further, instead of challenging specific areas of the research and hence meeting the issues head on, Biklen takes a backdoor approach, dismissing out of hand any and all research that casts doubt on the believability of facilitated communication.

Further, conceding only that differences do exist between his conceptualization of autism and that recounted in the autism research literature (but not attempting to explain them in any way), Biklen summarily dismisses any consideration of a relationship between the acquisition of language and the development of play skills even though such a relationship has been demonstrated in study after study across fields. In Biklen's opinion such a "presumption" would serve only as a barrier to successful facilitation

(Biklen 1993, p. 41). Thus in removing this major obstacle (i.e., the research findings), Biklen not only sets a dangerous precedent in favor of subjectivity but also clears the path to unchallenged acceptance of facilitated communication. The parallels to the psychodynamic era and autism's checkered past are inescapable.

In the area of communication and language, Biklen ignores the complexities involved in the generation of messages by reducing them to the trivial act of moving the hand up and down, thus ignoring the cognitive substrates that govern the selection of specific letters. Pantomiming this action during an interview on the television program *Prime Time*, Biklen stated before millions of viewers: "This is incredibly simple. We're asking a person to point with one finger and make some selections. And each choice, each movement is only slightly different than the other one. It's about as easy as teaching a person to do this [Biklen pantomimes a spoon being lifted to the mouth as in the act of eating]" (Sawyer 1992).

In reducing message generation to the simplistic up-and-down movement pattern associated with eating, Biklen ignores *all* of the myriad, intricately timed, cognitive decisions that are involved in the selection, retrieval, formulation, and eventual transmission of words to code one's thoughts in order to express one's intentions. That he does so before a vulnerable TV audience primed to witness an "awakening," if not a "miracle" (Sawyer 1992), and without the slightest regard for the substantial literature in the field of speech, language, and communication is incomprehensible, if not chilling.

Although seeing may be believing, what one sees does not necessarily represent reality. Examples exist throughout history of scientific objectivity being sacrificed on the altar of human subjectivity and experience. Vogt and Hyman (1979) cite the discovery of the *n*-ray as a striking example of the power of human experience to override scientific objectivity.

In 1902 French professor M. Blondlot "discovered" a ray that had no photographic effect. Notwithstanding the lack of scientific replicability of Blondlot's findings, the existence of *n*-rays was thereafter "confirmed" by several laboratories and several prominent scientists. That the phenomenon could not be reproduced anywhere outside of France did not keep well-respected investigators from applying *n*-rays to their own research. Nor did it keep *n*-rays out of prestigious scientific publications. Less than ten years after their "discovery," *n*-rays fell into scientific disrepute when an ingeniously designed experiment "clearly demonstrated that Blondlot's rays existed only in his imagination" (Vogt and Hyman 1979, p. 51).

By circumventing the scientific community and taking his case directly to the public, Biklen clearly defined the arena and charted the course for the FC debate. And so it was in this atmosphere that Biklen's simplistic view of language and communication went unchallenged even in the face of direct evidence against it. So too did his don't-confuse-me-with-the-findings-I've-already-made-up-my-mind stance regarding the appropriateness of facilitated communication for people with autism. Incomprehensibly, what was virtually ignored was the fact that FC was not only incompatible with the prevailing view of autism but also at odds with the prevailing research across several fields regarding the way in which play, social behavior, and language and communication develop in children. Thus if the FC culture was to fulfill its sacred mission to advance the cause of facilitated communication, it really did need to redefine autism! Consequently, autism was reshaped and repackaged to fit the contours of the new technology.

The Growing Discordance

There is an additional area of contention surrounding the use of facilitated communication with individuals with autism that goes beyond the discordance between the literature-based notion of the disorder and that advanced by FC enthusiasts. This area of controversy has clearly overshadowed all others, for it concerns one of the most volatile and abhorrent subjects of our time: sexual abuse.

Controversy over the origin of the unaccountable poetic elegance that seemed inevitably to emerge through FC was still raging when far more ominous facilitated messages began to appear on computer screens. These messages contained allegations of sexual abuse that were often rendered in explicit, if not vulgar, language and that almost always were directed toward parents and trusted caregivers. This development got not only the public's but also the legal system's attention.

In a particularly infamous court case in Australia, claims by a person with autism of sexual abuse were made against several members of her family through the medium of facilitated communication. What makes this case stand apart from others is that nine separate facilitators were involved, including the architect of facilitated communication, Rosemary Crossley. Even more remarkable is that all charges against family members were dismissed when an ingenious evaluation scheme revealed influence at the hands of all nine facilitators (Heinrichs 1992a). Although family members were vindicated, little could be done to eradicate their bitter memories.

Similar cases began to spring up in the United States. In a particularly noteworthy one chronicled on the television program *Front Line,* a close-knit New Hampshire family was split apart when facilitated accusations of sexual abuse were directed against the father of a young man with autism. That the charges could not be substantiated and were eventually dismissed could not erase that family's painful memories. Neither could dismissal of charges compensate for the court costs incurred or the doubts that inevitably remain in the minds of some regardless of outcome.

The growing number of court cases involving allegations of sexual abuse, and the devastation left in their wake, created a sense of urgency for validation studies of this increasingly controversial methodology. As a result, re-search on facilitated communication rapidly expanded.

Most of the validation studies employed a quantitative design, deemed particularly appropriate for courtroom use because it had the capability of providing information in an objective, straightforward, and time-efficient manner. In one of the most penetrating studies to emerge from the FC controversy, Wheeler and colleagues (1993) presented twelve subjects with pictures under three sets of circumstances. Condition 1 involved showing the pictures to only individuals with autism and then asking them to type the name of each picture with facilitation. In Condition 2, again only the individuals with autism were shown the pictures, but they were asked to type object names without facilitation. In the final condition, both the subjects with autism and their facilitators were shown pictures; neither group was aware of the particular picture being viewed by the other. In one-half of the trials the same pictures were shown to both sets of subjects; in the other half, different pictures were shown to each group. Results of the study indicated that individuals with autism were unable to type the correct object names—with or without facilitation—if the same picture had not also been shown to their facilitators. Further, the most striking finding stemmed from the final condition. Whereas ten of the twelve subjects were more accurate in their typing when presented with the same pictures as their facilitators, when different pictures were shown to each group, only those pictures shown to facilitators alone were correctly labeled by the clients. According to the investigators, the latter finding constituted evidence not only of facilitator influence, albeit unwitting, but also of actual facilitator authorship. Undaunted by the devastating results, proponents of FC remained steadfast in their defense of the technique.

Smith and Belcher (1993) explored the use of facilitated communication with adults with autism who were either nonverbal or possessed minimal verbal skills. They found that although some of their verbal subjects did demonstrate literacy skills with hand support, these skills "did not surpass their nonfacilitated literacy output" (p. 180). Their study pointed out the importance of determining prefacilitation literacy skills as a hedge against erroneously attributing such skills to the phenomenon of facilitated communication alone. According to Smith and Belcher (1993) their study "failed to replicate claims about facilitated communication with adults with autism, and as such raises questions about the ethics of its widespread use with this population" (p. 180). Though the finding regarding the interconnectedness of prefacilitation literacy skills and FC output provided important new information, it did little to dampen the enthusiasm of the true believers.

Green (1992, 1994a) focused her efforts on the ethical issues associated with the use of this technique, citing a number of objective evaluations of facilitated communication. She reported that of the 187 cases of FC she listed, only 3 had been confirmed. The latter involved a study by Calculator and Singer (1992) in which the Peabody Picture Vocabulary Test—Revised was administered with and without facilitation to five students. Results indicated that three of the five subjects evidenced "marked improvement" with facilitation (p. xiv). This study has been quoted extensively by proponents of facilitated communication as proving the validity of the technique, but Calculator and Singer (1992) themselves cautioned against an overzealous interpretation of their findings, noting that "it appears nothing short of irresponsible to claim newly discovered abilities before such skills are empirically validated" (p. xvi). Additionally, their study relates to facilitated test-taking as opposed to facilitated communication per se. At the 1993 International Conference on Autism, Calculator reported that in all of his subsequent investigations on facilitated communication, he has not been able to validate a single case.

Mulick, Jacobson, and Kobe (1993) addressed the complex linguistic performances that have been reported for individuals under facilitation. The results of their investigation lead them to make some of the strongest claims against the technique found in the early literature on FC. They state unequivocally that "at present, there are no scientifically controlled studies that unambiguously support benefits in expressive language function for people with mental retardation or autism by taking part in FC" (p. 275). As remarkable as it may seem in an age that appears to revere technology and the objectivity that goes with it, proponents of FC rejected outright scientifically controlled studies as a means of validating facilitated communication. Consequently, these studies with their devastating findings served to further polarize the scientific community and members of the FC culture.

No Longer a Matter of Choice

The growing number of court cases involving facilitated communication and the rapidly expanding literature base failing to support its efficacy created more than a crisis in confidence. They created a mandate for further, in-depth exploration of this increasingly controversial phenomenon. To test or not to test was no longer the issue. Now the bone of contention shifted to a consideration of the nature of such exploration. Since FC proponents were still staunchly opposed to the use of empirical procedures, I was hopeful that a qualitative research design would at least be met with less rancor, if not with greater confidence, by those who stood firm on the issue of facilitated communication. The qualitative investigation that forms the basis of this book represents my attempt to understand facilitated communication as it is experienced by its participants.

The study comprised two main areas of focus. The first consisted of a two-part document analysis, one part concerning client records and the other the facilitated messages. I felt that the latter focus was particularly worth pursuing because claims regarding the content of messages often fly in the face of much that is known about the development and nature of the communicative process in general (Arwood 1983; Bates 1979; Bruner 1990; Kaye 1982; Owens 1988; Prizant and Wetherby 1988) and the specific nature of the communicative impairment in autism in particular (Prizant 1983; Prizant and Schuler 1987; Schuler and Prizant 1987; Wetherby and Prizant 1992). Thus I considered a protocol to analyze both the specific semantic elements (i.e., the content and meaning) and the pragmatic components (i.e., the functional and social dimensions) of messages to be an important tool for determining the nature and source of the unexpected literacy skills reportedly demonstrated in facilitated communication.

The analysis of facilitated messages was also used to shed light on the desirability of directives by proponents of facilitated communication to ignore "interfering" verbal and nonverbal behaviors (e.g., echolalia and self-injurious or aggressive behavior, respectively) when they contradict the content or tenor of facilitated messages. Such directives are a particularly important area for examination because they are in direct contradiction to much of the pragmatically based literature that stresses the importance of nonverbal communication (Donnellan et al. 1984; Durand, Berotti, and Weiner 1993; Wazlewick, Beavin, and Jackson 1967) and emphasizes the meaning and function of echolalia (Prizant and Duchan 1981; Prizant and Rydell 1984). Finally, I undertook an analysis of the content of messages with respect to the presence of abstract, relational concepts and philosophical statements regarding the nature of disability as a construct. Such content has both generated controversy and polarized professionals because the level of sophistication in such messages is often in stark contrast to expectations based on reported functioning levels, to direct observation of clients, and to what is known about the nature of autism itself.

The second area of investigation concerned the nature of the relationship between clients and their facilitators. Since the facilitator is an inextricable part of this phenomenon (i.e., the key vehicle through which the message is conveyed), I also pursued additional lines of inquiry regarding the facilitators' knowledge and belief systems. Little was known, for example, about what they knew about communication in general and autism in particular. It was also important to explore facilitators' beliefs and attitudes concerning the major political issues involving those with disabilities (e.g., competence, inclusion, deinstitutionalization), particularly since these issues appear to constitute a significant proportion of the content of messages conveyed by many individuals through facilitated communication (Biklen 1992; Fox 1992). A closely related line of inquiry involved delving into the backgrounds of the clients themselves in order to discover patterns of experience that could shed light on the phenomenon Crossley and Remington-Gurney (1992) refer to as the "'caught not taught' view of literacy acquisition" (p. 35).

The Setting

In order to investigate the phenomenon of facilitated communication as it was experienced by participants, three facilitator-client dyads were chosen for study based on the following criteria: (1) evidence of successful facilitation between communicative partners as judged by the facilitators themselves, examination of previously generated transcripts, and my direct observation; (2) a functioning level in clients with autism in the range of mild to moderate mental retardation or below, based on information contained in client records and anecdotal reports; and (3) a level of manual support during facilitation ranging from less intrusive (e.g., support at shoulder or elbow) to highly intrusive (e.g., hand-over-hand support). Criterion 2 is particularly critical to the investigation of facilitated communication. First, it is difficult to reconcile the dual disability of autism and mental retardation with the sophisticated messages that FC proponents use to support their claim that autism is something other than what the research literature says it is. Second, this discrepancy is at the heart of the controversy surrounding facilitated communication. Whereas FC detractors cite the implausibility of such sophisticated messages from clients with these disabilities, FC proponents—in direct opposition—cite the implausibility of autism, as currently defined, in light of the sophistication of FC messages. Left with little choice, FC enthusiasts have called for both a redefinition of autism and, in some cases, the debunking of the concept of mental retardation. Consequently, the presence of both autism and mental retardation in the clients within this study was critically important.

The present investigation, begun in October 1992, took approximately twenty-five months to complete. It involved numerous full-day, on-site visits to a well-respected facility in the eastern United States over an eighteen-month period. I selected this site because of its recognized commitment to the concept of facilitated communication and its leadership role in furthering information about the nature and use of the technique via workshops, written materials, and training sessions. Prior to the start of this research project, I provided assurances that the names of both facilitators and clients would be held in the strictest of confidence. Further, I also acquiesced to the request of one of the facilitators to withhold certain information that he felt would serve to identify his client. This did not negatively impact the results of this investigation.

The Cast of Characters

The three facilitator-client dyads selected for participation in this study meet the criteria for inclusion listed previously. The first dyad, facilitator 1–client 1 (F1-C1), consisted of a twenty-nine-year-old female with a diagnosis of mild to moderate mental retardation and childhood autism and a male facilitator who was highly experienced in FC, having facilitated with well over 100 people prior to his participation in this study. This dyad had been facilitating together on a regular basis since January 1991.

The second dyad, facilitator 2–client 2 (F2-C2), consisted of a twenty-seven-year-old male with a diagnosis of moderate mental retardation and infantile autism and a female facilitator who had achieved successful facilitation with several clients at this facility. She began to facilitate with this particular client via typewriter in August 1991; however, she reportedly had begun using FC with him prior to that via a letter board.

The third dyad, facilitator 3–client 3 (F3-C3), consisted of a twenty-seven-year-old male with a diagnosis of profound mental retardation and autistic disorder and a female facilitator who had been using FC with him since August 1991. According to anecdotal reports and facilitator opinion, each of the facilitator-client dyads had achieved a level of success in facilitated communication.

Blocking Out the Action

In the tradition of qualitative research, I used multiple sources of data to elucidate the complex, multifaceted phenomenon of facilitated communication. Information obtained across sources not only promoted understanding of the various aspects of FC but also served as a means to verify the conclusions I drew. In qualitative research, this process is known as triangulation. Specific research questions were used to focalize, rather than limit, the investigation with respect to those areas considered integral to developing an understanding of facilitated communication. Table 1.1 provides a more detailed account of how data regarding these areas of investigation were obtained across sources.

The in-depth interviews with each of the facilitators provided both information with respect to the specific areas listed in Table 1.1 and valuable insights into the relationship dimensions considered so crucial to facilitated communication. Although two of the clients themselves responded to some of the questions posed through FC, it was not possible to interview them as such. In addition, because of the heightened state of anxiety observed in the third client and the relative paucity of his FC output, I did not consider him to be an appropriate candidate for interview. All interviews were taped to ensure greater accuracy and were then later transcribed for ease in data analysis.

The second method of information gathering consisted of observation of facilitated communication sessions for each dyad. In addition, I asked each facilitator to videotape an FC session with his or her client that each considered successful (i.e., typical of his or her customary FC activities) for comparison with the observed sessions. I also videotaped all of the in-person observations in order to provide a record for later review and analysis.

TABLE 1.1 Checklist Matrix for Information Sources

Research Questions	Observation	Interview	Document Analysis (Records)	(Messages)
Distribution of messages re pragmatic function				X
Congruence of messages with behavior	X			X
Level of manual support	X			
Content of messages re philosophical statements re people with disabilities				X
Content of messages re abstract relational concepts				X
Congruence of messages with background and functional level of clients	X		X	X
Knowledge of facilitators re Autism		X		
Beliefs and attitudes of facilitators about the abilities of people with autism		X		
Facilitators' explanations re what is happening in FC		X		
Facilitators' responses to questions re their influencing messages		X		

The final method of information gathering consisted of the two-part document analysis noted earlier. The first concerned an examination of client records with respect to the following: (1) diagnostic history, (2) reported level of functioning, (3) educational programming and placement history, (4) intervention history, and (5) medical and clinical history, particularly with respect to neurological and sensory information. As in the previous two cases, all excerpts taken from client records were tape-recorded and later transcribed in order to ensure comprehensiveness and accuracy. The second part of the document analysis consisted of an in-depth examination of specific aspects of the semantic content and pragmatic functions of facilitated messages. Detailed information regarding this protocol may be found in the appendix.

BOX 1.1   Facilitator Interview

Pattern Codes Delineating Recurrent Themes

Pattern Code 1:   The Nature of Autism

Pattern Code 2:   Relationship/Trust Issues

Pattern Code 3:   Philosophical Attitudes Toward People with Disabilities

Pattern Code 4:   Commitment to FC

Pattern Code 5:   Attitudes Toward Facilitator Influence

Pattern Code 6:   Issues Related to Competency/Literacy

Pattern Code 7:   Nature of FC

Elements of the Critique

Since the style and accoutrements of qualitative research differ substantially from those associated with quantitative investigations, a brief overview is in order. In general, the data analysis techniques I employed in this study consisted of both ongoing and end-stage analysis with respect to three main areas: data reduction, organization of information through the use of thematic clustering, and the drawing and verifying of conclusions. I analyzed the data frequently to keep it within manageable proportions and to render it more meaningful. The advantage of this procedure is that the data themselves guided the direction of the research. Thus, analysis during data collection represented the first level of examination and served the purpose of "stimulating critical thinking" (Bogdan and Biklen 1982, p. 149) about the observations in order to help focus the research endeavor.

Despite the use of these techniques for ongoing analysis, the amount of raw data generated from the major sources of information was too cumbersome to be considered meaningful without further data-reduction efforts and more precise systematization of information. Consequently, end-stage data analysis built upon refining the emergent themes and patterns within this study into coding categories of greater specificity (Bogdan and Biklen 1982; Miles and Huberman 1984). Early coding levels grouped data according to broad-based, general categories for the purpose of both labeling and more efficiently retrieving information. Later coding levels proceeded from the former to the delineation of more specific categories based on a distinctive pattern of recurrent themes that emerged from the interviews. This pattern was broken down into seven coding categories to reflect these prominent themes. Taken together, these themes reflect the prevailing view of the FC culture. A list of these categories and their respective pattern codes appears in Box 1.1.

In order to refine and verify my conclusions, I continually generated alternative explanations for phenomena. In qualitative research this serves to enhance the study's trustworthiness. With respect to the latter, I also attended to the transactional elements inherent in participant observation, as they not only helped to guide the direction of the research but also helped to provide validity checks throughout the investigation.

"Thickened observations"—that is, insights that come indirectly "in and through records" (Patton 1980, p. 286)—served to integrate the data by increasing sensitivity to the multiple perspectives and secondary relationships within the accumulated observations and materials.

I also employed more aggressive techniques for actively seeking out discomfirmatory information. In addition to generating alternative explanations for phenomena, these also included probing for negative findings. I used "bracketing" to control for researcher bias. In this qualitative research procedure, the investigator identifies his or her beliefs, biases, and assumptions. Finally, owing to the controversial nature of facilitated communication, I utilized peer debriefing throughout this study not only to invite challenges to the analysis of data but also to seek out different perspectives and interpretations.

2

The Emerging Portrait
of the Facilitator

We knew a lot of things we could hardly understand.

—Kenneth Fearing

The facilitators in this study represented various levels of educational and background experience in working with individuals with autism and other developmental disabilities. In that sense they mirrored the general population of facilitators in the United States. They also varied with respect to their levels of experience with FC, though this particular facility's commitment to the technique and the regularity of FC sessions suggests that the facilitators in this study were more experienced than most. Facilitator 1 (F1) was by far the most experienced in terms of both educational background and experience with the population. He held a master's degree in special education and had worked with individuals with developmental disabilities, including those with autism, for several years. At the time of the initial interview F1 had been facilitating with a variety of clients for well over two years. He estimated the number of such clients to be over 100. A trainer in facilitated communication techniques, F1 was also a leader in the advancement of FC theory and practice. When asked to estimate the percentage of time devoted to FC, he indicated that "in one way or another, writing about it and talking about it," he spent close to 100 percent of his professional time devoted to facilitated communication. He had also taken advanced courses on the subject.

Facilitator 2 (F2) had worked as a secretary for a number of years at the facility where the study was conducted prior to moving into her present position in service coordination. Thus in the early years, she had had little direct contact with the clients who were served by the facility. With respect to educational background, she was in the process of obtaining her bachelor's

23

degree in human services during the course of this study. F2 began facilitating with her client via a typewriter in August 1991, and according to the record, she facilitated with him "on a daily basis" for some time. At the time of the initial interview, F2 indicated that she was facilitating with three people on an ongoing basis. In terms of her experience with individuals with autism she noted, "I have never really done hands-on with people with autism at all until I started working with facilitated communication."

Facilitator 3 (F3) held a bachelor's degree in psychology. She began facilitating with her client in summer 1991, noting that she had "learned facilitated communication from watching F1" and from attending a few conferences devoted to the subject. When asked about her level of experience in working with people with autism she replied, "As I said, before I worked here I didn't know people like this existed." F3 indicated that she had worked at the facility where the study was conducted for a little over two years.

Sharpening the Focus: The Questions

What is the knowledge base of facilitators with respect to the nature of autism and autistic symptomatology?

Despite variation among facilitators with respect to their knowledge of both the nature of autism and its symptomatology, there were areas of commonality. Two of the facilitators viewed autism as essentially a motor dysfunction, a view that has come to be associated with proponents of facilitated communication (Attwood 1993; Biklen 1993; Hill and Leary 1993).

One of them, F1, agreed "completely" with the view expressed by many FC advocates that autism ought to be redefined as a movement disorder. He emphasized the neuromotor aspects of autism, specifically citing "problems with inhibition, and . . . in actually performing specific tasks." He characterized autism as a neurological disorder, volunteering that prior to beginning facilitated communication he "didn't have a clear view about what [autism] was, whether it was neurological or environmental or a combination." F1's response leaves little doubt that his view of autism was shaped by his experience with FC. It also leads one to question the wisdom of calling for a redefinition of a disorder in the absence of a clear understanding of its nature. Another facilitator, F2, expressed a similar view, characterizing the motor problems as neurologically based and, as such, not under the control of the client. The third facilitator, F3, presented views that superficially appeared to contradict those of her colleagues. A closer look, however, revealed the possibility that confusion in terminology may have created the appearance of differences that were more contrived than actual. This facilitator stated that she did not consider autism to be a motor disorder, citing her client's "incredible fine motor ability as far as picking up the tiniest little thing" as the reason for her opinion. In contradiction to this, however, she considered some of her client's behaviors to be both repetitive and compulsive and hence not under his control. Further, although she described autism as *cognitive* rather than neuromotor in nature, the examples she cited to support her viewpoint seemed more related to neuromotor function than to cognitive impairment. In fact, she seemed confused with regard to the nature of the two concepts. When questioned more definitively with regard to this issue, she indicated quite clearly that she was not referring to mental functioning when she characterized autism as a cognitive disorder. In summary, with regard to motor and movement issues, regardless of the terminology used, commonality was seen among facilitators in their perceptions of individuals with autism as manifesting a lack of *voluntary* motor control and hence needing assistance through facilitated communication.

In describing autism, none of the facilitators independently mentioned the problems in social behavior or the pragmatic communication deficits generally associated with the disorder even though these are considered its hallmark features. When specifically questioned about pragmatics, all of the facilitators readily admitted they had little knowledge regarding that element of communication. Despite this admission, two of the facilitators expressed specific views regarding pragmatics. F2, in contradiction to the autism research literature, indicated that pragmatic prowess has "always been there" and that FC has given individuals a way of expressing their pragmatic abilities. F1, in response to the question "Would you consider people with autism to have a pragmatic communication problem?" said, "I don't think they do. I think they just have, for whatever reason, the inability to get the words out." Later, he expressed concerns with respect to overgeneralizing and noted that some people with autism may have such deficits. The reader is reminded that of all of the symptoms associated with autism, there is nearly universal agreement on the issue of pragmatic deficits.

All facilitators expressed similar viewpoints concerning the nature of the sensory issues associated with autism. Interestingly, each discussed problems with sensation only in terms of overstimulation (i.e., hypersensitivity). None of the facilitators acknowledged the possibility of understimulation (i.e., hyposensitivity). Neither did they address issues related to the modulation and integration of sensation across modalities—aspects of sensory functioning often implicated in autism.

F1 described echolalia—the repetition of words, phrases, or sentences known to be associated with autism—as "an attempt at meaningful communication." He also stated, "I think that it's been demonstrated very clearly that it has a function." Both views reflect the current, research-based view of echolalia. At other times during the interview F1 referred to echoes as "perseveration," and he talked about the need to interrupt them—a view more reflective of the FC position on echolalia. F2 described echoic-like behavior in her client, attributing it to his "hearing voices." Despite this characterization, such behavior arguably fits the definition of delayed echolalia, that is, the repetition of utterances some time after they are originally heard. Lending credence to this characterization, F2 went on to describe instances of delayed echolalia in her client in which he would "fix on a phrase that he probably heard on TV." Regardless of their specific viewpoints concerning echolalic behavior, facilitators made it clear that should echolalia occur simultaneously with typing, they would focus only on the typed message.

In many cases, facilitators held viewpoints directly contradicting the autism literature. For example, F1 said he felt that individuals with autism "have a lot of empathy, sometimes so much that they have to withdraw because it is too much." He also noted that since FC, he has found people with autism to be more "perceptive" than he had originally thought. The latter view was expressed either directly or indirectly by the other two facilitators as well. F2 noted that her client "could pick up on things that were going on with [her] very easily, even though [she] tried to hide them." F3 raised the issue far more directly, stating, "I guess I think of people with autism as very perceptive people, just—it does seem to be like a person trapped inside like all these behaviors." None of these viewpoints reflect currently held beliefs about autism. They do, however, reflect the dominant theme of the FC culture. Finally, they are viewpoints born of the FC experience itself.

In summary, although facilitators had very definite ideas about the nature of autism and its symptomatology, they were consummately lacking in knowledge regarding the very elements that are recognized as the defining features of the disorder (e.g., the social pragmatic components). Consequently, their opinions did not generally reflect current thought on the subject. When asked to characterize the essence of autism, F1 said, "They have trouble initiating sometimes. They have trouble performing particular motor tasks. They have trouble speaking, and they have impulsive behaviors that they don't have a lot of control over which make it appear as though they have a cognitive deficit that may not be there."

F3 described the essential components of autism: "I think when people say that people with autism don't like to be touched, or don't like people near them, like to be on their own, I don't necessarily see it as that. I think it's more that the person wants to be in control when the touching is done or when they are, they'll choose when they want to be with a person."

F2 focused on the "stereotypes that have been written about [people with autism] not absorbing what is going on in their environment, and not caring and things like that." She went on to say, "That's not true. And if it is true about a person it's an individual characteristic; it's not the label of autism."

Finally, it was eminently clear with respect to facilitators' understanding and knowledge of autism that their views were not only at odds with current research-based views on autism but also singularly shaped by their individual experiences with facilitated communication. Their views were emblematic of the evolving FC culture.

What are the beliefs and attitudes held by facilitators about the abilities of persons with autism?

Facilitators were generally in agreement with respect to the related issues of competency and literacy development. F1 stated that prior to facilitated communication, he believed that "seventy percent of the people with autism have an IQ under . . . 80 or something." Since FC, however, his views had changed "very dramatically." He stated that "people with autism are much smarter than we ever thought." When asked to expand on the origins of such competence, F1 echoed a theme that has become emblematic of the facilitated communication movement, that is, the "caught not taught" view of literacy acquisition articulated by Crossley and Remington-Gurney (1992, p. 35). According to this viewpoint, simple environmental exposure is sufficient to allow people (even those challenged by developmental disabilities) to acquire literacy skills. Articulating this viewpoint, F1 stated, "Everybody is exposed to words. . . . And, you know, there are a lot of kids who have been exposed to Sesame Street, and the Electric Company, whose parents read to them." Although F1 was unequivocal in attributing "raw intelligence" to individuals with autism, he emphasized the need for specific training in spelling, vocabulary, sentence structure, and grammar, noting that "[people with autism] haven't used their knowledge before." He explained his client's "exposure to words" on the basis of her "somewhat more enriched environment"; however, he was careful to add that an enriched environment alone did not totally account for his client's ability compared to that of the other two clients in this study. Nevertheless, he did state that "the more enriched the person's environment is or has been, the more likely they are to have more knowledge of words."

F2 referred to the label of mental retardation in her client's record as "a misnomer"; she later noted that individuals "have to be under the label of mental retardation" to be served by the facility at which this study was conducted. In discussing her client's estimated reading level, F2 initially stated that had her client "had the opportunity through facilitation that kids right now are having I think he would be reading at about the fourth- or fifth-grade level now. I think he would be doing a lot more academically, so I think that score as far as the retardation would be different." A short time later she responded affirmatively to a question placing his present reading level at the fourth- or fifth-grade level, even in the absence of early

FC training. In commenting on the origins of such perceived competency and literacy development, F2 expressed the view that individuals with disabilities absorb information from their environments in much the same way that all people do: "So, what I mean, you've got people who have been sitting around for twenty-seven [or] twenty-eight years, or more, just soaking all this information in, and waiting for the opportunity to let it come out again. It's there. It's just there. It's been there. It's been growing. It's been developing."

Facilitator 3 described her client as "moderately high functioning" despite his diagnosis of "profound mental retardation" and an overt functioning level consistent with that designation. She did suggest the possibility of environmental retardation owing to "the way he has been brought up." She speculated that judgments regarding his mental functioning were difficult to make given his lack of education. She ventured the following opinion: "I would guess that maybe he is mildly mentally retarded, but I don't think of him as moderate." Her equivocation with respect to the issue of competency was clearly evident in the comment immediately following: "But I, but I, at the same time, I hesitate to say that because I think he's very smart." As with the other two facilitators, F3 attributed her client's perceived competency and literacy development to environmental exposure. This, of course, seems to conflict with her statement regarding environmental retardation. She stated, "I think a lot of it could be self-taught. I mean just by things that he sees the other people do, or hears what other people have said."

Many of F3's statements regarding her client's perceived ability either were not supported by the specific examples she cited or were in direct contradiction to them. When asked to estimate the level of her client's understanding, F3 indicated that he understood "a lot." She then went on to give the following contradictory example:

> I know like sometimes I wonder how he takes things in because, because I'll ask him to do something and he'll do something else that I always ask him to do as well, so I don't think he listens to the words, he just—maybe the inflection of my voice. Like if I—I'm trying to think—if I tell him to put his seat belt on, sometimes he'll wipe his face or like that. And I don't know if he's just anxious and not concentrating enough to listen to what I'm saying so he just does one of the things and hopes he's right, or something.

Although the client's inappropriate response may have reflected a lack of concentration or inattention, it is also reasonable to speculate that it may also have reflected a lower level of receptive language ability, in which comprehension is based more on the contour of the situation (i.e., that which is expected or customary) than on an understanding of the discrete linguistic elements. There was no attempt on F3's part to reconcile the discrepancy between her perception of C3's receptive language ability and his demonstrated lack of comprehension in practice.

Other instances cited by F3 of her client's general communicative ability were also inconsistent with the more sophisticated communicative ability attributed to him via FC. At the same time, they were consistent with the lower level of communicative functioning described previously. For example, she clearly described his use of contact gestures (i.e., physically taking the hand of the communicative partner and placing it on the object of his attention) to communicate specific intent. Further, she noted,

> He'll take your hand. I knew when I used to take him to the park on hot summer days he wanted to get back in the car because I had air conditioning. He would take me to the car and I would say, 'Not right now. Let's stay out.' ... And he did the same thing if we got back too soon from somewhere. He'd take my hand and put it on the key to make me turn the car to go back.

Contact gestures are considered to be at a lower level of competency than distal gestures (those that serve to indicate something at a distance) in the hierarchy of nonverbal communicative behaviors, since they represent intentional communication "outside the context of social interaction in order to achieve an environmental end" (Wetherby 1986, p. 305). Further, contact gestures, unlike distal gestures, are by definition tied to the immediate context in which the object or event is embedded. As such, they represent a more concrete (hence less abstract) form of indicating behavior. Consequently, their use would be inconsistent with the level of sophistication reported for this client with respect to FC.

Finally, although F3 noted that her client did know a few manual signs, he used the nonconventional and idiosyncratic gesture of patting the chest as his sign for *more* instead of the actual manual sign of placing the fingertips of both hands together as in American Sign Language. This example leads one to question the client's correspondence between the sign and the word, particularly if this idiosyncratic gesture is used indiscriminately. Further, as in the previous case, the low level of sophistication reported in this instance is consistent with a lower level of ability in language and communication than is reported for FC.

In summary, all facilitators reported a higher level of competency for their clients than was supported either by client records or by some of the examples given. Further, it appears that the judgment of competency in each case was not only presumed but based solely on the client's alleged ability to generate messages via facilitated communication. This clearly underscores the attitude-shaping power of FC. Finally, all facilitators subscribed to the "caught not taught" view of literacy development. Once again, facilitators' opinions were reflective of those advanced by the FC culture and were often in direct contradiction to the examples they cited to support their views.

What are the beliefs held by facilitators about what they think is happening in facilitated communication?

Two strands of information stemming from the interviews with facilitators provided insights into the phenomena underlying the concept of facilitated communication. The first ingredient seen as essential to the conduct of FC was trust between facilitators and their clients. The second integral element was the provision of some degree of manual support or physical guidance.

With respect to the former issue, all of the facilitators felt that the establishment of trust between facilitator and client was of paramount importance to successful facilitation. They used words such as *vital* and *essential* when characterizing the significance of the trust relationship to the phenomenon of facilitated communication. As such, they echoed similar sentiments expressed by other FC proponents (Biklen 1993; Crossley 1994).

In elaborating on the importance of relationship, F1 mentioned emotional support, confidence, and high expectations. He, more than the other facilitators, linked the relationship and trust dimensions to the issue of physical guidance. In addressing this perceived relationship he stated, "It is the confidence and the emotional support, but I think they are related because knowing that you are going to be prevented from engaging in some of those compulsive behaviors, whether they are motor or psychological, you gain confidence." F1 expressed similar views with regard to the issue of expectation, stating, "I think it's real clear that you mean you have to say I really expect you to be able to do this, and convey that not only in the words you say, but the way you act."

F2 characterized trust as "an extremely important component" of facilitated communication. She described people who are being facilitated as "putting themselves on the line, and putting their trust in you when they open up for facilitation." The use of such terminology seems to imply anticipation of highly significant information. In terms of the element of expectation, this facilitator too felt that it was necessary to believe in the client's ability to be facilitated in order to achieve success. F2's characterization of her relationship with her client seemed to extend beyond issues of simple trust and high expectations to those of a deeper "friendship." She spoke of his being *jealous* of her deeper personal relationship with a specific individual, stating, "I mean, he would see us together, other places too you know, in the building and stuff, and knew that we had some kind of a relationship and he didn't like it. He wanted me to like him as much as I like [the other individual] and it's just not possible." When asked to elaborate on this issue, she indicated that her relationship with her other two FC clients was different from the one with the client in this study, attributing that difference to the matter of gender (her other clients were both female). "He [her client] obviously likes attractive women and he likes to be around women. I think there are a lot of subtleties that are involved in all of this." The speculation that this client behaved differently around attractive women was raised by this facilitator at other times as well. Unlike F1, she did not link the relationship and manual-support issues. Rather, she addressed the latter as a technical (albeit important) and separate matter.

Like her colleagues, F3 emphasized the importance of a trusting, supportive relationship. Unlike her colleagues, however, she described her earlier interactions with her client as anything but indicative of a trusting, supportive relationship. She continually underscored the importance of giving as much emotional support as possible in spite of her client's off-putting responses to that support. For example, she described the initial stages of facilitated communication: "And for a while our relationship was that, he would just beat the crap out of me everyday. I had bruises all over, you know, and it was just hard to go to work but I was very determined to stay with him."

In response to the question "Now, what were you doing with him? Were you trying to facilitate with him during those times?" F3 said, "Yes. I had tried—I was—when I first started to try to facilitate with him he was so aggressive that I could barely get near him. I would bring the board out and he would go after me, you know, so that's where we were in the beginning."

In an attempt to avoid placing untoward emphasis on aggression as a response to facilitation and to avoid attributing confluence between the two where it may not have existed, I questioned F3 regarding other instances in which the client would exhibit similar behavior: "Okay, then it [aggressive behavior] wasn't just over-facilitated communication?" "No," she responded, "No, but if I even attempted, it would be even worse, so that's how it was." In spite of the rough start, both she and her colleagues believed this dyad had achieved a level of successful facilitation. Interestingly, F3 divulged that her client still engaged in intermittent acts of aggression during facilitation. She reported, however, that her own behavior had changed: "It doesn't scare me anymore, which is a wonderful feeling, but it's a very tense moment because he is out of control." At least for this facilitator-client dyad, trust appears to be a particularly unilateral phenomenon.

The facilitators all agreed that manual support was an essential ingredient in successful facilitation, although they differed somewhat in their rationales. In addition to F1's linking the relationship and manual-support dimensions, he emphasized the importance of the "technical" aspects of such support. He spoke about the need to provide "correction" and to "physically interrupt" the perseveration (echoes). In describing what happens in FC vis-à-vis the provision of manual support, he stated, "I think it slows people down, allows people to be more deliberate, think about what they're doing, and get beyond those stereotypical expressions. F1 also emphasized the importance of facilitated communication *training* as opposed to facilitated communication per se. He explained the former in the following manner, "So, I mean, the first thing we are doing is teaching. We're training them in that motor activity with the goal with most people that they become independent in their typing or in their pointing." According to F1, FC training teaches people a particular technique as opposed to an end in itself. In stressing the "training" aspect, F1 echoes the theme originally purported by Rosemary Crossley, the originator of facilitated communication (Crossley 1994).

F3 echoed F1's sentiments regarding the linkage between trust and manual support, noting that the mere act of touching may have a "calming effect" on the client. She also suggested a link, or at least concomitance, between manual and emotional support. As an extension of the latter, F3 also stated that facilitators "have to be genuine, and really believe in that person." In response to "Okay, so you feel that they would pick that up even if it's not stated, you know, overtly?" this facilitator responded, "Yes, definitely." Further, unlike her colleagues, F3 did not connect the presumed need for manual support to motor or movement disabilities: "And I think that might be part of it—that is the support. It's not necessarily that he needs any help with his fine motor coordination."

In addressing the technical aspects of FC apart from its relationship dimensions, F2 tied her client's motor problems to the need for manual support. When asked if she had ever tried to fade back the level of support from the wrist, she answered, "Yes, and it varies with him from day to day because of his radial ulnar instability, because I have to, even at this point now, I have to be right down here with him." F2 then demonstrated manual support close to the level of the index finger as opposed to at the wrist. Echoing F1's comments, she emphasized the need to "pull back" her client's hand after he typed a letter. She first stated that she would pull her client's hand back "after every letter that he types," noting that by so doing, it "really doesn't matter if I know the answer or not." Immediately following this comment, however, she stated,

> Actually, I mean, when we were talking about the level—now that I'm thinking about it, I'm not really pulling back a whole lot with him anymore. I mean, it's just a natural response, except if he starts to hover, you know, where he'll type a letter just a little and he just kind of hovers over the keyboard for the next. I'm pulling back and really what I'm doing is when I'm pulling back I'm cueing him to go to the next letter.

In summary, all facilitators emphasized the relationship and trust dimensions as *vital* to the conduct of facilitated communication. Further, all facilitators linked relationship issues to the controversial topic of validity testing, as will be elaborated elsewhere in this chapter. Two of the three tied the relationship dimensions to that of the need for manual support, ostensibly establishing a link between the latter and the engendering of emotional support. Further, two of the facilitators related the need for manual support to motor and movement issues, whereas the third, F3, did not feel that motor issues were operative for her client, having described him previously as demonstrating "incredible fine motor ability." Neither did F3 link the need for manual support to her client's problems with impulse control. Finally, facilitators either openly expressed or implied that expectation of success was critical to the FC experience.

How do facilitators respond to questions about whether they are influencing and/or actually producing the messages being communicated?

Possible facilitator influence is arguably one of the most contentious issues in the controversy surrounding facilitated communication. It is also a multifaceted one, intertwined with issues such as interpretation of facilitated messages, expectation, intensity of manual support, relationship and trust, and validity. Information derived from facilitators with respect to these subject areas is included here in order to more fully address possible facilitator influence and to elucidate ways they try to guard against it.

Facilitators evidenced wide agreement in their attitudes toward many of the issues related to facilitator influence. Although all acknowledged the possibility of such influence, they felt it was unconscious if it did occur. F1 stated, "I think people who do cue people, for the most part, are doing it subconsciously." Later in the interview he elaborated:

I think for a while—I think most of the people we typed with, especially early on, we had to—we went through, you know, periods of time where we didn't know. We didn't know whether we were doing the facilitating, and I think, whether we were cueing people or whether it was actually that. And I think there were times that afterwards, you know, we felt pretty clearly that we probably did provide some cues, especially as we were learning to do this. I think it is much less true now. I think it probably happens when I do it, but very seldom. I think we ask people, "Okay, just set aside, you know, the questions, set aside your skepticism, be aware of it, be aware that you can lead people, that you can cue people, but be very conscious of pulling the person back, providing that resistance."

F1 also conceded the potentiality of conscious influence by noting, "I think that there have been situations, though, where people were untrained and there were certain expectations that they would get results and I think in those cases it may have happened." As a trainer of facilitators, F1, more than the other two facilitators in this study, appeared to be eminently cognizant of the variety of ways in which facilitator influence might occur. When asked what he would caution other facilitators against vis-à-vis raising their levels of consciousness to the possibility of such influence, he gave the following comprehensive reply:

> First of all, I would tell them that they have to really concentrate on just pulling back, and be very conscious of any subtle movement on their part to the right or left or holding their hand a little bit longer so that their, so that they don't come down on a letter, *but come down on the one above it, the one that they might anticipate.* I would caution them to watch out especially toward the end of a sentence, or towards the end of a word when they have a pretty clear idea about what they think the person wants to type, so that if a person is typing a word and they are three letters into it and they think they know what the word is, I think that, that's the place where subtle guidance is much more likely to occur than at the beginning. I think also at the end of a sentence, somebody is typing a sentence, you know what the word is, and it would be much easier to lead the person at that point.

Note that my added italics point out a clear example of facilitator decision-making with respect to letter choice.

F1 also cautioned against the overinterpretation of messages. Despite this, in the follow-up interview he stated that it is all right to guess what the person is typing when he or she is several letters into the word as long as grammar issues are not being targeted. Following is an example of this "guess strategy" between F1 and his client:

> When we asked her why [she liked to be supported at her wrist] she said, "It helps me to find good." And I [F1] said, "Okay, there's a word missing here. What comes after *find*?" And she typed, *money*, which I *assumed* [italics added] was an echo, and I talked to her about that. I said, you know, "That really doesn't make sense here. Do you want to get rid of that?" "Yes." So she got rid of it. Then she typed *l-t*, and I said, "I'm going to guess at what you are going to type here. I'm going to guess that you are typing, *find letters*." And then I said, just to be sure, I wanted to really confirm to make sure that's really what she was saying, "Okay, I helped you a lot with this in getting this word in here. Is this really what you wanted to say?" And she typed, *"Truth."*

F1's response to "Is there any place for validity testing?" was "I think if it's done right." He went on to note that confirmation by "an independent facilitator, or a facilitator who doesn't know what the person said" is the type of validation that would be appropriate. F1 did feel that testing for validity is important in some situations such as "in cases of abuse [and] in cases of, where people want to make major changes in their lives, where they want to change medication, change where they live, or fire their personal care provider, and things like that. You have to confirm it with an independent facilitator, or a facilitator who doesn't know what the person says."

F1's initial response to "Do you think there is ever a place for the blind-fold or looking away?" was "If I did that with C1, I wouldn't get anything, because if she saw that I had a blindfold on, if she saw that I wasn't look-ing, her confidence would break down completely." When asked if it would work without the client's knowledge, F1 responded, "Yes. Yes. For a while and then if she started to perseverate, or if she had trouble getting to the letters, she would, it would start to break down. I wouldn't be providing the correction, her confidence would break down, and that would be . . . [he did not finish his sentence]."

Notwithstanding F1's ostensibly vigilant stance toward the possibility of facilitator influence, inconsistencies were noted in several of his comments and examples. One of these concerned co-construction, the phenomenon addressed by Duchan and Higginbotham (1992) that is the nonverbal ana-logue in FC to the verbal experience of finishing someone's sentence for him or her. In discussing this concept, F1 distinguished between "influencing what a person says and actually creating the word for them." He went on to say, "If you're putting words in their mouths, so to speak, because you're physically guiding them, I don't think that's co-construction. I think that's words coming from the facilitator or from the communication partner." In an attempt to clarify F1's intent regarding what he meant by co-construc-tion, I asked, "So, co-construction would be finishing a word you-they maybe start?" He responded, "Yes. I think, but also influencing what they're saying by, you know, your body language and, you know, whatever else." It would seem, then, that F1 considers some forms of influence ac-ceptable given that earlier he stated that co-construction as applied to FC was "all right" in order to "help a person become more efficient in their communication." F1 gave the following descriptions of interactions be-tween facilitator and client as an example of how to avoid giving in to pre-conceived notions regarding *expected* responses. The first interaction in-volves facilitation with respect to a picture of a person named Bill. The client was directed as follows:

Let's spell his name, and he went, I've done enough of this that I can anticipate some of the stuff, you know, he went for the *w* and normally in this situation I would pull him back. I was thinking maybe he was spelling *William* and that is what he went on to spell. Another kid who was in his first session—"What do you like?" We were giving him some set work. "Do you like the board better or the computer?" He went for the *i*. A lot of sentences start with *I*. Okay, you know, instead of—because he didn't go for *b* or *c* and pulling him back, I am going to let him go for the *i*. "I like computer." So, there is a judgment a lot of times and *the more a person facilitates the more adept they get at being able to understand when they need to pull back and when just to let go* [italics added].

This entire description clearly reveals the extent to which facilitator decisionmaking is allowed before it is considered influence. It also seems to contradict some of F1's other comments regarding the technical aspects of facilitated communication training and the need to pull back after every letter.

Finally, since the issue of mental telepathy has been raised by responsible professionals in the field of autism as an explanation for some of the studies that have revealed facilitator influence (Haskew and Donnellan 1992), F1's opinion was sought on this topic as well. He summarily dismissed the idea of mental telepathy in FC as "crap." He also felt that raising the issue of telepathy is "going to be incredibly harmful." F1 elaborated: "I think people have to state up front whenever they do trainings and be really clear about it that you can lead people to letters, you can be influencing with communication. There is absolutely no question that that can happen and you have to be aware of it to make it not happen."

F2 came at the issue of facilitator influence from the relationship standpoint, emphasizing that any such influence would be, in her opinion, "unconscious at both levels." She explained,

> I mean, if you have this relationship with somebody, and you're typing with them, and you have asked some question, "How are you feeling today?" or whatever, or, "Did you get over your problem you were having with so-and-so yesterday?" they don't want you to, sometimes they want to please the individuals they are typing with, or they don't want to disappoint them, or they just don't want them to know, you know, it's none of their business or whatever. So, the attitude, you know, might influence the answer of the person being facilitated. I really don't think that someone could type the answer for the individual by forcing them to do that typing. It's impossible.

In response to "Why is that?" F2 responded, "Because that person who is being facilitated is making that movement toward the letter and it would be pretty obvious to manipulate somebody who was going for an *a* over to the other side of the keyboard to give the answer the facilitator decided they wanted to put down instead. So, I think the influences are because of that, again because of that personal relationship."

At first glance it appears that F2's acknowledgment of the possibility of facilitator influence, albeit unconscious, contradicts her clear assertion that physical guidance in FC is impossible. A closer look, however, reveals that F2's description of unconscious influence is more reflective of normally occurring transactional elements (i.e., the reciprocal influences that are part of normal interaction patterns) or the client's mental attitude as opposed to the less wholesome influences that could occur as a reflection of preconceived notions and expectations in the mind of the facilitator. Thus it appears that F2 really does feel that unwholesome influence is not possible, a position that is diametrically opposed to that of F1. Moreover, F2's position is also inconsistent with recognizing the need to take precautions against providing undue influence, for people don't usually guard against events they consider unlikely.

F2's response to a question concerning comments made by detractors of FC that facilitators may be influencing or actually producing the messages was decisive, if not hostile. She stated, "I think they're pretty ignorant." In elaborating, she said,

> I would have to consider the source. You know, what's in it for them by dis-agreeing with, you know, by saying that this isn't valid. What is your experience in it, you know, and things like that. I think people, a lot of people that have said this is garbage, or whatever, haven't tried it, haven't, are probably angry because they didn't develop it. You know, professional jealousy or whatever.

She later added that it would make her "pretty angry" if she were accused of "influencing [her clients'] replies."

In contrast to the definitive nature of her feelings toward charges of facil-itator influence, F2's response to a question concerning the possibility of mental telepathy was far more ambiguous:

> Well, I think, when you have a relationship like I have with C2, I mean we were typing every single day—I mean, yes, some of what you are typing about is going to be dependent upon the mood that either individual is in. I mean, [he] could pick up on things that were going on with me very easily even though I tried to hide them. In typing with him for a long time, *sometimes I even know what he is going to say* [italics added], depending, I mean—unless he gets into a sentence or whatever, what the next word might be. So, I think a lot of it has to do with the facilitator herself as far as when you are talking telepathy or any of that stuff. I'm just too concrete of a person to ever think that somebody was reading my mind or I was reading somebody else's mind. I think that there are people out there who are involved in that type of study or they talk of mysticism. You know, they get some type of spiritualism out of that in their lives and I think it probably would come through in the individ-ual's, it might, it might. I don't think it is intentional.

She went on to say,

> It may be that it comes through because like I say somebody is picking up on the different ways that I express myself. If you have a facilitator and somebody who is being facilitated typing, the person who is being facilitated sometimes is going to very much be in awe of the individual, the normal person who gets to do all these wonderful things, you know, to get involved and knows so much about whatever and will try to emulate them.

With respect to the issue of validity testing, F2 expressed sentiments similar to those of F1. She stated, "The validation that I have done is by having somebody else type with [him]." When asked whether she had ever tried to close her eyes or look away, she responded,

> No, I have never tried closing my eyes. I have a real hard time with typing with him anyway because I usually can't see the left side of the keyboard, so to me that's validation. He goes for letters on that side just because of the reach and stuff because a lot of times I back off because I just can't go that far. So, he is pulling me over there. So to me that's validation, but as far as trying to do any of these things, no, I always have somebody else type with him.

Although the subject of overinterpretation of messages was not addressed directly during the interview, a review of several of the preexisting typed transcripts of F2's client revealed multiple instances in which specific meaning was attributed to what appeared to be unrelated, ambiguous strings of typed letters. The following excerpt is one example taken from a transcript dated August 20, 1991. The parenthetical statements refer either to the translation of the message by the facilitator or to F2's response to the typed message.

> gmoupk (Still don't understand. Talked about using words so I could understand)
> ji1/2iu (Try again)
> your juojip (Try again)
> ukkghkj; (Are you trying to say I'm yucky?)
> yes
> yucky [typed by facilitator] (this is how it's spelled. Let's type it.)
> hyour yucky

In another transcript, dated August 13, 1991, and concerning a baseball discussion, F2 was assisted by an additional facilitator who often served as a co-facilitator with her client. The following excerpt further illustrates the ambiguity regarding the meaning attributed to the typed messages vis-à-vis their letter configurations:

> yds (In response to, "do you want to tell me something?")
> yugot into ohiki (The other facilitator typed, in response to this, "ohio cincinnati reds" and F2 asked the question, "Are you trying to type this?")
> yes
> yesuhm,
> you unjinh (In response to, "Do you want to type something?")
> you jhmm,
> ilike baseball (In response to, "Make a sentence about baseball.")

In contrast to F2's contention that overt facilitator influence in the form of physical guidance is "impossible," F3, agreeing with F1, expressed the view that such influence is indeed possible: "But I have watched other people and I'm convinced that they're helping the person, and it looks like they're helping them point and, and there's just, and I have seen someone type with C3 who was just starting out and had him point to a letter down in the left hand corner. I just know for a fact that he jumps down to it."

With regard to prior knowledge of content, F3 stated, "I think it's hard when you know what the person is about to type sometimes, but I think after a while I got very comfortable with not helping at all and just pulling back. So maybe at first I helped more than I realized, but I think you train yourself not to."

F3's reaction to charges of facilitator influence by detractors of the technique was more tolerant than F2's. She declared that she understood people's skepticism, stating, "And it's understandable that people would feel that way, especially when you let go and then they [the clients] don't type or they think that's all part of why the facilitator is there." Further, F3, like F2, seemed to subscribe to a "seeing [or more to the point, *doing*] is believing" standard with respect to mitigating against skepticism: "I think that they [the skeptics] would have to try it themselves. I think that some people wouldn't, might not believe it until they tried it themselves." When asked how she felt about mental telepathy as an explanation for some of the content of messages, she said, "I feel like I sometimes know what he is about to say, or type, but I'm not always right either."

F3's attitude toward validity testing mirrored that expressed by F1. It was important, she said, to do it in a way "that it is not so insulting." She stated, "I think there are ways to test and I think it is important to know if you are, if they are the ones typing or if you are helping." She described one approach that she felt had been successful with her client: "I think that throwing things in to keep a check or like having [colleague's name] and C3 type, which he did the other day, the same thing that he typed with me, you know, months ago. You know, that right there, you know, how could you deny that there was something there, you know?"

Insight into F3's interpretation of her client's messages, which could have implications with respect to the issue of facilitator influence vis-à-vis message interpretation, was gleaned from an answer she gave to a question regarding the juxtaposition of literacy skills and aberrant behavior in her client:

> He was getting really angry and I was asking him what was going on. And he started to type, "I hate Jeff" and "Kill Jeff" and stuff like that. I went through lists, you know, "Who is Jeff? Does Jeff live at your house?" "Yes." "Does Jeff work with you at day program?" "Yes." And just everything I could think of so it wasn't leading at all. And finally it came out that Jeff was him, like part of his behavior. And that makes sense because a lot of autistic people use either a name or something to describe their behaviors that they can't help.

Following additional questions to ensure understanding of F3's interpretation of her client's message, she continued, "Jeff did finally turn out to be part of his behavior, and he said that he can't help it. And when I go to visit him sometime, he'll type that Jeff is dead. And before I left, or stopped working with him, he typed—now what did he type—oh, something that I was leaving because of Jeff. So, I felt that he was saying that Jeff is dead so that I would think that's all over." In the absence of supporting documentation, it would seem that F3 takes great liberty in interpreting her client's facilitated message.

Finally, a comment by F3 seemed to crystallize a pervasive, albeit subtle, undercurrent among all facilitators with respect to the feeling that testing for validity was somehow inimical to a trust relationship with their clients. In response to a question regarding the types of validity checks she had utilized with her client, F3, referring to a kind of "shell game," responded,

> That's what it was—it was more he could type on the board what the number was but he couldn't, he didn't point to the actual cup and that was what—and I talked to F1 and he said, "Maybe he didn't trust you." You know there are a lot of reasons why—it was like a trick, it was like a game. Maybe he thought I was fooling him or something, you know so, but he would type out the right number.

Here, F3 explains away a clearly erroneous response with speculation regarding trust. The belief that validity checks of this type would be detrimental to the facilitator-client relationship is widely held by proponents of the technique (Biklen 1993; Crossley 1994) and hotly contested by skeptics (Green 1994b; Palfreman 1994; Shane 1994). It has been a consistent battle cry since the earliest days of FC.

Other Lines of Inquiry

Additional areas of investigation germane to developing an understanding of the phenomenon of facilitated communication surfaced during the course of this study. One of these concerned the philosophical issue of attitude toward people with disabilities. Because the number of collected facilitated messages varied considerably among clients, ranging from a paucity of available documents for one client to a significant number for another, it was not possible to meaningfully compare the specific portions of the messages that may have involved philosophical statements about the nature of disability and society's attitudes toward persons with disabilities. But since commonalities with respect to this issue did surface both in the review of client records and in some of their facilitated messages, I sought facilitator opinion on this important subject. I found a distinctive pattern of opinions among facilitators that was consistent with the commonalities already noted.

Each facilitator was specifically questioned regarding his or her personal philosophy with respect to people with disabilities. Paralleling the commonalities found in the review of documents, widespread agreement was discerned among facilitators with regard to their own attitudes on this issue. F1 stated, "I'm totally in agreement with what is happening in [name of state] which is that they are closing down the State institutions, and they have as a way of dealing with that a crisis network. I think that if it is planned and you give the support when people need it, there is no place for institutions."

He also indicated that he was "very strong" in his support for integration and inclusion of people with disabilities. Finally, F1 echoed a familiar sentiment associated with the FC movement—the importance of involving clients in crucial decisionmaking affecting their lives:

> People can tell us more reliably what they want to do, where they want to live, what kind of work they want to do, you know. . . . Probably the biggest change, the biggest benefit is that people perceive the person with the disability differently. They treat them with more respect. They talk to them as if they understand. They stop treating them like children.

F2, like her colleague F1, expressed favorable feelings toward deinstitutionalization, noting that "people have the right to be able to access their community and to not live sheltered, isolated lives." She was also in favor of integrated settings under certain conditions:

> I think that's right and it's fair. I think people have to have the supports that they need in order to do that [be in integrated settings], not only for their protection—not protection so much—it is protection. We are talking sexual abuse and all kinds of things that are going on out there—for their protection and also for somebody who is self-abusive for the protection of people who also exist in that environment.

F2 indicated through her response that for her, deinstitutionalization goes far beyond mere living arrangements. Although she conceded that "we are learning," she added, "I don't think the treatment of the people with disabilities is something that our society should be proud of, you know."

When asked whether FC would be helpful, not helpful, or a total nonentity in the community integration process, F2 stated that she thought it would be "very helpful." Like her colleague F1, she also mirrored a sentiment that has come to be associated with the facilitated communication movement, stating, "I think it opens up the world for the individual that is being facilitated. It also opens up the eyes of everyone involved around them to know that somebody has something to say. It is important that it be heard and that just because it is an alternate way of being able to express yourself it is very valid." Finally, F2 felt that it was a good idea for clients to be involved in decisions affecting their lives (in this case participation at team meetings) as long as clients were comfortable in doing so.

F3's views on community integration were tempered by concern about her client's being accepted in such settings: "In the ideal world, I think that we all should be able to go wherever we want, you know, C3 and everyone included." She was circumspect, however, citing her client's aggressive behavior as a major factor in needing to proceed slowly with integration.

Early on in the initial interview F3 raised several issues that have become associated with the FC movement. Also typical is that when discussing these issues, proponents often attribute high-level judgment skills to individuals with autism. Citing the use of primary reinforcement with her client by the individuals who originally trained him in FC, F3 disapproved of the practice: "They were giving him chips like he was a dog or something like that, and he wouldn't cooperate. I think that that was why. It just was so insulting that he was asked to do some really inane things."

F3 also raised the issue of clients commenting on how they and others perceived their disabilities. Her client had typed with other facilitators that "he felt retarded." F3 stated, "That was the first consistency we had because he typed with me the same thing. He typed that he felt dumb, you know, stuff like that or people thought he was stupid." Facilitated messages containing similar content have been associated with the FC movement since its inception in this country (Biklen 1990; Biklen 1993; Haskew and Donnellan 1992). When I asked if she thought that FC had changed people's attitudes toward persons with disabilities, F3 responded affirmatively: "Well, I think that more people will watch what they say in front of autistic people or other people that type and [unclear audiotape, approximately one second] and talk directly to them *'cause now there's a person there'"* [italics added]. Referring to her own experience in this regard, F3 went on to state, "I mean before—I think that's when my relationship with C3 got so good because there was a person that I could relate to in there with the same words and feelings that I could feel, you know, and that's something that I could understand. So I think that that's a big part of it." (But for FC, there is something disconcerting about the implication that one's *personhood* was somehow in question.)

In response to the question "What do you think is the best thing about facilitated communication?" F3 stated, "The person can take more control of their lives." When I asked what she thought FC had done in general for people with disabilities, she responded, "I think it protects them against victimization." Here, as in the case of F2, one sees an expectation of victimization with respect to people with disabilities.

In this study I also explored the matter of sexual abuse, a subject that also revealed similarities among facilitators. I felt that facilitator opinion regarding sexual abuse was important because this subject not only has been frequently raised by FC users throughout the country (ASHA Technical Report 1994; Rimland 1992) but also has been perhaps the single most volatile issue raised in court cases regarding facilitated communication. Interestingly, facilitators gave responses that were almost identical regarding why the issue of sexual abuse comes up so often in facilitated communication. Each one expressed the sentiment that the issue was raised frequently because the population that uses facilitated communication is at risk for sexual abuse. F1 stated, "So, I think first of all, it is a very vulnerable population. People never thought they would be able to speak. I know that we aren't getting the incidence of it at the rates that other people are talking." F2's response was even more definitive, even chilling, and left no doubt as to where she stood on the issue: "Because I think people were sexual and a number of people who were disabled or mentally retarded or autistic have been abused since they are perfect targets for that. People who are offenders know the professions to go into to offend, and this is a perfect place for them—to work in an institution." F3's reply to the question echoed the sentiments expressed by her colleagues: "Because I think it happens a lot, especially with clients who are nonverbal." In the follow-up interview she elaborated on her initial response: "I think especially being in institutions— which a lot of people here have been in institutions and it seems like it's just bound to happen when somebody can't speak or they are victims ready to happen."

Clearly, all three facilitators viewed individuals with developmental disabilities as candidates for victimization with respect to sexual abuse. In so doing, they echoed a familiar theme of the FC culture. Given the literature on the powerful effects of expectation on behavior, one cannot help but wonder what effect the expectation of victimization may have on the interpretation of facilitated messages.

Commitment to Facilitated Communication

An additional pattern that emerged from the interviews with facilitators seemed to cut across all other patterns in the sense of encapsulating a pervasive notion about the preeminence of facilitated communication not only in the lives of FC users but also in matters where inconsistencies or incongruities in its use were apparent. Within this study, in virtually *every* instance in which FC use may have been legitimately questioned owing to its specific discordance with other relevant factors and information, not only was it *not* questioned but FC itself was often used to explain away inconsistencies. So striking was this proclivity in favor of the preeminence of facilitated communication that the pattern code used in this study to address this issue is labeled *Commitment to Facilitated Communication* to underscore the high esteem in which facilitators held this technique.

The tendency among facilitators to uphold FC use even in the face of specific incongruities and inconsistencies was seen across several subject areas. One of these concerned discrepancies associated with what is known about autism itself. Despite studies that specifically link nonverbal behavior with communication (Donnellan et al. 1984), F1 disregarded the possible message value of nonverbal behavior, attributing the occurrence of self-injurious behavior as the client types a neutral message to the client's "having a bad day." When I asked, "What would lead you to look at the verbal [typed] message over the nonverbal message?" F1 said, "They told us. Pay attention to what I type, not to what I say." A short time later he went on to state, "C1 has very unreliable yeses and nos in her speech, but in her typing it's pretty accurate. When she types, 'Yes, I want to do something,' you can be sure that she definitely wants to do it." When I asked, "How do you judge that it's more accurate when she types?" F1 contradicted his earlier statement discounting nonverbal behavior. He replied, "Yes, and this may sound a little bit inconsistent, but, I guess, you know, there seems to be less anxiety after she types yes and no. There I am paying attention to the behavior." In probing this apparent inconsistency, I asked, "Would you pay attention to nonverbal behavior when they are not typing, but if it is not congruent with what they are typing pay attention to the typing?" He responded, "Yes." To the additional request for clarification of his intent, "Would that be a fair statement?" he responded, "Yes, yes, yes, yes." Thus F1 appeared to sanction a double standard by which to judge nonverbal behavior—one for FC and one for all other situations! In response to a question concerning the incongruity between his client's relatively impoverished verbal behavior and her more sophisticated typed messages, F1 noted, "With her it's really interesting because over time what we've seen is that her typing and her speech have become more consistent. And, you know, where before she used to type one thing and say something else quite a bit—now that doesn't happen nearly as often." In addition, he noted, "Although there have been times when C1 does very sophisticated things, when there have been, there has been an increase in her behavior problems while she is typing." This would seem to contradict those studies that have demonstrated a decrease in behavior problems in the face of increased communicative ability (Carr 1982; Carr and Kologinski 1983; Layton 1987). Once again, this discrepancy went unchallenged, if not unnoticed, so strong was the commitment to facilitated communication.

F2 noted that she had never seen any behaviors in her client that would be considered incongruous to the typed message, emphatically stating, "There is not a discrepancy at all." She then went on to say, somewhat contradictorily, "If he is typing and all of a sudden he reaches up and hits his forehead, something is going on." F2 also attributed motives to her client that are not consistent with much of the mainstream autism literature. She talked about his telling "wonderful stories—these fantasies." Later in the interview, in attempting to explain the inconsistencies between her client's typed messages and actual occurrences in his life, F2 stated, "It took me a long time to figure out that C2 is a very professional liar." The attribution of lying is specifically contradicted in the autism research literature (Sodian and Frith 1992, 1993). In elaborating on her statement she said,

> [He would] go on and on and on, and make up—oh, what he did over the weekend—oh, man, that guy had a social life that I would die for, you know. And I just assumed that it was all true. I would talk to his foster parents and say that C2 had an interesting weekend. "Well, if you call stacking wood interesting." "Wait a minute, he went [square dancing[1]], and he did this." "Oh, no he didn't." So, we had to discuss the fact that it's okay to have these wonderful dreams—things that you want to do.

Incomprehensibly, even *erroneous* information is somehow explained away in service to FC. In response to a question concerning where this client would have come up with something as specific as square dancing, F2 responded, "Who knows. They [the foster family] might have had a distant cousin who came to visit who talked about it, or he got it from somebody walking in the hallway." Two things should be noted here. The first is that F2 made no attempt to determine how her client might have come up with this information even after she found out that it was erroneous. Second, several months after the initial interview I learned that square dancing was the hobby of this client's other regular facilitator.

F3 also described instances in which her client's nonverbal behavior was incongruent with the typed message: "When he is laughing but he's typing that he is really angry—that would be a great example of that." When asked which would be the more appropriate communication, F3 responded, "the typing." She elaborated on her response:

> He does that laughing, but sometimes he is really upset. It's just his behavior. I guess with autistic people they say you can never really tell what's next, you know, because of the way they are acting. I think that's a good way to explain it because he does that with his laughing or with his behavior and then he'll turn around and hit you when you have no clue, but he types that he is angry and then it makes sense, but don't look at the smile on his face. Look at what he is typing.

In the follow-up interview F3 discussed some of her client's uncooperative behavior during FC: "I think with the typing like, like what he was doing today was curling his finger, or he would start to try and pinch me almost at a point; and I really thought it more a matter of him being resistant to it [FC] or playing a game or something like that, but I don't think he has a problem doing it [referring to the physical act of pointing]." Incredibly, even though F3 actually attributes her client's nonverbal behavior to his being resistant to facilitated communication, she still manages to ignore (sac-

---

[1]In the interests of confidentiality, the type of dancing has been changed.

rifice?) its communicative intent in service to FC. In answer to the question "What might be going on with somebody who now is given this powerful tool—communication—and yet resists it?" F3 responded, "Right. I think that maybe he fears that if he—if people knew he was capable of doing a lot more, then they might expect him to take care of himself or that he would lose the support that he has now. . . . Or, there's also the other side where he might just feel like he's in a helpless, hopeless situation and why would it do anything for him anyway, which is possible." Here again, F3 takes great liberty in her response to what her client *might* be feeling, explaining away his ostensible resistance to FC as stemming from his greater concern for the ramifications it would have in his life.

Facilitators' commitment to FC sometimes led to definitive judgments in situations that were easily open to other interpretations. For example, F1 described a situation with his client:

> Sometimes when she is typing she just wants to type, you know, stuff that is very similar to what she says. "How do you feel about all these people having so much control over your life?" "*Good*," she types. Or she says "*Good*" and goes for the letter *g*. I say [to client], "I'm not going to let you do that because every time I ask you how you feel about anything *you say and you type good. I want something different*" [italics added]. She types, "I feel secure when you ask."

F1 gives no consideration to the possibility that receptive language difficulty or auditory processing problems may have caused C1 to misinterpret the question. If this were the case—and given the length and complexity of the question, it is indeed possible—she may well have *intended* to type the word *good*. The congruence between her verbal and typed expression of the word would lend credence to this position, but it was not even considered by F1.

F3 described a situation in which she attributed aggression in her client to his overhearing plans for his future living arrangements. She stated, "They were doing it right in front of [him] and [he] was aggressive for the next three days, and I am sure that had something to do with it." One would have to question the source of such certainty, especially in view of the extended time period involved (i.e., three days) and the complete disregard for other plausible explanations.

Commitment to facilitated communication has also led facilitators to make assumptions, implied or stated, that are either unsupported or actually fly in the face of the professional literature across several fields. For example, F1 stated, "I think among kids I've known who seem to be hyperlexic they seem to have an understanding of it when they're given a way of expressing themselves." The attribution of comprehension to the phenomenon of hyperlexia is specifically contradicted in the literature. According to

Silberberg and Silberberg (1967), hyperlexia is the "ability to recognize words . . . on a higher level than their ability to comprehend and integrate them" (p. 41). (Will it be necessary to redefine yet another term to mold it to the specifications of facilitated communication?)

An additional observation that F1 made on differences in the client's ability to retrieve words verbally and when typing is not only unsupported by the literature but seems contrary to logic: "I think people have word-finding problems regardless of whether it is in speech or their typing, but I think that with typing they are able to get around it a little bit more easily and they are able to communicate more reliably." F1 was at a loss to explain why he felt that word-retrieval difficulty was somehow ameliorated by typing. Further, although F1 believed that echolalia has a function—a notion supported by the autism literature—he completely disregarded its function when it came to facilitation, referring to the need to provide correction by pulling back his client's hand when she typed what he termed an echo.

Finally, in many instances commitment to facilitated communication clearly approached blind faith acceptance. F2 typified this when she responded to a question regarding what is specifically happening in FC: "What's happening? It's just doing it—it's just happening. It is just giving that person support."

F3's belief in FC was so strong that it led her to resolve all issues of incongruity in favor of facilitated communication. For example, F3 listed drinking from the toilet bowl as one of her client's problem behaviors, a behavior that would be inconsistent with her characterization of him as "moderately high functioning" and with his alleged concern regarding people's reactions to him (i.e., people fearing him or thinking that he was retarded). Given this apparent inconsistency, I asked the following question to further delineate F3's thinking on the subject: "Wouldn't C3 extract from society that drinking out of the toilet bowl is a no-no?" In F3's simplistic response to the question she not only minimized the significance of the behavior but also made no attempt to consider it in the light of the sophistication that C3 had allegedly shown in his typing:

> Right. His dad says that he does, or he thinks he does, things like that just because the opportunity is there. It's a game. Maybe his standards aren't the same as our standards. He doesn't think of that as socially unacceptable in his mind, you know, but he obviously has fun when he does it. He thinks it is very funny. He laughs when he does it, and if the opportunity does arise—if you walk out of the room for a minute—he knows he has to get something in before you get back.

As can be seen, F3 manages to explain away a behavior that is highly inconsistent with the view of her client as having sophisticated perceptions. Her comments are similar to those of F2 when she went to great lengths to believe the facilitated message allegedly typed by her client *even in the face of specific evidence to the contrary:* Her client was "lying" rather than responding with erroneous information.

Finally, a remark made by F1 with respect to an FC demonstration that both he and I had witnessed in another forum with a different client encapsulates the strength of the FC commitment. Both of us were in agreement regarding the highly questionable validity of the particular demonstration; however, F1 stated, "I guess what I was disturbed about is that they would put her [the client] in a public situation like that where at this stage it could be so questionable." F1 went on to say, "And, I think the important thing with her is, that *even if she was being cued, even if all the communication wasn't hers, even if it wasn't valid what she was saying, it doesn't mean that she can't do it*" (italics added). This comment illustrates clearly that F1's concern is not for the validity of the client's message but rather for the potential well-being of facilitated communication as a technique (i.e., an entity in the disability field). Interestingly, F2 expressed a similar notion regarding FC. She noted that "even if all of this was a sham, which I don't think it is, there are other gains which have been brought about for clients because of the phenomenon of facilitated communication."

Such sentiments demonstrate both the strength of facilitators' overriding commitment to FC and the consequent *invincibility* of the technique, for even in instances of *recognized inveracity,* facilitated communication stands inviolate. Such sentiments also represent the prevailing view of the FC culture. In addition, they come curiously close to some of the more extreme views of some disability rights advocates with respect to the inclusive-education movement. One has to wonder about the effect such an intense commitment to FC has on the judgments facilitators are called upon to make in their interactions with their clients. Likewise, one can't help but speculate that the "everything for the cause" mentality that characterizes both the FC and inclusive-education movements may be less a matter of coincidence and more a matter of mutuality of purpose, for how better to demonstrate the remarkable learning ability of individuals with disabilities and thus ensure their place in the mainstream than through the medium of facilitated communication.

3

A Portrait of the Client

The longer you can look back the further you can look forward.

—**Winston Churchill**

One of the most perplexing aspects of the facilitated communication phenomenon is the astonishing degree of competence that is attributed to many clients by their facilitators. Stories abound of remarkable academic feats by individuals who, prior to FC, were considered too low functioning to be served in mainstream settings. Not only was FC their gateway to inclusive education, it was the magic carpet on which many of them flew past their typical peers straight to the head of the class! Even more remarkable was the "official" response of FC enthusiasts. Instead of maintaining the healthy degree of skepticism ordinarily reserved for truly incredible achievements, proponents accepted these accomplishments at face value with nary a thought to other possible explanations for the extraordinary happenings. Skepticism would have engendered closer scrutiny with respect to probing for the source of the unexpected competence. But unquestioning acceptance left no other alternative than to redefine autism and to disregard the symptoms, and all other information, that interfered with such full acceptance of facilitated communication.

Because my goal in undertaking this study was to meet the controversial issues that plagued FC head on so that I could develop a true understanding of the use of this technique with individuals with autism, I had specific requirements in choosing clients. Since the degree and extent of competence attributed to FC clients previously classified as low functioning was most remarkable as well as most controversial, I felt it was important to select clients who carried the combined labels of autism and mental retardation. In addition, I took a purist approach to the phenomenon of unexplained literacy in such individuals by choosing clients who, despite demonstrated literacy through FC, had come from backgrounds where such competence would not have been expected. I felt that these criteria would offer the best opportunity to elucidate a phenomenon that was largely inexplicable.

This chapter provides an in-depth look at key aspects of these clients' lives prior to their experience with FC. An understanding of what each of them brought to the table as FC clients is critically important because it provides a meaningful and relevant context within which to view the conduct of facilitated communication. It will also enable the reader to view FC holistically, that is, not as an isolated "splinter" skill but rather as part of the entire pattern of behaviors and events that shaped these clients' lives.

Diagnostic History

F1's client, C1, was a female twenty-nine years, four months of age at the time this study was initiated. Her diagnosis of record was mild mental retardation and infantile autism. The statement in her record in reference to the "mild" designation further elucidated her level of functioning: "The full scale I.Q. score of 50 is at the lower most limits of that range of function." The next placement level would obviously be moderate mental retardation. Thus this client's full-scale IQ places her at the boundary between the two functioning-level designations, at mild-to-moderate mental retardation. By report and by observation, this client was the highest functioning of the three clients in this study.

Symptomatology associated with the diagnosis of autism in F1's record included self-stimulatory behavior in the form of vocal noises and self-injurious behavior in the form of slapping herself on the face and forehead. She also engaged in "impaired interpersonal interaction, and perseverative and stereotypical behaviors such as rocking."

F2's client, C2, was a male of twenty-seven years, six months, at the time this study began. His diagnosis of record was moderate mental retardation and infantile autism. Notwithstanding a reference to his "functioning on a severe level of retardation" in the past, the "moderate" designation would seem to be the one most consistent with both formal testing and with his designation over time. One of his examiners suggested that the diagnosis of infantile autism be changed to "infantile autism residual state." This judgment was not rendered as a result of specific evaluation but rather on the basis of the following opinion: "He may have been autistic by definition earlier but at the present time he is functioning quite well in the situation he is in." The fact that this client may have been "functioning quite well" would not be sufficient to overrule a diagnosis made by several different examiners on the basis of prior cogent observations; nor did it change this client's diagnosis of record, which remained infantile autism.

Unlike C1, C2's record contained numerous references to motor difficulty and to various diagnostic procedures for the purpose of determining the nature of such impairment. A hospital evaluation of 1969 contained the following information: "Findings of this study were microcephaly, question of eighth cranial nerve deficit and deafness. X-rays of skull revealed a defect in the frontal bone. Views of the hands and wrists showed marked shortening of the middle phalanx of the left hand." A neurological consultation at the time not only confirmed these findings but also speculated on the presence of "mild cerebellar dysfunction." The latter, if present, would undoubtedly contribute to movement difficulty and as such would probably have implications for facilitated communication use as well as for the possibility of independent typing in the future. Diagnostic history also included an oblique reference to the possibility of cerebral palsy. Although deafness was later ruled out, issues related to the exact nature of the motor involvement were never satisfactorily resolved.

An additional area of interest in this client's diagnostic history is a request for a psychiatric evaluation "for possible diagnosis of multiple personality." An April 30, 1991, letter from a state agency reviewer noted that the request had been "turned down . . . on the theory that 'There does not appear to be any effective treatment at this time for Multiple Personality Disorders that would be useful or accessible to [C2].'" This denial was based on input from a physician who, according to the reviewer, stated, "It would be questionable if someone of low intellectual function could participate in that type of therapy." The latter characterization of C2 is decidedly inconsistent with his reported level of sophistication in facilitated communication activities. Further, there was no attempt to rectify this judgment based on his performance in FC. Finally, as noted in Chapter 2, the type of verbal behavior described for this client as an example of multiple personality disorder could arguably also be used to describe delayed echolalia.

Some of the behaviors associated with autism listed in C2's record over time include head banging, self-injurious behavior, difficulty with transitions, tantrums, and pica. The latter refers to the ingesting of inedible objects. The following notation in his record articulated the seriousness of the latter issue: "Records indicate that [C2] has a history of maladaptive behaviors which include pica behaviors. This necessitated surgery in 1983 due to small bowel obstruction." In March 1993, during the course of this study, C2 was admitted for similar emergency surgery for ingesting plastic, an incident that will be covered in the next section of this chapter.

By report and by observation, C2 was considered to manifest a greater degree of mental retardation than C1 and a lesser degree than the third client in this study, C3. In addition, C2 was the most motorically involved of the three clients.

At the time this study began, F3's client, C3, was approximately three weeks shy of twenty-eight years of age. His diagnosis of record was autistic disorder and profound mental retardation. Unlike the other two clients, he was nonverbal. After two unsuccessful attempts in 1983 and 1985, psychological evaluation was completed in December 1988 owing to "[C3's] improved demeanor and willingness to participate in the evaluation." A notation in C3's record indicated, "Combined with results of the Vineland Adaptive Behavior Scale, the outcome of the evaluation is considered valid in terms of diagnostic purposes." This seems to suggest concordance between day-to-day functioning and test results. This client's performance on the Stanford Binet, fourth edition, fell "below the norms of the scale." His record further indicated that "his task completion and the age he obtained for the specific sub-tests suggest a level of intellectual functioning which is within the range of profound mental retardation."

Behaviorally, "records note periodic episodes of maladaptive behaviors which include self-injurious behavior, agitation and aggression." A July 1991 program note contained greater detail with respect to maladaptive behaviors:

> Some problem behaviors include screams, yells and loud nonsense sounds, thigh slaps, hopping on his knees, and biting his forearms. When frustrated, [C3] will hit, slap, pinch, or bite staff and other residents. [C3] will also attempt to bolt from the residence or van if given an opportunity. Rocking with his back hitting the shower wall, or in the van, also occur. [C3] will take every opportunity to drink anything he can to excess and will urinate.

In stark contrast to the previous description of this client is the day program narrative completed at the same time (July 1991) by his facilitator, F3. She wrote,

> [C3] is making remarkable progress using facilitated communication. In the past three months he has typed sentences concerning his basic needs, self-perception, and perception of others. I have witnessed a noticeable decrease in [C3's] maladaptive behavior once he has communicated his thoughts and they have been acknowledged and understood by another person. He can type simple sentences coherently and *with almost no spelling errors*. (italics added)

July 1991 would have been very close to the time this dyad (i.e., F3 and C3) began facilitating together, according to information obtained from F3 during the interviews. Consequently, the reference made to the client's progress over "the past three months" most likely summarizes C3's earlier work with his other facilitators. What is particularly significant in F3's description of C3's use of facilitated communication is that it directly contradicts her portrayal of that early experience when "he would just beat the crap out of me every day."

Developmental History

C1's early development with respect to the achievement of developmental milestones was somewhat delayed, reflecting consistency with her diagnosis of mild-moderate mental retardation. Her mother began to suspect a problem when C1 was approximately one year old; her daughter "made no effort to play with toys or other objects." With respect to speech and language development, C1's record states, "She made no sound or attempt at speech with the exception of loud screeching. By the time she reached the age of three years, [C1] had a speaking vocabulary of three words." This pattern of development seems not only significantly delayed but also atypical given her disinterest in toys and the lack of sound/speech attempts. It is, however, consistent with the pattern of development often reported for children with autism. Regarding behavior, C1's record noted, "[C1] rocked in her crib for long periods of time and did not sleep well."

C1's current level of functioning with respect to both speech and language ability and behavioral symptomatology appears to be consistent with what was reported in her record. A speech and language evaluation of May 1986 delineated "the presence of behaviors which are a reflection of autism. Specifically, [C1] was noted to repeat the same repertoire of about ten sentences all day long, and ask questions to which she already knew the answers." Such verbal behavior has been linked to a variety of problems associated with autism (Twachtman 1996). Additional symptomatology associated with autism reported in her record included the use of echolalia, although C1 was reportedly capable of generating simple novel utterances. An assessment of her adaptive behavior in January 1990 further elucidated this client's level of functioning with respect to speech and language and social behavior:

> In the area of social skills, [C1] is able to initiate and respond to greetings. She establishes and maintains eye contact in response to statements. [C1] maintains an appropriate social distance. She usually listens during a conversation without interrupting, and uses appropriate expressions, social amenities, and gestures to convey meaning.

C2's developmental history is significantly more involved than that of C1, as would be expected given his more complex diagnostic picture. Both speech and language and toilet training were reportedly significantly delayed. His record contains the following description of him at age four years, three months, "The child speaks only a few words and is not toilet trained at present." In terms of social development, his record notes, "There is a history of social deprivation and some question of maternal incompetence regarding loving and caring for [C2]." The significance of this alleged deprivation may be seen in the additional notation within this client's record: "His abnormal behavior may be a manifestation of generalized brain damage or may be secondary to social deprivation at an early age." The following July 2, 1974, behavioral description of C2 reveals a picture of him as a young child: "[C2] will force large amounts of food into his mouth if not supervised. He knocks his plate off the table without provocation at times. He swallows mouthfuls of food without chewing. His attention span is limited. [C2] demands constant attention and will do temper tantrums to gain attention. He appears puzzled with a change in his routine."

Specific descriptions of C2's early behavior appear to be consistent with his present-day functioning. Noteworthy, however, is the lack of congruence between the presence of aberrant (and in one case, life-threatening) behavior and the level of sophistication that has been attributed to this client via facilitated communication. Such lack of congruence is an accepted phenomenon in FC (Biklen 1993). As noted previously, pica behavior continues to be a significant issue for this client, as evidenced by his March 1993 hospital admission secondary to the ingesting of plastic. The following excerpts serve to illuminate the stark disparity between this client's perilous overt behavior and the triviality ascribed to it in the facilitated message that addresses it. The first excerpt is from the hospital admission note:

> The patient is a 28 year-old autistic male who approximately ten years ago was explored for intestinal obstruction secondary to ingested foreign bodies. . . . The patient's present admission was required because of increasing vomiting associated with fever and leukocytosis, and at presentation the patient was noted to have an acute abdomen and was taken to the O.R. for exploration. Surgical findings revealed a perforation of the distal jejunum secondary to ingested plastic and other foreign bodies. . . . Postoperatively the patient was placed on total parenteral nutrition [feeding tube]. However, he discontinued this and *ate his triple lumen catheter* [feeding tube; italics added] on his 5th post-operative day, and TPN [total parenteral nutrition] was therefore not restarted.

The next excerpt is from the progress notes for March, April, and May 1993 in this client's record: "[C2] went to the hospital in March for emergency surgery for ingesting plastic. . . . Once out of the hospital, we typed about why he ate hazardous wastes. Basically, he said that he liked the taste of plastic, oil, dirt, etc. and he did it to 'get his way.'"

The facilitated communication literature is replete with similar inane explanations aimed at accounting for the oft-seen inconsistencies between overt behavior and the content and sophistication of typed messages (Biklen 1990; Biklen et al. 1991). Indeed, one of the tenets of the FC movement is the perceived primacy of the facilitated message over the behavior that accompanies it (Biklen 1993).

It is particularly noteworthy that there was no written or verbal report on this client that he had indicated through facilitated communication that he was ill prior to his being admitted to the hospital. One would have to question the benefit and effectiveness of a communication system that would not enable the client to communicate about such an important and potentially life-threatening situation.

In terms of C2's speech and language development, the following was noted, "Most of the time he mumbles words and his speech is high pitched, nasal sounding and very hard to hear. However, at times, he will speak in short sentences and phrases very well." C2's overt speech and language behavior appears to be consistent with that described in his record. Of particular note in his record is C2's ability to verbally generate novel sentences. A 1989 speech and language evaluation note provides additional insight into the nature of his verbal expression: "[C2] used oral expression to answer questions. 'Yes'/'no' questions were very easy for [C2] to answer. His response was clearly understood, *though not always accurate in content*" [italics added]. His record further revealed that C2 tended to use telegraphic speech (i.e., abbreviated verbal responses containing only the main words). The longest verbal utterance reported by that examiner was five words containing two thoughts: "Christmas tree, then buy flowers."

C3's record did not contain information regarding the specific ages at which he achieved important developmental milestones. The record does note, however, that "the first fourteen months of [his] life were normal." Such a developmental pattern is more consistent with the diagnosis of autism than with that of mental retardation per se. Thus given this client's diagnosis of profound mental retardation, one would expect to find a delay in the development of the important milestones that demarcate functioning level. That pattern is certainly true for both C1 and C2 even though their levels of retardation are, by report and by observation, less severe than that attributed to C3. A possible explanation for this and one that would be consistent with both C3's developmental history and his current level of functioning is that the severity of his autism is far greater than that of either C1 or C2 and could account for his more significant impairment in adaptive behavior. It could also contribute significantly to his ability to take in, process, and interpret information from his environment in order to respond appropriately. C3's lack of verbal language, his use of primitive and idiosyncratic gestures, and his reported and observed difficulty in two-way, reciprocal social interaction support this conclusion.

According to diagnostic reports in this client's record, severe deficits were found in both receptive and expressive language behavior. In addition, his functioning in the domains of play and socialization were reportedly at a "sub-domain [level of] zero years" and a few months. A December 1985 description of this client summarized his level of functioning across socio-communicative domains:

Little interaction with others is demonstrated, rarely establishes eye contact, but he will do so if he wants something. Sometimes seems to distinguish individuals who are familiar from those he does not know. Does not demonstrate an interest in his peers, and does not show desire to please caregivers. Will sometimes participate in a group situation (i.e., playing catch) but he will not self-initiate this type of activity. Rarely self-initiates the use of manual communication.

Reported Functioning and Intellectual Level

As noted, each of the clients in this study was reportedly functioning on a level of mental retardation (MR), and the degree of retardation varied considerably among them. Classification of MR status for each client was conferred as a result of psychological testing. Overall consistency in functioning levels for each client was seen across evaluations over time. In addition, general concordance was seen between test results on demonstrated skills and on the functioning-level designations (i.e., mild, moderate, or profound).

C1's designation of mild (or mild to moderate) retardation was consistent with various examiners' descriptions of her. One of these noted, "On both the verbal and performance scales, [C1] was not able to complete tasks which involved the analysis and manipulation of abstract and/or symbolic materials. [Her] adaptive behavior is consistent with the overall measure of her learning ability." In addition, verbal and performance scores were very similar, indicating that "in terms of a global measure, verbal and nonverbal areas of functioning are similarly developed."

The following description of strengths and weaknesses is also in C1's record:

> In the area of social skills, [C1] is able to initiate and respond to greetings, she establishes eye contact and smiles, but is unable to maintain eye contact or to maintain an appropriate social distance. [C1] responds to a statement and uses appropriate expressions, social amenities, and gestures to convey meaning. She does not listen during a conversation without interruption, her speech is not always clear, or at an acceptable rate or volume. [C1] *is able to read and write her name* [italics added]. She can indicate her full name, but is not able to specify her address, home phone number, or the name and address of significant others. In terms of functional academics, [C1] is able to recognize numerals from one to ten, but is not able to count. *She reads and writes simple phrases* [italics added].

This description was written in 1987. Thus C1 was reportedly capable of some degree of reading and writing activity (i.e., literacy skills) prior to the initiation of facilitated communication in early 1991. Further, it appears that she was able to write independently; there is no reference made to facilitation of any type. C1's prefacilitation literacy skills would take on greater significance as the study progressed.

Since C1 is judged to be at the low end of the mild range, the degree of difference between the functioning levels of the two clients may not be as disparate as the labels mild and moderate suggest. A review of C2's record revealed some noteworthy inconsistencies with respect to speech and language and social functioning. According to a December 1989 assessment, "His use and understanding of speech and language skills were at the young three-year level." This description is basically consistent with an evaluation two years earlier that specified an age equivalence of three years, six months, for receptive language using the Peabody Picture Vocabulary Test—Revised. This evaluation included the following with respect to his performance on a verbal-reasoning subtest:

> [C2] was able to name all but one of the fourteen picture vocabulary items. In response to verbal items, [C2] provided some associations, (i.e., he responded penny when asked to define the word dollar); but was not able to earn credit for accurate descriptions or definitions of the words. [C2] frequently repeated the stimulus words in an echolalic fashion. On the comprehension sub-test, [C2] correctly identified various parts of the body by pointing to a picture of a child. He was able to respond correctly to some items which involve the practical use of information (i.e., what do people do when they are hungry?).

The foregoing responses would seem to be consistent with what might be expected given earlier test results.

C2's professional parent (i.e., professionally trained foster parent) appeared to significantly overestimate speech and language ability if one compares her description to the previously noted test results. Based on information provided by the professional parent for the Vineland Adaptive Behavior Scale, the following was reported: "Within the communication domain, [C2's] performance level for receptive language is adequate. He functions at a low level for expressive and written communication." Adding to the confusion, there is a notation at the end of these descriptions: "When compared with a group of mentally retarded adults who reside in a community setting, [C2's] overall adaptive behavior is average and at the thirtieth percentile." Based on this note, C2's placement "within community and day treatment settings" was considered appropriate to his needs.

This client's record contains additional inconsistencies between the reported summary of his skills and the depiction of him by his professional parent. The following excerpts of September 1991 stand in proximity (and in stark contrast) to each other in his record:

> Skill summary: Was not indicating address; name; phone number; name or address of significant other. Did not recognize functional words (except with help). Did not understand numerical relativity. Does not do at all well with identifying coins or knowing the value of coins. Does not recognize months or associate times with specific routine activities or tell time on hour; half hour; quarter hour; or at five-minute points.
>
> Comment by professional parent: [C2] is much more intelligent than he appears by first impression. He seems to have good reasoning skills and a very good "grasp" of what's going on in his immediate environment.

With respect to C3, as noted earlier, completion of a psychological evaluation in December 1988 after two unsuccessful attempts revealed the presence of profound mental retardation. C3's scores on the Vineland Adaptive Behavior Scale for the communication, daily living skills, and socialization domains were all in the range of "profound deficit," as was his overall functioning. At that time, evaluators were not able to obtain responses on the Peabody Picture Vocabulary Test—Revised.

In summarizing the results of the psychological evaluation, the examiner made the following observation: "In comparison with supplementary reference groups, [C3's] functioning is average in terms of a residential, (i.e., institutionalized population) and below average for a nonresidential adult mentally retarded group." Unlike the other two clients in this study who resided in professional parenting homes, C3 resided in an intermediate care facility for persons with mental retardation (ICF-MR), a placement that is typically reserved for less able individuals. His record indicates that although a professional parenting home was considered a goal, the "placement in the ICF-MR is considered appropriate to his needs." This placement notation was consistent with this client's relatively greater degree of impairment. It was also consistent with his reported overall functioning level.

In summary, each of these clients was functioning in the range of mental retardation according to psychological testing, anecdotal record, and demonstrated skill development across several areas. Significant differences may nonetheless be found among clients in the specific degree of intellectual impairment, the overall ability level, and the extent of behavioral disturbance. There is, however, a good deal of internal consistency within each client concerning these three factors. Specifically, each client's record revealed the following pattern: the higher the degree of reported intelligence, the higher the degree of demonstrated skill development and the lower the incidence of maladaptive behavior. Conversely, the lower the degree of reported intelligence, the lower the degree of demonstrated skill development and the higher the incidence of maladaptive behavior. Such a pattern both can be reasonably expected and was consistent with my own observations over time. Thus when viewed according to this yardstick, C1 would be placed at the high end of the scale, C3 at the low end, and C2 somewhere between the two. But this pattern stands in stark contrast to the facilitators' perceptions of their clients—as notably more intelligent than indicated by either their records or their demonstrated skill levels across a variety of areas.

Educational and Environmental History

The educational backgrounds and environmental milieus of the three clients in this study reveal important similarities as well as notable differences. I saw the same pattern of internal consistency noted previously with respect to educational and environmental variables. Specifically, the more capable the client, the more generally "hospitable" was his or her background. Current knowledge as well as conventional wisdom certainly lends support to this observation.

C1's early placement in a day care center would have afforded her exposure to typical children from an early age, a practice that today is highly recommended by many professionals for children with autism. Subsequent to this placement, for three years C1 spent her weeks living with a family while her mother worked. She went home on weekends, however. This arrangement was a stable one for C1. The record notes that C1's mother "felt that the [family's name] had special concern for [her daughter] and that the large family environment was beneficial." This notation not only speaks to the perceived quality of this arrangement by the mother but also underscores her commitment to providing her daughter with what was, in her opinion, a wholesome environment.

C1's initial placement in a special education class was short lived. Her record indicates that she entered residential treatment at a state hospital at approximately eight years of age and remained there until she moved to another residential facility at age seventeen. Programming at the state hospital was described as follows: "Services were provided to address skill acquisition for areas of daily living, pre-academics, prevocational training, and self-care." Placement in the new residential facility at age seventeen afforded C1 the opportunity to attend a high school special needs program at which "programming was instituted to address community, self care, and leisure time skills." An oblique reference in C1's record indicates that prior to attending this program, she participated "in a self-contained, special education classroom for autistic youngsters" at another school. Despite placement in residential facilities, it appears from C1's record that she continued to have an ongoing relationship with her mother.

Placement in residential facilities ended in 1983 when C1 was placed with a professional foster care family in a rural area. This setting ostensibly offered her a more family-oriented and less institutional living arrangement. She moved from that professional parenting family to another after approximately six years so that she would have "a more urban location where she would have access to more community services and activities and would have the opportunity to increase her independence in the use of the services."

Undoubtedly the greatest difference between C1's background and those of the other two clients in this study is the richness of her pre-FC environment. The following description of this client, taken from the residential narrative completed in January 1992, testifies not only to the number and variety of opportunities that were available to her but to her broad-based competence in being able to take advantage of them.

In her leisure time, [C1] enjoys downhill skiing, which she does regularly with her mother. . . . She is an avid swimmer and is a member at [name] Health and Fitness Club where she swims laps for a half mile. . . . She is very skilled at putting puzzles together. She works with sewing cards, and for Christmas she received a touch tone computer from her mother which she also enjoys using. She likes to look through or read magazines and especially loves music and dancing. [C1] goes out to restaurants with her family, with her mother, with her co-workers, and with her friends.

Other references to such activities as horseback riding and bike riding as well as to attendance at recreational classes for special needs adults give one an appreciation of the relative richness of this client's environment. They also speak to the type of care available to her from both her natural mother and her foster care family.

In contrast to C1, C2's early environment was socially impoverished. The record states that his mother "appears to be a dull individual and overwhelmed by the care of her retarded child." It further states, "She has a reputation for being promiscuous and has lived with several different men." A notation in C2's record reveals that he "was cared for by the maternal grandmother until May of 1968 when the mother took over his care. Previous to this the mother had worked, but in May of 1968 became concerned that the grandmother was not giving proper care." Support for this belief was found in C2's record: "There is also some indication that due to [C2's] retardation and mal-behavior, that the grandmother could not handle him." The father "never supported or has shown any interest in [C2]." The summary of C2's family history notes, "All of the maternal relatives are of low socioeconomic level and of poor reputation, and have been all supported by the state."

On a recommendation from the Department of Social Welfare and based on a diagnosis of infantile autism, C2 was admitted to a state residential training school when he was six. Initial enrollment at the school was in a "preschool recreation and self-feeding program." After approximately two years at the residential facility, authorities investigated placement with his family (his mother had remarried) but did not recommend it because of perceived "problems of supervision, consistency, and stimulation" in the home. At one point, C2 was assigned a foster grandparent; however, he was "too difficult and was dropped after six months." A notation within C2's record of a May 27, 1975, visit to his home by a social worker lists the following problems: "speech, temper tantrums, self-care skills, the family's lack of training (education ability to provide stimulation)."

At the age of twelve C2 was admitted to an intermediate care facility for the mentally retarded (ICF-MR). His record notes, "He remained there for ten days and was subsequently re-admitted [to his former state training school] due to a variety of maladaptive behaviors within the ICF-MR, and the community." Over the years this client spent a good deal of time in a variety of intermediate care facilities as well as in special education classes either in the state hospital or in the public schools. These school programs varied with respect to classification. At times C2 attended programs specifically designated for "autistic youngsters"; at other times the program designation was "multi-handicapped." In all cases, his programs were housed within segregated, special education environments. This was true for the other two clients in this study as well.

Residential placement ended in 1982 when C2 was placed in a professional parenting home. He moved to another foster care home in 1985 prior to arriving at his current placement in 1989.

Information regarding C3's educational and environmental background was obtained from both his record and his natural father. Given that this client was, by report and by observation, the least able of the three clients in this study and given that many of his facilitator's attributions with respect to his abilities were in stark contrast to the data sources, I sought additional information concerning his early educational programming history and his environmental milieu. According to his record, C3 began attending a preschool program run by his area mental health service when he was four and one-half years of age. His parents were reportedly dissatisfied with that program and were consequently referred to the state hospital for services. According to his father, C3 lived at home until the age of eight and was then placed at the state hospital, where he received services for the next "six or seven years." These services were described in his record as addressing "the acquisition of self-care skills." It was also reported that "gains were noted." C3's father described this program as a special education program with *"no exposure to academic information"* (italics added). C3's record notes that after discharge from that residential facility, "his parents assumed the role of primary caregiver." Respite services were reportedly provided for them through the local mental health service, which may indicate a level of severity with respect to this client's overall functioning.

In 1979 C3 entered a special education program through the public schools. His record notes that "school history also includes the provision of in-home instruction." In-home programming is often recommended in cases of severe behavioral disturbance or when intensive programming is felt to be necessary. His record reveals progress, but he "regressed quickly when program schedules were disrupted for any length of time." This pattern of regression and lack of generalization and maintenance of skills is associated with autism. Records documenting this period indicate that C3 was taking Mellaril, a "heavy duty" neuroleptic drug often given to control behavioral excesses. At age seventeen C3 was placed in an ICF-MR "on an emergency basis." This client was eventually transferred to his present intermediate care facility in 1984 "so that he could reside with clients of similar age level, and because of the availability of more appropriate behavioral models." At the time of this study he was "attending day programming" on a regular basis.

During my pursuit of information regarding C3's educational background, his father independently volunteered,

> I remain quite skeptical about facilitated communication, and there are a couple of reasons. There may be something going on, but it would have to be like a savant. I am convinced that he [C3] has a great deal of receptive language, but I haven't seen anything that would personally convince me [of his son's ability to use FC]. There's a caution here, *my biggest fear is that an injustice could be done to him in the name of facilitated communication. For example, "he told me he wants this."* That's my biggest fear [italics added]. Caregivers have to render good judgment and humanity.

I copied the preceding statement verbatim and read it back to C3's father to ensure accuracy.

In summary, each of these clients had spent several years in segregated facilities for both educational and residential purposes, but there were notable differences in their backgrounds. Even within the state hospital school it appears that C1's program, though aimed at the development of functional skills, afforded her some exposure to preacademic information unavailable to the other two clients. Their programs were more exclusively geared to the development of self-care activities and the like. These differences seem to be a reflection of functioning level and the degree to which interfering behaviors may have impacted learning ability. Environmentally, there is no question—given the reported social deprivation and maladaptive behaviors reported for C2 and the apparent overall severity of impairment and behavioral excesses noted for C3—that C1 had the benefit of many more enriching opportunities than were available to the other two clients in this study.

Intervention History

> Autism, by definition, includes behavioral symptomatology related to:
> (1) Disturbances in the rate of appearance of physical, social, and language skills
> (2) Abnormal responses to sensations
> (3) Speech and language are absent or delayed, while specific thinking capabilities may be present
> (4) Abnormal ways of relating to people, objects, and events (Definition of autism 1994)

Given the number of areas of functioning that may be affected in autism, I sought information regarding the types of intervention procedures to which each of these clients had been exposed. I was particularly interested in information regarding referrals to occupational or physical therapists for evaluation of the sensory system. I also sought information related to referrals to speech-language pathologists for evaluation of language and communication needs.

A great deal of commonality was seen among clients with respect to intervention history. In short, none of the clients, according to their records or to information derived from their facilitators (and C3's father), had been evaluated for their overall sensory needs. Indeed, there seemed to be a lack of recognition that some of their so-called aberrant behaviors may have been related to their abnormal responses to sensation. For example, C2's pica behavior may have reflected the need for increased sensation to the mouth and/or hyposensitivity to taste or texture, just as C1's rocking behavior may have indicated the desire for increased vestibular input (i.e., stimulation of the balance centers in the inner ear) (Ayers 1979). Similarly, many of the behaviors attributed to C3 by his facilitator, and those I observed myself, may have reflected a variety of sensory needs. These behaviors included "tight hugging," smelling hair, bolting, and hopping. I also observed C3 run from one wall to another, literally thrusting himself against the walls at a velocity high enough to cause discomfort to a person with a normal pain threshold. Consequently, one would have to speculate not only on the nature of this client's response to pain but also on the possible sensory need this behavior may have satisfied. Many of the behaviors described and observed in this client are the same behaviors that have been found to be associated with abnormal response to pain and the need for proprioceptive input (i.e., stimulation vis-à-vis the muscles and joints) (Ayers 1979).

In C3's case, one specific, isolated sensory area did receive attention. His facilitator reported that in the recent past, he had received auditory integration training (AIT) for his alleged hearing sensitivities. AIT made its debut on the autism scene at approximately the same time as FC. Although the bravado surrounding this technique was far more subdued than the evangelistic fervor accompanying facilitated communication, AIT did nevertheless have its day in the spotlight. Touted as a miracle on the television news magazine and talk show circuit, auditory integration training certainly caught the attention of the American public. The pursuit of this sensory treatment technique for C3 in the absence of specific knowledge regarding many other aspects of sensation may indicate a predilection on the part of FC enthusiasts to "sort" for the spectacular—that is, to support techniques (like FC itself) that promise the hope of transformation. Regardless of the particular reason for seeking out this type of intervention, AIT was the only treatment technique devoted to problems with sensation that was tried.

In contrast to the lack of evaluative data regarding sensation, all of the clients in this study had had speech and language evaluations throughout their lives. Remarkably, however, prior to facilitated communication none of them appear to have had the benefit of any type of assistive technology or augmentative system for the purpose of supplementing speech or serving as an alternative communication mode. This void was particularly dramatic in the case of C3 because he was nonverbal. Moreover, with the exception of FC messages attributed to him, this client did not possess a reliable, consistent means of conventional communication. Rather, communication was at a primitive, idiosyncratic level. Further, this client would often use aberrant behavior to express his needs. In addition, even with facilitated communication, C3 did not have an alphabet board available except when it was presented to him by an adult caregiver. I asked his facilitator, F3, "Now has anybody thought about having available this alphabet board so that he could just walk over and like lead you to it?" She responded, "Well, I think part of the problem is where he lives. I don't think they use it very often. Yes, I think we keep saying that and then we never do it as far as like putting boards everywhere." One would have to question the functionality and effectiveness of a communication system that is available to a client *only* when some other person deems it to be the appropriate time and place for him to speak!

Medical and Clinical History

I was particularly interested in obtaining information related to the clients' neurological functioning given the numerous references to movement disturbances found in both the FC literature (Atwood 1993; Biklen 1993; Donnellan and Leary 1995; Haskew and Donnellan 1992; Hill and Leary 1993) and the interviews with facilitators. There was nothing in the records of C1 or C3 that would lead one to suspect motor deficits of the type attributed to FC users both in the literature and in the interviews, including references to a lack of motor control, radial ulnar instability, or apraxia. In fact, C1's record contains the following statement, "[C1] has no physical limitations, nor does she require any special accommodations." The list of activities in which C1 participates (i.e., skiing, puzzles, etc.), noted elsewhere in her report, appear to corroborate this assertion given that such activities would seem to require adequate motor planning ability and an adequate degree of fine and gross motor coordination. There is even a reference in C3's record that contradicts attributions of motor control problems in FC users. The record states, "[This client demonstrates] ability to coordinate simultaneous movements of both hands; that is bi-manual coordination." The following example was used to support this statement: "[C3] can catch a ball when playing catch. *Using verbal cues* [italics added] he is capable of bi-manual coordination." C3's ability to execute movement patterns on command argues against a motor planning problem (i.e., apraxia or dyspraxia).

Only in C2's record did I find clear-cut evidence of significant motor difficulty, which was also evident when I observed him. A 1975 evaluation for the purpose of determining whether there was a neurological basis for his "persistent abnormal behaviors (i.e., hand wringing, frequent temper tantrums, hair pulling, head banging, and speech impediment)" revealed the following: "Finger dexterity was limited but he had an adequate pincer grasp. He had difficulty with balance when he walked (i.e., shuffling gait); difficult time walking on his heels. Bending over to pick up something was difficult because his body was somewhat rigid."

A 1990 neurological consultation underscored the lack of diagnostic certitude regarding the exact nature of C2's motor involvement:

> Impression: His veering tendency when walking probably is the same problem noted when he was four as "a cerebellar problem," representing a bit of gait ataxia. Because of difficulty doing a careful examination in this patient, it is hard to demonstrate that this abnormality is cerebellar, as opposed for example to vestibular, so it's hard to make a really clear diagnosis.

Moreover, unusual physical findings listed by the neurologist seem to have implications for this client's use of facilitated communication. These included "shortened digits, [and] finger clubbing."

In summary, regardless of the cause of this client's motor deficits, they were apparent in his difficulty with oral-motor control and with fine and gross motor functioning. Further, the degree and extent of his long-standing motor problems clearly mitigate against the feasibility of independent typing in the future.

Commitment to Facilitated Communication

The category label Commitment to Facilitated Communication applies equally well to both the interview segment of this study and to the review of client records. It also epitomizes the FC phenomenon and reveals its preeminent place not only in the lives of these clients but also in the minds of their facilitators. I found commonality both in the esteem in which FC was held by facilitators, as revealed during the interviews, and in the prominent notations of FC success documented in clients' records. This was particularly apparent with respect to important decisions governing their lives. Furthermore, I found the same tendency to ignore possible contraventions to FC in clients' records that I had found in facilitators' responses during the interviews. For example, testimonials extolling the remarkable progress made by clients through facilitated communication often stood in stark contrast to other record notations that clearly repudiated them. In addition, there was no sign that such discordance was even acknowledged, as there were no accompanying commentaries aimed at accounting for the apparent inconsistencies.

I found the least amount of discordance in C1's record with respect to information reportedly derived from FC output and her day-to-day functioning. For example, the following reference in C1's client record seems to be consistent with information about her life prior to facilitated communication: "One notable happening that has come out of this facilitated communication is a burgeoning social life." The concordance I found between information in the record and C1's use of FC was further corroborated by her verbal responses to an interview by her professional parent in January 1992. The type and quality of these responses were also remarkably similar to those I observed during FC sessions.

> When asked what she liked about her home, she said, "like my room, pretty room, music, doing puzzles, eating snacks, Mark, Mary, Jenny."[1] When asked if there was anything she would like to change, she said, "go out for ride." When asked if she liked living with a little child, she said "yes." I asked her where she thought she might live when she got older; she said, "the hospital." I said, "Would you want to live more independently someday?" and she said, "Yes." When asked, "What do you want to learn?" she answered, "Go out for dinner." I said, "You want to go out for dinner more? What does that teach you?" She answered, "To be quiet." "Would you like to do more facilitated communication together with me?" She answered, "Yes. I do. Yes."

I found two main areas of inconsistency in this client's record that I felt had significant implications for the attributions made regarding her performance with facilitated communication. The first concerned the discordance between the specification of C1's literacy skills documented in her record and the level of literacy skill development attributed to her by her facilitator. A report apparently written in early 1986, prior to the introduction of FC, notes, "Although her enthusiasm coupled with her skills and imitated/approximated types of behavior indicate mastery of many tasks or programs, closer inspection shows that [C1] lacks the capability in many cases to complete a job which requires a degree of sophistication." Later in this report she was described as having "poor language skills" and as requiring the services of a speech-language pathologist to help her carry "her communications beyond a purely superficial level." A behavior checklist completed at the same time noted, "[C1] does not always articulate well. She is unable to describe situations and events well. She speaks in phrases, and not in sentences. She can imitate new words and ask appropriate questions." The same behavior checklist described her reading and writing skills:

---

[1]These names refer to the client's professional parents and their child and have been changed for confidentiality.

[C1] is able to follow picture cues. She recognizes safety and functional words. She cannot read books or information on packages. She cannot break words down phonetically. Writing skills—[C1] is able to spell her name. She can copy and trace letters. She is able to print simple messages. She cannot use a dictionary for spelling, and is unable to write letters. [The word *write* may refer to cursive writing.]

The second main area of discordance I found concerned a report, written somewhere between 1985 and 1986, that "recommended that protective supervision be provided in all areas of the Protective Service Act." Several matters were delineated as being beyond this client's understanding. One of these concerned medical and surgical procedures, the specific area for which protective supervision was sought: "I do not believe she has sufficient insight to make informed decisions about medical/surgical care. She responded that she would 'hide' if a doctor suggested surgery." Authorities granted protective supervision, and a surgeon subsequently performed an operation with the consent of her guardian. No one, either in this client's record or within the context of the interview with her facilitator, made any attempt to reconcile differences between perceived ability as a result of FC and contradictory references to her lack of competence contained within her record.

I found even greater discordance in C2's record with respect to his reported level of functioning prior to FC and his perceived level of ability as a result of his experience with FC. A September 4, 1991, interview with this client via facilitated communication served not only to illustrate the degree to which FC had changed the way in which his caregivers viewed him but also to underscore the importance of perceiving him as competent, a basic tenet of the facilitated communication movement (Biklen 1993; Crossley 1994; Haskew and Donnellan 1992). His record notes, "It's hard to put into words the great change FC has had in [C2's] life. His possibilities for future growth in this area cannot be realistically stated because it has no limits." The record describes this client's ability to express his wants and needs: "He does much better expressing himself through FC than doing it verbally. You can't always trust what he says verbally, unless it pertains to food." The final notation from this interview reveals a prevalent theme in the FC culture, "I told [C2] that now that we knew he wasn't retarded, that he was a smart person, and that we now knew he could read, was there anything else that he would like to learn or something we could help him with? 'More,' [he replied]. I said, 'Do you mean more of everything?' 'Yes!'"

The following excerpts from C2's record not only clearly delineate his remarkably rapid progress with facilitated communication but also illustrate FC's preeminent place in important decisionmaking governing this client's life:

September 1991:

As trust and friendship with facilitators has grown, [C2] has moved to a new level of communication. He is typing about feelings, wants, desires and has demonstrated his great sense of humor! He has also identified ways for people to help him from aggressing toward himself. These approaches have been adopted by staff as they are less restrictive than the behavioral plan currently approved.

October 1991:

[C2] continues to "open up" about feelings and concerns. He has asked to learn more about sex and [staff member's name] has been educating him on this through readings and discussions about sexual matters. His feelings about people in his life are being explored. [C2] has asked that his behavior management program be revised to include what he feels he needs from others when he becomes aggressive (hold his hands, talk to him, walk with him, and type with him after he has calmed down).

November 1991:

During the month of November, [C2] participated in the development of a new behavior program to be implemented in the event of his becoming self-aggressive. Once his needs for treatment were identified through facilitated communication, they were presented to the [name of committee]. [C2] participated in the meeting with facilitation and communicated his desire to have the procedures outlined be approved by the committee, which they were.

The November 1991 progress note also included the following reference to proper technique in FC: "Facilitators have emphasized spacing between words in a sentence with [C2] to make his typing clearer. Also introduced the delete button for [C2] to correct spelling and change words. He is grasping these concepts and will frequently space between words independently, but must be prompted to correct words."

Judging from his FC transcripts of this period, the progress that C2 made in terms of spacing and spelling is nothing short of extraordinary, albeit inexplicable. For example, the FC transcripts from November 5 and 6 contain no spaces between words and numerous spelling and typing errors. In contrast, the very next transcript given to me—a four-page transcript from November 12 (a mere six days later!)—demonstrates appropriate spacing between virtually all of the words. In addition, spelling and legibility are both vastly improved. Given C2's impoverished, institutional background and his significant motor compromises, one is hard pressed to understand how he was able to accomplish such rapid learning and such a skilled performance. Such accomplishments would be impressive even in people without impoverished backgrounds or motor problems.

December 1991: "In December [C2's] typing skills have continued to improve. His sentence structure is becoming more complete, and he is *independently* [italics added] initiating the use of the space bar as well as the delete key to correct misspellings."

The following entry for the same month seems to contradict the reference to C2's being able to "independently" access both the space bar and the delete key: "Arm support continues to be at the wrist level. [C2] has experienced some difficulty with index finger isolation this month, and support has been dropped to the hand level on occasion to increase his proficiency when this occurs." In contrast to the previous month, this entry indicates a highly intrusive level of support during facilitated communication.

January 1992: "[C2] expressed his desire to have facilitation become a more integral part of his daily life. We discussed how this can happen and [C2] suggested that we have a meeting with people that played a big part in his life." Further on in this particular excerpt C2 reportedly stated, through facilitation, that he would like to have speech therapy. An evaluation by a speech-language pathologist took place subsequent to this request.

February 1992: "[C2] continues to express himself about many aspects of his life through facilitation. In February he was interviewed by a reporter from [a national magazine], both with another individual and individually. During these interviews he stated his thoughts on facilitation and his views on his years of living in institutions." There is an interesting reference later on in the progress note to C2's earlier input with respect to his behavior program:

> We have been exploring [C2's] thoughts on his current behavior program, which he designed for himself in November. It appears that this program is not always successful and may be in need of review. [C2's] thoughts on what approach to use when he is upset appear to vary, which is understandable, as most of us can't predict in advance what will work to calm us when we are upset. We will continue to discuss this with [C2] and note the cause of aggressive behavior toward himself.

The February 1992 entry is significant from several standpoints. For one thing, this entry clearly indicates that [C2] continued to manifest self-injurious behavior in spite of his alleged suggestions regarding ways to address it. It also illustrates the disparity between his overt behavior (i.e., aggression toward self) and his sophisticated typing skills. The latter is particularly puzzling given C2's reported ability to "open up about his feelings and concerns." Here again one sees the familiar disparity between overt behavior and the level of sophistication in typing reported in FC. Again we see the tendency to decide all matters of incongruity in favor of facilitated communication and no speculation on disparities.

A more cogent illustration of this overriding commitment to facilitated communication, even in the face of conflicting information, is seen in the following excerpt:

> We spent time on helping [C2] to provide truthful answers to the questions asked on the discussion at hand. [C2] often types about things that he would like to have happen rather than what really took place. Through discussion and example we went about explaining the importance of both truth and dreams/wishes. (Example, this is what I really did, but I would have liked to have done this instead.) This provides us not only with *validation* [italics added] but ideas on what [C2's] hopes and dreams are to assist him in realizing some of his wishes.

Clearly, even erroneous responses are used to justify the validity (and hence the sanctity) of facilitated communication. The previous excerpts from C2's record stand in stark contrast to other notations in his record that underscore his similarity to adults with mental retardation. And as noted previously, the disparities stand unchallenged.

I found the most glaring discrepancies between C3's reported (and apparent) level of functioning and his reported level of success with facilitated communication. The residential narrative of September 1991 notes, "The depth and intensity of [C3's] feelings have startled all of us." This comment also illustrates the predominance of FC in the minds of caregivers, since it demonstrates their unconditional faith in the veracity of the facilitated messages even in the face of contravening information in the client's record. Further, commitment to the practice of using this technique to involve this client in decisions affecting his life is clearly seen in the following comment in the same summary: "Our perception and understanding of [C3] have been greatly enhanced by this program [FC]. His ability to communicate in a written format will make him an active participant in program development." The day program narrative completed by his facilitator at the same time as the residential narrative states,

> Antecedents to [C3's] maladaptive behaviors based on my experience with him, are his allergies acting up; being around other people, especially other clients; his father not visiting him on days when he is expected; feeling ignored; being excluded from conversations, especially when conversations are about him; being asked to stop doing something that he doesn't want to stop doing; and being stared at when he is out in the community.

This narrative contains a blend of comments that not only represent statements attributed to C3 by his facilitator but also embody the genre of thoughts and opinions that F3 expressed during the interviews. Later in this same narrative F3 delineated C3's strengths: "He can spell simple words and sentences, capable of following simple verbal and gestural cues, reasoning ability, adaptability, perceptiveness, highly energetic, affectionate, good sense of humor, strong relationship with his father, excellent dining habits when in the community." This description stands in stark contrast to the September 1991 assessment of this client's skills:

> 1) In the personal management section he scored 7.6% overall. This score is identical to the 9/90 assessment. 2) Social development: a score of 12%. This score shows a drop from the 9/90 assessment of 16%. 3) Household management score was 13%. Again, this is a drop from the previous score of 16%. 4) Academic skills show a slight improvement—3.4% current in 9/91, and 1.1% on the last evaluation in 9/90. *This increase in [C3's] score is directly due to his participation in the facilitated communication program* [italics added].

Given that every score but the last was either identical to the previous score or lower, the definitive statement attributing the less than 3 percent increase in academic skills to facilitated communication is yet another example of the indomitable faith the technique has instilled in the minds of those who support its use. It is also indicative of the extremes to which FC enthusiasts will go to confer upon the technique a status that is simply not borne out by either observation or the record.

The stark contrast between C3's perceived ability via facilitated communication and the descriptions of him in other records are no more apparent than in the following petition for guardianship filed with the court in 1986:

> He is a twenty-one-year-old man who is functioning within the profound range of mental retardation. [C3] does not comprehend the concepts of choosing a suitable residence or day habilitation program, entering into a contract, or money matters. He is unable to express when he is sick and cannot make knowledgeable judgments concerning medical matters. I therefore, recommend a total guardianship be appointed for [C3].

The record entry goes on to enumerate the specific areas over which the guardian should have control. Again, as for the other clients in this study, there was no attempt to reconcile the ability level attributed to C3 as a result of FC and the profound deficits across several areas of functioning reported in his record. Further, there was no attempt to bring his daily activities up to the level of his alleged newfound capabilities. Given the unsubstantiated attribution of credit to FC for patently obscure gains in C3's academic skills (concomitant with a complete disregard for the level of deficiency that both cited academic scores represent), it is eminently obvious in C3's case, as with the other clients in this study, that the commitment to facilitated communication evidenced by proponents represents a wholesale endorsement of the methodology and a blind faith acceptance of the veracity of facilitated messages even in the face of significant contradictory information. Once again one must question how objective judgments can be rendered in so subjective (symbiotic?) an atmosphere.

PART TWO

The Drama
Unfolds

If the essence of qualitative research may be reduced to its lowest common denominator, then surely it would be *immersion*—in this particular case, the act of embedding oneself in the FC culture in order to obtain an insider's view. Chesterton (as cited in Sacks 1995) spoke eloquently of the benefits of such an intersubjective approach at the same time that he poked fun at its more elite, empirically based "sister":

> Science is a grand thing when you can get it; in its real sense one of the grandest words in the world. But what do these men mean, nine times out of ten, when they use it nowadays? When they say detection is a science? When they say criminology is a science? They mean getting *outside* [italics added] a man and studying him as if he were a gigantic insect; in what they would call a dry impartial light; in what I should call a dead and dehumanized light. . . . I don't try to get outside the man. I try to get *inside* [italics added]. (p. xix)

In Part 2 of this book I attempt to get inside the phenomenon of facilitated communication by focusing on its essential elements: the client, the facilitator, and the message itself. Here, as in all human encounters, one finds that the whole of facilitated communication is indeed greater than the sum of its individual parts. First, a word about the approach to message analysis in this study.

The examination of facilitated messages could have proceeded along several different pathways. For example, I could have selected for scrutiny elements of form (e.g., grammar, syntax, length of utterance, etc.). Instead, I focused on pragmatic function (i.e., the intentions of the "speaker") and semantic content (i.e., the meaning elements of language). I selected these particular features of message generation because they have been at the heart of the FC controversy since the beginning, understandable given the well-recognized difficulty individuals with autism have with these aspects of language and communication. The appendix provides detailed information regarding the general protocol, including the specific coding categories, that I used for the pragmatic and content analysis of facilitated messages.

I do not intend the pragmatic analysis of facilitated messages in this study to serve as an in-depth, exhaustive account of all of the possible pragmatic elements that help to convey meaning but rather as a general overview of some of the more common pragmatic features. Although there are many perspectives from which the communicative intent of an utterance may be judged, I arbitrarily broke down utterances according to three pragmatic elements. First, I examined the utterance for specific utterance function (SUF), that is, with respect to the purpose for which it was intended (e.g., to make a request for a particular object or action or to gain attention), based on the work of Twachtman (1990). Second, I determined the most appropriate placement of the utterance in terms of its broad pragmatic category (BPC), that is, whether it was interactive, imaginative, and so on, based on the work of Halliday (1975). Finally, I looked at the use of linguistic devices (LD) (e.g., deixis, topic maintenance) based upon the work of Owens (1988). More detailed information concerning each of these parameters may also be found in the appendix.

Although the main focus of message analysis was on pragmatics, the content of facilitated messages was also examined with respect to three specific areas that often relate to the themes of these messages: the presence of abstract, relational concepts; philosophical content; and the expression of introspective thoughts.

Initially, I had intended to analyze only those messages generated during the sessions I actually observed. As the study progressed, however, it became apparent that I could gain a richer understanding of these clients' alleged semantic and pragmatic abilities by examining FC transcripts from the past. The addition of previously generated transcripts not only allowed comparison in terms of representativeness but also increased the number of message units available for analysis.

The selection of specific preexistent transcripts depended on a variety of factors: the number made available to me; identifying features in the transcripts that might breach confidentiality; and the need to probe highly specific areas related to the research questions. I also endeavored to integrate data across information sources in order to derive a cohesive picture of facilitated communication. All of these factors made message selection and analysis a complex and multidimensional process.

The disparity in the number of messages available for each client, combined with corresponding concerns regarding issues of confidentiality, presented naturally occurring limitations. Issues of confidentiality were most prevalent for the F2-C2 dyad, the team that had also generated by far the greatest number of transcripts. Thus removal of several transcripts for reasons of confidentiality brought this pool of messages in line with those for the other dyads in this study.

I also employed the "critical incident" technique in the selection of specific transcripts. This qualitative-research technique is used to ensure that information critical to the research questions is attended to (Miles and Huberman 1984). Its use in this study encouraged sensitivity to threads of commonality among the sources of data, generating a more cohesive, overall view of facilitated communication.

In addition, I asked three speech-language pathologists with specific expertise in autism to review the coded preexistent transcripts as a means of checking my own coding decisions regarding message analysis. I took their input into account with respect to the final coding decisions, thus further enhancing the study's trustworthiness with respect to message analysis. Further, I analyzed the transcripts of messages generated during the observed FC sessions in light of the relationship dimensions that emerged, as they represented the contexts for these sessions. My analysis also took into account my opinions and insights, recorded at the time of the original observations, as well as those stemming from the in-depth analyses of the videotaped records of the interactions across multiple viewings. As a check on my own judgments, I also solicited opinions from an additional speech-language pathologist with a great deal of experience in autism regarding those segments of videotaped footage selected for illustration. The specific nature of this input concerned impressions regarding the match or mismatch between verbal and nonverbal behavior; the emotional reaction of the client; and where ambiguous, the specific content of clients' verbal behavior. A portion of the analysis related to this segment of the study includes overt interactions between myself and each of two clients, C1 and C2. Finally, I asked all of the facilitators whether the observed sessions were, in their opinions, representative of their typical FC sessions with their clients. Each of them responded affirmatively to this question. One of them, F1, even planned to use segments of some of the footage obtained during this study as illustrations of positive practices in facilitated communication.

Finally, a word of caution is in order. The exploration of communicative intents (i.e., the pragmatic elements) is a complex, multidimensional process that ordinarily involves looking at the variety of behavioral and paralinguistic features (facial expression, gesture, body language, etc.) that co-occur with vocal or verbal expression. Facilitated communication, however, specifically recommends *against* the use of *any* behavior other than the typed word for the purpose of conferring intentionality. Given this constraint and the fact that little information is available concerning the manner and surrounding circumstances (context) in which the various *preexistent* transcripts were generated, the pragmatic analyses of the latter should be viewed with caution. The pragmatic and content analyses, and the accompanying messages representing the preexistent transcripts, may be found in the appendix in Tables A.1–A.7. Further, despite the fact that some facilitated messages were generated and videotaped in my presence, these too were constrained by facilitators' adherence to FC proscriptions with respect to disregarding the behavioral and verbal/vocal contexts in which messages were generated. The pragmatic and content analyses, and the accompanying messages representing the sessions I observed, may be found in Tables A.8–A.11 of the appendix.

Despite the aforementioned caveats and limitations, the narrative descriptions of the dyadic interactions in Chapters 4, 5, and 6 provide a window on the contextual world in which the facilitated messages were imbedded. They also offer a glimpse of the many meaning-enhancing elements that are ignored in FC's artifactual adherence to considering as intentional only a small portion of the message (i.e., the actual words typed). In the interests of presenting information in a cohesive, lucid, and comprehensive manner, each of the three chapters is devoted to a different facilitator-client dyad. Chapter 7 provides additional information on the facilitated messages as well as a synthesis of the observations and judgments concerning the nature and dynamics of the relationship between client and facilitator.

4

At All Costs:
The Messages of F1-C1

We shape our tools, and thereafter our tools shape us.
                                        —Marshall McLuhan

I observed the F1-C1 dyad on three occasions. The first observation session took place one year and eleven months after this pair began facilitating together. The second and third sessions took place approximately five and five and one-half months later, respectively. I felt the level of experience to be more than satisfactory for this facilitator-client team. I saw concordance across all three sessions with respect to the degree of manual support provided, the concomitance between C1's verbal and nonverbal behavior, the general level of competence in using FC, and the relationship dynamics underlying the interactions. Transcripts for this dyad may be found in the appendix. Tables A.8 and A.9 contain transcripts of the observed sessions; Tables A.1 and A.2 contain this dyad's preexistent FC transcripts. Portions of some of these transcripts are described here, particularly as they relate to important aspects of the FC experience.

What You See: Outside the FC Experience

Of the three clients in this study, C1 required the least intrusive manual support during facilitation. Generally, support was provided at the level of the mid- or upper forearm just below the elbow, although on some occasions support was at the shoulder. As will be discussed later, C1 could also type independently under certain circumstances. Unlike the other two clients in this study, C1 demonstrated clear-cut, albeit rudimentary, literacy skills by reading words, phrases, and short sentences aloud from the computer screen. Other manifestations of literacy awareness included appropriate reciprocal referencing of the screen and keyboard during typing as a means of monitoring output; ability to make appropriate, *independent* use of the delete key and space bar; and both the recognition of her own errors and the ability to type specific letters dictated by others. Even so, this client clearly evidenced specific problems in recognizing some consonants and vowels phonetically, selecting specific words to type, and spelling longer words. There were also instances in which her reactions to verbal input appeared to indicate the presence of some language comprehension or processing difficulty.

C1 demonstrated the most consistency overall with respect to her observed and reported functioning level and the degree of competence she exhibited during facilitated communication sessions. The verbal and nonverbal behavior, pragmatic communication ability, autistic symptomatology, and literacy skills I observed during the sessions were all absolutely consistent with reports written prior to FC that addressed these issues. They were also consistent with her reported educational and environmental background. Because the issue of consistency among such parameters is pivotal to an in-depth understanding of facilitated communication, I sought additional information regarding C1's literacy skills and environmental background from her natural mother, who confirmed judgments on the consistency between reported and observed functioning levels. In fact, in elaborating on her own observations of her daughter's literacy skills, she stated, "She [C1] likes to type by herself, *but she only types the same things she says*" (italics added). She went on to cite specific examples, all of which apparently correspond to actual people and events in her daughter's life. I noted during observation sessions that the content and sophistication of the messages C1 typed *independently* were indeed congruent with what would be expected given this client's diagnosis and history. I did not observe the disparity in the level of sophistication between verbal ability and typed messages that is often reported in facilitated communication. Nor was there a lack of concordance between verbal and nonverbal behavior. In fact, the match between C1's verbal and nonverbal behavior was remarkably consistent across all observed FC sessions. This is certainly consistent with the pragmatic communication literature, which holds that all behavior communicates (Watzlawick, Beavin, and Jackson 1967).

Impressive Concordance

From a pragmatics perspective, C1 was able to establish and maintain joint attention to a common referent, that is, to an item of interest to her and another person. She also demonstrated *verbal* use, albeit on a relatively basic level, of the following specific utterance functions (SUF): requesting, accessing, protesting, answering, commenting, questioning, greeting, and inform-

ing. Although she evidenced the ability to express a number of broad pragmatic categories (BPCs), the majority of her verbal utterances were classified as instrumental (i.e., intended for the purpose of satisfying needs), an
observation consistent with what is known about autism (Prizant and
Schuler 1987). C1 also demonstrated the ability to initiate interactions and
to maintain topics for several conversational turns. Even more impressive
from a social communication perspective was C1's burgeoning ability to
utilize persistent repair strategies (i.e., techniques to mend communicative
breakdown) and to make appropriate use of pauses and persistence strategies to get her verbal messages across.

Concomitant with C1's fundamental pragmatic ability was her *consistent*
use of appropriate, accompanying nonverbal behavior in the form of gestures and manual signs to support *both* verbal communication and typed
messages. In fact, with only a few noteworthy exceptions, C1's general demeanor (i.e., affect) and overt nonverbal behavior were entirely congruent
with the communicative intent of her verbal message. For example, in
word-association tasks, C1 would often give the manual sign as she both
said and later typed the word, demonstrating absolute congruence among
the parameters of typing, speaking, and nonverbal behavior. In one such instance, consistent with the lack of regard for both verbal and nonverbal behavior that was both observed among facilitators during FC sessions and
acknowledged by them in the interviews, F1's response to his client's
multidimensional communicative message was, "We're not signing now,
we're not talking, we're typing." This comment clearly illustrates both the
predilection that facilitators have for typing over *any* other form of communication and the lack of regard for other forms of communication when
they do occur. Even more significant, however, is the possibility that this
propensity for the typed message may cause facilitators to overlook or
misinterpret important communicative information that the client may be
trying to convey through other means. I will elaborate on the word-
association example further on because it illustrates several important aspects of facilitated communication while underscoring the relevancy of the
concerns regarding possible misinterpretation. The transcript for this session (dated 5/12/93) may be found in Table A.8 of the appendix.

What You Get: Inside the FC Experience

In one word-association task, F1 asked his client to give an association for
the word *work*. After both signing and saying the word, she went on to deliberately pantomime an action that looked as though she was pulling
something up from the floor (ground?). She then said, "grass," and although the audio portion of the videotape is somewhat unclear, it appears
that she went on to further refine the utterance to "pull grass." Given this

context, I construed the motion the client pantomimed as that of pulling weeds. Ignoring *both* his client's verbal and nonverbal behavior, F1 repeated the following directive twice: "I want you to type a word." At this point the client seemed somewhat frustrated, as judged from the fact that she started to rock back and forth. Next, with support at the level of the upper forearm just below the elbow, C1 typed a *y*. F1 immediately depressed the delete key and said, "Not yes or no."

There are many disturbing aspects about this interaction, not the least of which is the facilitator's complete disregard of what appeared to be on-task, appropriate, understandable, and *congruent* verbal and nonverbal communication on the part of his client. In addition, F1's demonstrated lack of regard for C1's verbal and accompanying nonverbal behavior appears to have caused this client some frustration. More disturbing, however, is the possibility that F1 may have totally misjudged his client's communicative intent with respect to what she had typed on the screen. That is, it is conceivable, given the verbal and nonverbal context, that C1 may have been trying to type *yard* and not *yes*, the word the facilitator obviously had in mind when *he, not she,* deleted the *y*. This possibility took on greater salience after a conversation with the client's natural mother. During the final phase of data analysis, I contacted her and asked about the nature of her daughter's work experience in order to determine whether there could have been some possible contextual relevance to C1's nonverbal behavior (i.e., what appeared to be the gestural equivalent of pulling weeds). In response to an open-ended question regarding the nature of her daughter's work experience, the mother indicated that her daughter had indeed performed yardwork for a local park as one segment of her vocational experience.

The interaction continued with C1 typing two letters from the bottom row of the keyboard. After typing the third letter she looked at the computer screen and said no in an agitated voice, at which point F1 deleted the letters and directed her to start over. After typing four letters, she looked up at the screen and again said no in an agitated voice. This time she *independently* hit the delete key to remove the letters. At one point F1 read aloud the letters she had typed, after which, *without consulting the client,* he deleted them. C1 reacted with even greater agitation, saying, "No, no" while shaking her head and covering her face with her hands. After F1 directed her to "think about it and type *i*," she typed a letter toward the bottom of the keyboard. Again, F1 deleted it. He said, "Try to relax. Whenever you don't think about what you're typing, you hit the *b* or the *n*. Almost every time today when you typed a word that didn't make any sense, you started with a *b* or an *n*." He went on to say, "I'm going to pull your hand back from that from now on, okay, unless *I think that's what you're really trying to go for*" (italics added). This clearly indicates that the facilitator made judgments about the selection of letters and words irrespective of input from the client. In addition, F1's liberal use of the delete key, concomitant with the specific content of his verbal remarks, seems to indicate that he had a specific word in mind for this association task. Also, during F1's reproval, the client seemed to be whimpering in a manner suggesting that she was sorry she had disappointed her facilitator.

This interaction continued with C1 typing *gol*. Verbally, she said, "Good job." It is conceivable, given both the verbal context and the physical proximity of the letters *l* and *o* on the keyboard, that C1 may have been trying to type the words *good job* as her association for the word *work*. Regardless of this possibility, she then went to the top right-hand side of the keyboard. She typed a letter, looked at her facilitator, and with her left hand again pantomimed a gesture that suggested upward movement. F1 ignored this gesture and said, "I don't think that's a word" and pressed the delete key. They tried again. This time she typed an *m* followed by an *o*. She moved toward a letter at the top right-hand side of the keyboard. Before she could type it F1 said, "You tried to type that before and then you think it's not what you wanted." Eventually she typed the word *money*, after which she pointed to the screen and said it aloud. Manual support during this entire interaction was at the upper forearm just below the elbow. Given the length of time that this dyad had been facilitating together and given the level of sophistication F1 had reported for his client during the interviews, the numerous inaccuracies and laboriousness of this simple word-association task was indeed surprising.

A Matter of Influence?

After the dyad completed this word-association task, F1 made several comments that were both revealing and quite disturbing from the perspective of possible unconscious facilitator influence. He said, "Let me explain to you what happened. You have a tendency to follow your *o*'s with *p*'s." He cited the following example: "You typed *mo* and then you had a tendency to type *p*." Obviously, that word would have been *mop*, a perfectly appropriate association for the word *work* and one that is also consistent with this client's work experience both as reported by her natural mother and as noted in her record. Interestingly, C1 responded to F1's explanation by saying no in an agitated voice. F1 responded to this by answering, "[C1] it's all right. You did fine."

This interaction illustrates an important, and somewhat obscure, point about possible facilitator influence. That is, many of the studies that have addressed the issue of authorship suggest that when facilitator influence can be shown, it seems to imply a lack of ability on the part of clients to generate their own messages. In the current situation, however, the client may well have generated her own message (i.e., *mop* as the word association for *work*). It is possible that the facilitator failed to recognize C1's word as a valid association because he was too focused on his own word. The fact that this type of influence is unconscious does not exonerate it but rather insulates it from acknowledgment and, hence, remediation. The important thing to keep in mind is that *influence related to facilitator mind-set, even if unconscious, has the power to violate the client's communicative intent and negate the message he or she desires to convey.*

The Seeds of Frustration

The match between C1's verbal and nonverbal behavior was remarkably consistent across the three observation sessions given that mismatches between the two behaviors have often been reported in facilitated communication (Biklen 1993). Indeed, there were several instances in which verbal and nonverbal behavior matched typing behavior as well. An example of this is C1 saying no while shaking her head and then typing *no*. As noted earlier, however, there were what appeared to be noteworthy exceptions to this verbal and nonverbal concordance. These occurred during times of stress and were quite puzzling from a contextual viewpoint. For example, there were several instances, across sessions, when C1 was obviously frustrated or agitated but would nonetheless say, "More please," ostensibly as a request to continue typing. The following description from the first observation session clearly illustrates this point. It is described in some detail, since it also covers issues related to the dimensions of relationship, communicative intent, language comprehension, and facilitator mind-set. (See Table A.9, transcript 12/9/92, in the appendix).

I had asked C1 what she liked best about facilitated communication, inadvertently pausing after the word *best*. Before I could finish the sentence, C1 verbally answered with a word that appeared to be either *eating* or *skiing*. Not picking up on the confusion immediately, I completed my question, saying, "about facilitated communication." I then attempted to clarify my intent by saying, "What do you really like about it?" C1 responded, "Go out." She then *independently* set out to type, at which point F1 took her arm at the mid-forearm level, a curious move given that the goal of FC is purported to be independence. She typed the word *going* and depressed the space bar. As she typed, with support as noted, she said, "Go out." She then deliberately referenced F1 and said a two-syllable word that sounded like *mountains*. She repeated it twice. Given that her original answer to the question may have been the word *skiing*, *mountains* (if that was in fact the word she said) would have been contextually appropriate; and skiing is an activity in which this client regularly participates. Articulatory problems made it difficult to make a definitive judgment, however, even given the contextual considerations and the input from a peer reviewer on the videotape analysis.

Also, C1 did appear to be looking to her facilitator for help and approval, perhaps for spelling and/or for help in generating the specific word. He responded by repeating the original question without a pause after the word *best*. C1 became agitated. F1 read the word *going* from the computer screen with a questioning tone in his voice. C1 verbally filled in with "home," an appropriate automatic fill-in response for the word *going*. She typed the word *out*, however. This word, too, was an appropriate automatic fill-in response. The words on the screen now mirrored what C1 had uttered verbally moments before. F1 said, "Going out for what?" The client verbalized a name that appeared to be either that of her house parent or a person who has also been mentioned in C1's record. According to C1's mother, both individuals have taken her out on several occasions. Consequently, both names would have been appropriate to the context of the client's verbal utterances. F1 responded, "[C1], right now we're talking about FC."

The Tension Mounts

The client became extremely agitated at this point and clasped her left hand over her mouth. It is possible that C1 was responding to the violation of her specific communicative intent or reacting to the realization that she had, once again, disappointed F1 by not performing as expected. By this time I had figured out that C1 had probably misunderstood the intent of my question. I informed the facilitator that my inadvertent hesitation after the word *best* may have caused C1 to interpret my question as, "What do you like best?" F1 responded by rephrasing the question: "What do you like best about typing?" He directed C1 to type a sentence. She typed, with support just below the elbow, *I like to*. She looked down and said, "Help me please." F1 replied, "Put a space in." She complied. She typed another few letters with the same degree of manual support. She stopped, looked at her facilitator, and again said, "Help me please." Since C1 was already receiving her customary level of manual support, I viewed this request as her attempt to obtain assistance with word selection, ostensibly to meet expectations. F1 read from the screen, "I like to say." She repeated the word *say* and seemed to balk at it.

As the interaction surrounding this question continued, the client began to evidence increasing signs of frustration. At one point she put her head down and said something that sounded very much like, "Don't know how to." According to my sense of events and the demeanor of the client, this would have been clearly appropriate to the situation. F1 said, "Go ahead. Go ahead." She continued to type additional letters, looked at the screen, and ran her index finger under the word. She said, "today"; however, F1, reading what was actually on the screen said, "I like to say nice thoughts." The moment she heard this her facial expression changed from neutral to

clear displeasure. She buried her head in her hands and said no in a very agitated manner, repeating it six times in rapid succession. F1 responded by
saying, "Let's try again." She would not type, however, until F1 deleted
what was on the screen. With manual support just above the mid-forearm,
C1 smiled and extended her index finger, obviously pleased that the word
on the screen had been removed. The first word she typed was *good*. F1
read, "I like to say nice good." The typing continued. She read, "I like to
say good now." She was calm, smiling as she read this. What was actually
on the screen was, *I like to say nice good lot now.* F1 seemed displeased
with what was on the screen, pausing with his hand on his chin before saying, "I'm a little confused." Upon hearing this C1 said no and put her
hands over her ears. It appeared that although the client had seemed to be
pleased with what she had typed or was happy that she had finished the
question to her satisfaction, she also seemed upset that she had, once again,
displeased F1. This impression that C1 was reacting to her facilitator's
mood was quite consistent across sessions whenever F1 evidenced displeasure toward either the client or the typed message.

F1 did some deleting and said, "How about we go back?" He typed out *I
like to say* with C1 referencing the screen as he did so. When he typed *I
like*, C1 calmly read this off the computer screen. As soon as he started typing *to say*, however, she became frustrated. She put her head in her hands
and said no, perhaps realizing the constraint the words *to say* placed on the
content of the message or perhaps protesting against words that she did not
intend to convey. Clearly, it was obvious from what had transpired that she
had wanted to type about the things that she liked best. I did not construe
her apparent disinterest in typing about facilitated communication as reflecting a negative attitude toward the topic. I felt that perhaps she may
have perceived the task as difficult. After all, naming things that one likes is
a far more concrete and hence easier task than rendering an opinion about
a technique. Whatever the reason, it is certainly possible, given the degree
of congruence noted previously and the overall consistency of her reactions,
that C1 was protesting against words, thoughts, and messages that were
not completely her own. The ability to do this not only was clearly within
her demonstrated level of competence but would also have been compatible
with both the consistency of her behavioral responses and her perseverance
over time. Unfortunately, according to the tenets of FC, unless such protestations are rendered through the medium of facilitated communication,
they are not considered valid!

From Stress to Despair

The next time F1 said, "What do you like to say?" C1 verbally responded,
"mother." With assistance at the forearm, she typed four letters and then

said no very agitatedly, covering her eyes. She depressed the delete key and went on typing. She was clearly having significant difficulty typing her message. She looked at F1 and repeated, "mother," after which she pointed to herself. She could have been referring to her mother or could have been informing him that that was what she wanted to type. In any event, I construed the gesture as adding force to her verbal utterance. C1 looked back at the screen and again said, "mother." F1 responded, "You type it out. I don't know what ... " (he did not finish his sentence). He then depressed the delete key because C1 seemed clearly at a loss as to what to type next. He said, "Let's start the word over. I like to say what?" She looked at me briefly and then turned her attention to F1, saying, "mother, mother." Her level of persistence, inflection pattern, repetition of the word, and general demeanor suggested exasperation with the lack of understanding (help?) available to her. F1 pointed to the screen and said, "The question was what do you like most about ..." Before he could finish the sentence C1 put her head down and kept saying no in a manner suggestive of despair. Ignoring this behavior completely, F1 matter-of-factly repeated, "That's the question. What do you like most about typing?" At this point, C1 put one hand over her eyes and wrapped her other arm over her ears. She mumbled something that sounded like, "I don't know" and became even more frustrated. With her right hand and arm over her right ear and her left hand covering her face, she said, "No. More please. More please. More please. More please" in rapid succession. She then bolted in frustration, went behind a room divider, and started to cry. She continued to say, "More please" in rapid succession. She also said, "Okay, okay, okay, no."

Although her level of agitation was eminently clear, its specific cause was less obvious. Her discomfort could have stemmed from frustration over F1's lack of response to her obvious communicative intent and/or his insistence that she answer the question as worded. It could also have been related to her genuine need for assistance with wording that placed a high degree of constraint on message generation. Further, given C1's apparent desire to please her facilitator, she could also have been upset over having disappointed him. Finally, C1's level of agitation may have reflected a combination of one or more of these factors. Regardless of its source, it is clear that if this client's verbal utterance was indeed "more please," it was patently incongruous with her extreme frustration and high level of anxiety. An additional scenario is even more plausible given the client's level of agitation. It is possible that C1 had intended to convey the message "*no* more please," but given her stress level, she may have gotten caught up in simply repeating the last two words of the utterance. This explanation would certainly be more in keeping with the contextual elements of the situation.

After a few moments F1 calmly said, "Whenever you're ready, [C1]. We have about five more minutes." She replied, "Yes" while still standing behind the screen. He repeated, "Whenever you're ready, [C1]." She said, "Ready now"; however, she made no move to come out from behind the screen. He said, "When you're ready just come over and sit down and we'll finish." She took a step or two forward, just barely coming out from behind the screen. She said, "Ready now." F1 replied, "All you have to do is come over and sit down and we'll get back to the typing." He said, "Let's go." She then came out from behind the screen very sheepishly with her head hung very low and her hands held limply at her sides. She was clearly dejected. She walked over to the computer in this fashion and sat down. As she was seating herself, she turned her head toward me, still holding it down, and definitively said, "Finished." I interpreted this as a clear, verbal request to stop typing. F1 completely ignored this and said, "I like to say, the question was." After he repeated the question a second time, he took her arm at the mid-forearm level. She put her index finger out, but she repeated the word *finished*. He responded by saying, "Can we finish that word?" She said yes. Then he said something that sounded like, ". . . and then we can finish, but let's finish this sentence." F1's ambiguous use of the word *finish* may have created some confusion for this client, since her use of the word *finished* was an obvious request to terminate the activity. Notwithstanding some whimpering, C1 kept her index finger extended. F1 repeated the question, "What do you like to say when you're typing?" C1 began to type with manual support at the mid-forearm level. The interaction continued. At one point she said, "Good, okay?" seeming to ask either for F1's permission to type the word or for his approval of her choice of words. At another point she put her head down and said, "Help me." The session continued for several more minutes even though there were other instances when the client expressed agitation and frustration. This included the manifestation of mild self-injurious behavior at the end of the session.

F1 did keep his commitment to C1, asking her if she wanted to finish after she completed the message for which he had originally directed her back to the computer. She said no. Even F1 appeared surprised by this response, as her entire demeanor suggested that she wanted to stop typing. I attributed her response to the ambiguity of the question. Specifically, F1 asked, "Do you want to finish now?" C1 could easily have construed such wording as an invitation to finish typing, especially since F1's use of the word a bit earlier was associated with *typing* as opposed to *finishing* (i.e., stopping). A less ambiguous question would have been, "Do you want to stop typing?"

Unexplained Discordance

Interpretation of language input seems to be an important consideration in determining this client's sense of communicative events, especially since she demonstrated a proclivity for literal interpretation on several occasions.

For example, C1's invariable response to questions such as, "Can you type my name?" or "Can you type the color of your nail polish?" was yes. Performance of the task would ensue only when such questions were followed by explicit directives to type. This may have been why C1 made no attempt to come out from behind the room divider when F1 said, "Whenever you're ready . . ." because he had not *explicitly* directed her to do so. This proclivity toward literalness is a well-recognized feature of autistic language symptomatology. It represents the person's failure to understand the speaker's actual communicative intent.

In addition to evidencing literalness, C1's use of verbal language was often idiosyncratic and reflective of autism. I observed her using reenactment strategies, ostensibly to try to bring about desired ends, that is, engaging in behavior that in the past had resulted in the outcome that she wanted (Schuler and Prizant 1987; Twachtman 1995). In C1's case she used this strategy when frustrated. For example, on one occasion C1 became so agitated over a particular typing sequence that she whipped around in her chair, looked pointedly at F1, and put her left hand up to her ear and said decisively, "Phone call." She paused and repeated the sequence two more times. F1 ignored her and said, "[C1] what are the next letters in this word?" She made a moaning sound but persisted with "Phone call, [F1]," uttered with some degree of agitation. It was obvious to me that C1 was reenacting a situation, both behaviorally and verbally, that in the past had terminated, or at least interrupted, facilitated communication sessions. Given the context of the situation, I construed it as an almost desperate attempt by C1 to bring about an end to a highly frustrating experience. Specifically, if she couldn't extricate herself from the situation, she would try to remove her facilitator!

Interestingly, this client also evidenced some difficulty with verbal perspective-taking that she did not demonstrate in her facilitated typing. "Help you?" and "Help you, please" are instances of verbal pronominal reversal that illustrate this phenomenon. In both instances C1 was asking for assistance regarding typing, substituting the pronoun *you* for *I* or *me*. Pronominal reversal is a well-recognized problem in autism, representing the failure to shift from a listener-appropriate pronoun (i.e., *you*) to a speaker-appropriate pronoun (i.e., *I* or *me*). I also observed C1 using pronouns correctly, but correct use appeared to occur in stock phrases such as, "Help me, please." Usually she either omitted the personal pronoun or referred to herself by name. Thus, it would appear that C1 has some difficulty with deixis (i.e., shifting referents), at least in her verbal behavior. But one needs to ask, If she has this difficulty in her verbal behavior, why does she not demonstrate it in her typing?

An additional aspect of her verbal behavior that was not reflected in her typing concerned the issue of syntax. C1 customarily spoke telegraphically (i.e., omitting the connecting words), for example, "Store please, store," "Store, store. Ride a please. Ride a truck." Sometimes her syntactical structure was clearly disordered. On one occasion she said, "Feeling better [C1] is." The following utterance was a request to try on one of my rings: "One? Try on? [C1]?" In the latter example, I observed that this client used a rising intonation at the end of the word or phrase to indicate a question. She also pointed to herself, thereby enhancing the meaning of her utterance with appropriate nonverbal behavior.

C1 also reverted to the use of echolalia (i.e., the repetition of utterances verbalized by others) when it appeared that she had difficulty processing oral language. This phenomenon, a well-recognized feature of autistic language behavior, has been documented in the autism research literature. (Prizant and Duchan 1981; Prizant and Rydell 1984). C1's echolalia tended to be mitigated (i.e., altered from its original form) as opposed to an exact duplication of the original model. For example, on one occasion when she clearly indicated that she did not want me to facilitate with her, I said, "If you change your mind, let me know." She immediately responded with "change mind." This appeared to be accompanied by a head nod. She then repeated the phrase adding, "Okay." I said, "I can type with you?" She said, "No." She looked at the screen and said, "No want to." I said, "Okay," and she added, "Don't want to. No want to." I said, "Maybe later." She echoed, "later."

I also observed C1 engage in rote, repetitive verbal behavior, a characteristic of language use highly associated with autism. Much of her social language was highly routinized and reflective of a learned ritual consisting of phrases and sentences such as, "How are you today?" which she uttered repeatedly. These were sometimes used as conversation starters or as fillers to maintain conversational turn-taking. She also engaged in this type of verbal behavior when stressed. For example, in a typing sequence in which she became quite anxious, she moaned a bit and repetitively uttered, in an agitated voice, the out-of-context social routine "How are you today?" This was particularly reminiscent of the "Who's on first?" routine uttered by Rainman, in the motion picture of the same name, during times of apparent anxiety.

Finally, there were also instances in which it appeared that C1 had difficulty in both verbal and reading comprehension. In questioning where she had learned to read, F1 said, "You told somebody or other that you learned to read at the state hospital." C1 repeated the word *hospital*. This may have been an echoic response, as her demeanor suggested that she did not understand the question, which referred to C1's early schooling. C1's response suggested the possibility of receptive language difficulty; she said, "Yes. Teeth out," while pointing to her teeth.

Even though C1 was able to independently read many of the words she had typed, she evidenced specific comprehension difficulty on a few occasions. The most notable in terms of her behavioral reaction occurred when she responded to the question of what she liked best about typing. As noted, she ran her finger under the word *thoughts*, reading it as the word *today*. When F1 read the sentence as it appeared on the screen, substituting the word *thoughts* for *today*, C1 clearly reacted negatively, saying no several times and burying her head in her hands. C1's extreme reaction brings up an important and disturbing question. Why did she react so negatively to the word *thoughts* if she had indeed authored it? Furthermore, it is difficult to reconcile the obvious lack of concordance between typing and reading. Specifically, how was it possible for C1 to type, without error, a word with a complex spelling configuration (i.e., *thoughts*) and then not be able to read it a moment later?

The Blurred Boundaries Between Help and Influence

The matter of possible facilitator influence is arguably the most significant and the most controversial issue in facilitated communication. Notwithstanding F1's professed (and presumably sincere) interest in taking specific steps to avoid such influence, these were not generally demonstrated during the observation sessions. In fact, there were many instances in which I observed this facilitator engaging in behavior that he had specifically cautioned against during the interviews. For example, he had warned against the overinterpretation of messages. Yet in an example cited previously, F1 interpreted the client's intended message as *yes* based on her having typed only one letter (i.e., *y*). There were other instances in which overinterpretation occurred as well.

During the interview F1 acknowledged that influence can occur "if a person is typing a word and they are three letters into it, and [the facilitator] think[s] they know what the word is." Despite this acknowledgment, I observed F1 not only making a judgment with respect to word choice in a situation remarkably similar to the hypothetical situation he had cited but also applying more intense "facilitation" in that situation than would be considered appropriate even by his own standards. In this case, C1 was asked to give a word association for the word *summer*. It appeared on the videotape that with support at the forearm just below the elbow, F1 very decidedly pushed his client's arm toward the left side of the keyboard. He then put his left hand on her shoulder and seemed to push in the same direction. After C1 typed *swi* she pointed to the screen, shook her head, and clearly said, "*i*, nope no *i*." F1, ignoring her completely, responded, "*That letter belongs there*" (italics added). Thus not only does the facilitator reveal a specific mind-set toward letter selection, that mind-set is obviously in direct contradiction to the communicative intent of his client! As proof of this, a short time later he said, "What's the next letter in swim?" Interestingly, *after* he said the word, C1 pantomimed swimming gestures. When he asked for the next letter in *swim* once again, C1 turned her right hand over, palm up, in a gesture that I interpreted as indicating "I don't know." Eventually, she typed the word *swimming*. Although the latter is an obvious association for the word *summer*, so are the words *swing* and *sweat*, among others. Finally, despite the fact that the client had indicated *both* verbally and behaviorally that she did not intend to type the letter *i*, F1 nonetheless saw fit to violate her clear and specific intent in favor of his own.

I considered most of the instances of possible facilitator influence to be either unconscious or construed by the facilitator as appropriate to FC training. For example, F1 often interpreted instances of relatively clear-cut influence as appropriate ways of *helping*, rather than *influencing*, his client. The following example clearly illustrates this point. On one occasion when C1 was particularly frustrated, F1 responded, "To give you a start, let's type the word *to*." This type of "help" fails to recognize that the choice of a particular word constrains those that follow, thereby *implicitly* influencing message generation. To summarize, then, I observed F1 exercising far greater liberty with respect to facilitator influence during FC sessions than he had advised during the interviews. He was also clearly *unaware* that influence could occur simply as a result of his own mental predispositions and liberal interpretations.

Most of the instances in which I questioned unconscious influence in this dyad concerned the mind-set (i.e., expectation) of the facilitator. F1 manifested his influence in different ways depending upon the circumstances. Given the contextual elements in the example that follows, it is possible that the client's poor articulation may have caused F1 to inadvertently misinterpret her verbal answer, thereby creating an expectation for a particular response. In soliciting information with respect to how C1 had learned how to read, F1 asked, "I learned to read from what?" The client's verbal response seemed to be either "wordbook" or "workbook." The typed message, however, said *world book*. F1 then typed out and read the following question, "Do you mean encyclopedia?" C1 responded, "No." The verbal answer was *ignored* and she was directed to *type* her answer. He repeated, "Do you mean encyclopedia?" She said, "No. No," persevering in her original answer. Agitated and whining, she then typed *No* after which she said, "More please, more please." Here again, I saw an incongruity between verbal and nonverbal behavior during stress.

In an attempt to better understand the communicative intent of this client, I contacted her mother regarding how her daughter had learned to read. She replied that she would have learned to read in one of two ways. The first was through the *Richard Scarry Word Book* and the second was through workbooks available to her in her educational program at the state hospital. In either case, C1's verbal response to the question regarding whether she had learned to read from an encyclopedia was obviously correct. It also supports my own interpretation of C1's verbal response to the question of how she had learned to read.

The Consequences of a Mind-Set

Questions regarding the possibility of facilitator influence are, by virtue of the observational and descriptive nature of this study, for the most part speculative. Still, I can speak with some degree of "expertise" to my own involvement with this client. Although C1 refused all of my attempts to facilitate with her, she did type without facilitation (i.e., independently) at my request. At one point I asked if she wanted to ask me a question. She nodded yes. I asked if she'd like to type her question. In literal fashion, she said yes. I said, "Go ahead." She hesitated momentarily and said no in a kind of moaning voice. My impression was that she did not feel she could do it on her own. Next she said, "Store, please, store." She put her index finger over the *w* and then moved over to the right of the keyboard before depressing it. I said, "*w*? That's a good question word." I obviously anticipated a *wh* question! She immediately went back to the *w* and depressed the key. After that, she calmly and easily typed the rest of the letters in the word *want*. I read each letter after she typed it and said the word aloud when she finished it. She replied, "Store, please, store. [pause] Store, store, rider, please. Ride a truck. [pause] Rider, please [as she referenced me] Rider, please." At this point she placed her index finger over the letter *r*. I said, "Go ahead." I said, "*r*" and then she typed it. She moved her finger to the *d* next. I said, "What comes before that?" Obviously, I had decided what word C1 was about to type. I said, "*r*" and "ride" while emphasizing the long *i* sound. She went immediately to the *i*. As I said the name of the letter, she pressed the key. She then moved to the *d* on her own and looked at me for direction. I nodded, and she pressed the key as I said, "*d*." She then went to the *e* on her own, and I said, "*e*." At one point I said, "What did you type?" She pointed to the screen with her index finger and said, "I ride. I ride. Want ride to." She then said, "please," even though it wasn't on the screen. A short time later she added the word *truck* to her verbal repertoire. I directed her to type it. She put her finger over the letter *k*. She then independently moved it to the letter *t*. I nodded and said, "*t*," after which she depressed the key. I said, "What's next after *t*?" She typed an *h*. Anxious to follow her lead I said, "You're writing *the*?" She shook her head and said no at the same time. Despite her negative response, my desire to have her be successful with her typing was apparently so strong that I *ignored* her clear and congruent verbal and nonverbal message and said, "Well, you can do *the*. What comes after the *h* in *the*?" She typed *e*, and I said, "Good." She used the space bar independently, and I said, "Now, let's do *truck*." She put her index finger over the *k* and named the letter. I exaggerated the first letter in *truck*, and she typed a *t*. She pointed to herself with her left hand while very deliberately looking at me and said, "with you?" Inexplicably, I completely *ignored* this and said, "You're doing a beautiful job, [C1]." She nodded in response to this but immediately moaned in frustration. It was not until I reviewed the videotaped footage several times that it became clear to me that I was so caught up in the typing that I did not even realize that she may have been requesting either my help or that I take her for a ride when she said, "with you?" Neither did I realize until many viewings of the videotape that while I was *fashioning* her typed message into one thing, she was actually trying to request, both verbally and through typing, something quite different. The latter (i.e., *ride in the truck*), I learned later, was often the phrase this client used as a request to terminate the session. Finally—and this is a crucially important aspect of the FC experience—I had no sense at the time of the extent of my "help" (influence?) in her "independent" typing. Nor, in the heat of the FC moment, did I have any sense that I had completely—time and time again—missed C1's communicative intent!

One of the most revealing aspects of this interaction was the effect that my wanting the client to succeed had on the behavior I exhibited. That desire not only caused me to ignore a clear verbal and nonverbal signal with regard to the word *the* but also caused me to ignore the various ways in which my verbal and nonverbal prompting enabled C1 to be "successful." What is perhaps most enlightening is the lack of concordance between my impressions at the time of the interaction, recorded a short time after the session took place, and my impressions after *multiple* viewings of the videotaped footage of the session. At the time, I viewed the interaction as extremely positive, focusing on the impressive literacy skills evidenced by this client and the lack of manual support with respect to typing. I actually encouraged her facilitator to use the videotaped footage as an example of *independent* typing! My present viewpoint, although I acknowledge the significance of the client's skills, also recognizes the fine line between help and influence and the degree to which decisions to include words unintended by the client (i.e., *the*) not only may place constraints on the utterances that follow but also may cause the client undue anxiety by violating her specific intent. Most of all, however, I understand just how a passion to believe can obscure common sense and distort one's judgments in favor of the *preferred* "reality."

Getting a Different Message

The F1-C1 dyad was characterized by several unique features not found in the other two pairs in this study. The underlying basis for these differences is very much related to the level of acquired skill development I observed in this client. Of the three clients in this study, only C1 demonstrated specific literacy skills (i.e., reading aloud and independent typing) outside the confines of actual facilitation (i.e., manual support). Further, only she demonstrated a basic grasp of a wide variety of the pragmatic functions of communication and the ability to utilize specific linguistic devices (e.g., repair strategies and supplemental use of gestures and manual signs) to modify or add force to her utterances. She also evidenced the ability to persist in her communicative attempts. Persistence is considered to be an important marker for intentional communication (Bates 1979).

Because of the previously noted combination of factors, specific aspects of facilitated communication not generally available with less communicatively competent individuals were brought to light. This client's level of skill development gave me the opportunity to view the use of facilitated communication with an individual who not only had a clearly functional communication system *prior* to the initiation of FC but also evidenced prefacilitation literacy skills.

Definitive judgments are always risky, but the consistency of specific observations over time with this dyad makes certain conclusions difficult to avoid. For one, there is no question in my mind that C1 is a far more *effective, efficient, reliable,* and *flexible* communicator when she uses a combination of verbal and nonverbal communicative means than when she uses FC alone, especially when one considers such factors as level of stress, intentionality, and the use of pragmatic communicative functions and linguistic devices. It is also clear that she seems to *prefer* verbal and nonverbal means (gestures and manual signs) to express herself, as these are the forms that she characteristically accesses first. This may be because they *work* for her; that is, they get across the messages that she *intends* to convey.

Conditional Synchrony

Two findings for this dyad run counter to claims made by proponents of facilitated communication. The first concerns the contention that the client's motor difficulty necessitates the use of manual support. Initially, an analysis of this client's behavior did seem to favor this explanation, as C1 did on several occasions hover over keys with her index finger and look to her facilitator for greater physical support, often tugging at her sleeve or arm while looking at F1 to "request" support. This behavior initially caused me to question the presence of possible mild apraxia, a disorder associated with difficulty in initiating voluntary movements. Closer scrutiny over time, however, revealed that such behavior occurred only under one or more of the following circumstances: when C1 seemed concerned that she might displease F1; when she seemed unsure of letter selection, word choice, or spelling; and when she genuinely did not appear to have a response in mind. In addition, my initial speculation regarding the possible presence of apraxia is inconsistent with both this client's ability to *independently* type specific letters named by others and her reported adroitness in a variety of motor activities, including the demanding sports of cross-country and downhill skiing and swimming.

The second finding that appears to be at odds with claims made by proponents of facilitated communication relates to specific aspects of the relationship between facilitator and client. The dimension of relationship is considered by proponents of facilitated communication to be integral to the conduct of the technique. There were several occasions on which I was specifically struck by the lack of synchrony existing between F1 and C1, particularly with respect to trust and emotional support. However, I observed asynchrony between the two *only* in situations in which C1's verbal or nonverbal behavior seemed to run counter to the conduct of facilitated communication. For example, C1 reacted to the facilitator's disapproval of her verbal and nonverbal communication with varying degrees of frustration. It is difficult to comprehend how the facilitator's indifference to the client's obvious and intentional communicative behavior, especially considering the degree of frustration this client experienced, would be consistent with providing an atmosphere of trust and emotional support. Could it be that the highly touted alleged synchrony between facilitator and client occurs *only* when the client is performing in the manner that is intended by the facilitator? If so, the following question must be asked: What price does conditional synchrony exact?

5

An Unreal Reality: The Messages of F2-C2

What we perceive comes as much from inside our heads as from the world outside.

—William James

I observed the F2-C2 dyad on two occasions. The first observation session took place one year and nine months after this pair began facilitating together. The other session took place four months later. An additional session had been scheduled; however, the client was ill on that occasion as a result of complications stemming from surgery for the removal of foreign objects he had ingested. I considered the level of experience for this dyad to be more than adequate, especially since F2 and C2 had reportedly facilitated on a daily basis in the early stages of their work together. I saw concordance across both sessions with respect to the degree of manual support provided, the client's verbal and nonverbal behavior, the general level of competence in using FC, and the relationship dynamics underlying the dyadic interaction. The transcript for this dyad may be found in the appendix, Table A.10. Preexistent transcripts for this dyad may be found in Table A.3.

What You See: Outside the FC Experience

Because of this client's significant motor compromises, under most conditions he required a fairly intrusive amount of manual support during facilitation. According to his facilitator, however, there were times when the level of support varied considerably. When asked if she had recently decreased support from the index finger to the wrist she replied, "Well, no. It comes and goes." Here she was making reference to the intermittent need to increase the level of manual support because of difficulty with index-finger isolation, a problem repeatedly cited in C2's record. F2 confirmed that manual support was, for the most part, at the wrist; however, she did indicate that she tried to decrease support to the lower forearm when she deemed this to be feasible. She attributed the need for different levels of support to C2's "going from very floppy to being very stiff."

This client's difficulty with index-finger isolation was apparent across FC sessions and seemed to coexist with a tendency to drop his remaining fingers onto the keys while typing. Further, he did not appear to be frustrated by the latter occurrence even though it caused numerous errors and confusion in his typing. Owing to his motor problems, C2 was not yet typing independently, a goal that may not have been realistic given the extent of his motor problems.

This client did not demonstrate the same degree of competence as C1 with respect to either the verbal expression of pragmatic communicative functions or literacy skills acquisition. In terms of his *verbal* use of the pragmatic functions of communication, I observed C2 make only simple requests. I inferred protest behavior from his nonverbal communication during times of apparent stress. On one occasion this included mild self-injurious behavior in the form of hitting himself on the side of the neck. On another occasion, this was manifested by a kind of tense, hyperventilated sound production that suggested a high degree of agitation. Although C1 engaged in similar types of nonverbal protest behavior, she did so only *after* her more conventional verbal responses had been ignored. C2 did use some verbal language, but unlike C1, he generally used nonverbal protest behavior as his *predominant* communicative strategy. Thus C2's verbal and nonverbal behavior was at a lower level of communicative competence that C1's. Further, by report and by observation, C2's verbal expression mostly involved private soliloquies that were often unintelligible and seemingly unrelated to present events. As noted previously, some of his caregivers felt these were "psychotic" in nature and indicative of multiple personality disorder. I felt they were more indicative of delayed echolalia, which is characterized by memorized "chunks" of language that are uttered some time after they are assimilated, ostensibly as a manifestation of a gestalt, as opposed to an analytic, style of language acquisition (Prizant and Schuler 1987). Delayed echolalia is a well-recognized feature of autistic language behavior (Prizant and Rydell 1984).

C2 did not demonstrate the ability to read during FC sessions. That is, unlike C1, he did not read aloud any of the words, phrases, or sentences from the computer screen. Indeed, he did not at any time evidence behaviors that would be consistent with literacy awareness, such as reciprocally referencing the screen and keyboard during typing to monitor the generation of messages and/or correct errors. Unlike C1, C2 evidenced *no* interest in the computer screen, looking up at it, with rare exception, only when his facilitator directed him to do so. Even when he did reference the screen, attention was fleeting and reaction to errors was nonexistent. Further, on numerous occasions, I observed C2 typing letters *without actually looking at the keys*.

Remarkably, the content and sophistication of this client's messages were the most impressive of the three clients in this study despite the absence of behaviors associated with literacy awareness, the lack of demonstrated literacy skills outside the confines of actual facilitation, and his impoverished environmental background. His transcripts stand in stark contrast to the verbal, nonverbal, and affective behavior that he demonstrated during FC sessions. His FC transcripts read like a social-affective lexicon, demonstrating a high degree of social awareness and perceptiveness with respect to even subtle social information. They also reveal an ability to express feelings, elaborate utterances, initiate and appropriately maintain topics, use appropriate deictic (i.e., referential) language forms and linguistic devices, and engage in good-natured social banter. All of these behaviors are inconsistent with what is seen in autism.

Overall, C2 demonstrated little consistency between his reported (and observed) functioning level and the degree of competence attributed to him with respect to message generation during facilitated communication sessions. For example, none of the relatively advanced language behaviors enumerated previously were demonstrated or reported outside the confines of the FC sessions. In fact, this client's verbal and nonverbal behavior, general affect, reported functioning level, environmental and educational history, and autistic symptomatology stood in stark contrast to the level of sophistication evidenced in the typed output generated through facilitated communication.

What You Get: Inside the FC Experience

On the day of the first observation, the session began in the customary manner (as judged from previous transcripts), with the facilitator and client exchanging social amenities. After a short time F2 addressed me: "He's offered you an invitation." She went on to say that she had asked him, through typing, if there was anything that he wanted to ask or say to me. She reported that he typed, "Yes, please type with me. I open the open door to typing with me." I sat next to him and took his arm at the level of the wrist. As I did this he began to type. My impression at the time, recorded a short time after the session, was that his response appeared to be a kind of knee-jerk reaction. Even though I had not yet said anything to him, C2 was randomly typing letters in the general vicinity of the lower-middle part of the keyboard. F2 interrupted this behavior and said, "Why don't we let Diane ask questions? That would be best. Okay?" She then pulled his hand back and repeated the question, directing him to type the *y* for *yes*. His hand went to the general vicinity of the letter. F2 said, "You're close." The next time he attempted to type the letter he got it correct, and his facilitator said, "There you go." During this time I had my palm against the underside of the client's wrist. In addition to the support I was providing, F2 was supporting the client beneath the elbow. I took direction from F2 regarding the degree of manual support to provide and with respect to other technical aspects of facilitated communication. At this point, with both F2 and me providing manual assistance, support was highly intrusive.

F2 directed me to begin with yes-no questions because they are easier. Once again C2 began to type as soon as I started to ask him a question, again evidencing a knee-jerk reaction. F2 placed her hand more securely under the client's forearm at this point. It seemed to me at the time that she was applying more pressure than was advisable given the fine line between help and influence; however, F2 may have done so in her desire to instruct me in the technique of facilitated communication. C2 typed a *y*, to which I responded, "Okay. Yes."

As I started to ask the next question, C2 again dropped his hand to the keyboard to begin typing. This time his hand was pulled back by F2 as she continued to provide support beneath the elbow. The question was repeated. This time he (we?) hit the *y*, to which I responded, "Terrific. Okay." On reviewing the videotape of this point in the session, I was struck by the position of F2's hand on the client's arm. Instead of simply resting her palm against the *underside* of C2's forearm, F2 had repositioned her hand so that her palm rested against the *top* of the client's forearm. This more aggressive placement would seem to accommodate both a stronger grip and increased pressure, and it did appear on the videotape that the tension in the facilitator's hand increased.

While I was trying to think of additional questions, C2's finger came down on the space bar. My next question was, "Do you have a favorite television program?" C2 went for the *y* again with the same degree of manual support by the two of us. I clearly felt that I was being moved along the keyboard, though I did not have a clear sense of who was guiding whom at that point. I then asked C2 to type the name of his favorite television program. After he was four letters into it, he sat back in his chair and put his hand in his lap. I said, "You're taking a rest, are you?" In response to a comment from me with respect to the client's arm or wrist dropping, F2 explained that she was providing support to him as well in order to "stabilize him." My notes, written shortly after the session, describe the client's arm and hand as feeling very limp in my hand. I used the term "low tone" to further characterize the experience.

When we began typing again, F2 moved her hand back somewhat closer to C2's elbow. At this point he put his head down and seemed to be staring at his lap as opposed to the keyboard. He rubbed his eye with his left hand. Even though he was not looking at the keyboard at this point, he did type a letter. F2 pointed to the screen with her index finger, saying, "[C2] look; *mh* is not a word. You want to fix that up?" The facilitator repeated that as she held *all* of our hands up to the computer screen—hers, the client's, and mine. She again said, "Do you want to fix that up?" He nodded slightly and said, "mmmmm," but he made no movement. F2 continued, "So what have you got to do?" His hand dropped down to the space bar. I said, "Oh, you're going to start a new word?" After he used the space bar, he did look up at the screen. This was one of the few times that C2 referenced the computer screen independently. Next, he typed two letters. F2 said, "*bj? bj* is not a word." She prompted C2 to do something about the incorrect letters. He moved his head and his hand toward the keyboard, but I did not have the sense that he had a specific course of action in mind. F2 then positioned my hand so that it was actually under C2's wrist. She then held on, tightly, to both my hand and his wrist, and I felt distinct, unmistakable pressure from her hand. My clear impression at this time was that both my and C2's hands were being moved around the keyboard. F2 said, "You feel the pull?" I responded, "Yeah." To the present time, I'm not sure of the meaning of F2's question. I am, however, quite certain of what I intended to convey with my answer: the feeling of being led from letter to letter on the keyboard.

This "double facilitation" continued for many letters scattered throughout the keyboard and continued for what appeared, under the circumstances, to be an interminable length of time. At one point F2 said, "*nd* is not a word." After pointing to the computer screen she said, "You took Diane's word, huh? Easier than thinking of your own?" The meaning of this remark is not clear from the transcript; however, the only verbal remark I made that C2 could have picked up on was a comment about the Brady Bunch. F2 may have been referring to it with her comment. After this, I tried facilitating on my own without additional manual support from F2.

Providing support at the wrist, I began to ask the client a question. In stimulus-response fashion, before I could get the words out, he began to type. He hit the same letter twice and appeared to be going for it a third time before F2 intervened and pulled him back. Once again, my impression both at the time and on review of the videotape was that this reaction was an automatic response pattern; that is, taking the client's hand was the *stimulus* that ushered forth the *typing* response. F2 placed her hand under my hand, ostensibly as a means of holding C2's hand back to prevent him from typing before I finished my question. Having learned my lesson from the constraints one of my FC questions had placed on C1, I asked C2, "What do you like to do best of all?" At that point F2 let go of his hand, which dropped limply to the keys. I said, "Whoops." The client laughed. He then, with support at the level of his wrist, began to jab at the same area of the keyboard. His hand was in a limply held closed-fist position with very little index-finger isolation.

My notes describing that session indicate that I was quite surprised at the difficulty C2 evidenced in typing given his level of experience with facilitated communication and the fact that index-finger isolation was within his motor capability, according to notations in his record vis-à-vis FC. A short time after this session, I recorded additional impressions regarding what I termed a sense of "purposelessness"; that is, I had no idea and C2 seemed to have no idea of where he was going with respect to the keyboard!

F2 intervened at that point. She pulled his hand up, deleted the letters he had typed, and said, "[C2], let's start this letter with an *i*. Diane asked you what you liked best of all." At this point, F2 placed her fingers more gently under my hand, presumably trying to reduce the amount of physical guidance. She then seemed to guide him (us) to a particular part of the keyboard, withdrawing physical support at that time. Because C2's hand was close to the letters, it did not come down as precipitously as it had previously. However, the action appeared as purposeless as it had earlier. F2 reached over, took C2's hand, and said, "You're typing nonsense." I recorded my impressions a short time later:

> I had no sense of where this client was going, or what he was doing. He was really like dead weight in my hand, and I remember thinking as I facilitated with him that I must be doing something wrong, because nothing was happening. I also remember thinking, "how can he possibly be moving to the various letters to spell out a message, since I don't get any sense at all that he is able to do that from the way his arm rests so limply in my hand."

Feelings of Incompetence

F2 deleted a couple of letters and directed C2 to go back to the *i*. Feeling distinctly incompetent at this point and willing to accept responsibility for the difficulty we were encountering with message generation, I commented, "Don't forget. I'm real inexperienced." With facilitation at the level of the wrist, C2 began to rhythmically jab at keys in the same general area of the keyboard. I said, "Let me space it out for you. Let's start again." Again, F2 intervened. She said, "When he starts that, pull him back and kind of take a breather, just to let him know that you're serious. He's such a jokester." C2 was not smiling and did not exhibit any other behavior that would lead one to believe he was joking. Nor was the situation in any way jovial!

After deleting a couple of letters, F2 said very matter of factly, "*You might want to lead him to the letters when you first start*" (italics added). I was incredulous at the comment, since it blatantly solicited facilitator influence, albeit only as a form of helping "when you first start." She then made an adjustment aimed at isolating C2's index finger. I assumed the position of providing manual support at the wrist. His finger was over the letter *k*, and he came down on it. I said, "*k*," and then following F2's directive, I actually led him in the general direction of the *e*. Once there, I said, "Close." Obviously, I had had a word in mind! I was not conscious of this at the time, however. His hand then drifted toward the lower middle of the board. At this point F2 said, "*You should sort of go to the area where he should be going*" (italics added). Not only did this comment imply that it was acceptable to make a judgment with respect to letter choice, it granted permission to directly influence the client in getting to the "area where he should be going." Finally, it either implied an *a priori awareness* of the communicative intent of the client, or it sanctioned a violation of it in favor of one's own! My commentary at the time indicated that I clearly felt the client move away from the area where the *e* was and that I felt I should be following his lead rather than influencing him to follow mine.

I felt increasingly incompetent and responsible for the client's lack of success in generating intelligible messages. I was at a loss to understand how something that seemed so simple and straightforward could give me so much difficulty. At the same time I was also struck by the awesome amount of pressure on the facilitator to generate messages.

I continued to facilitate with this client, providing support at the wrist. At this point C2 seemed to hover over the keys, after which he sat back and put his hand in his lap. I commented (really in my own defense) that C2 seemed to have trouble getting his hand far enough up on the keyboard. F2 attributed that to *radial instability*, a term often used by proponents of FC to justify the need for facilitation. My observation, of course, clearly conflicted with F2's assertion during the interview: "He goes for letters on that side just because of the reach and stuff because a lot of times I back off because I just can't go that far. So, he is pulling me over there."

After a short time, F2 picked up C2's hand and tapped her hand against his index finger, ostensibly to isolate it. I changed the subject, asking him to type the name of the person with whom he prefers to facilitate. His finger randomly dropped to a key. F2 directed me to "pull all the way up" on his hand. F2 intervened again when C2 began to type random letters in the same area of the keyboard. She said, "Let's delete." Feeling very sheepish at this point, I said, "Do you want to do it?" Perhaps sensing my uneasiness, she very graciously said, "I want you to. The whole part of learning is being able to pull back. There are a lot of things to remember at the same time." I said to C2, "Ready? What was the question?" F2 repeated it. C2 typed *carnly*, which was interpreted as Carol, the name of one of his caregivers. As this configuration of letters was typed, I had the clear sense that something was different this time. It seemed to me that F2 may have been providing some manual support to the client, unbeknownst to me, as the client's movements appeared to be more definitive. It was not possible to make this determination at the time, however, owing to my level of involvement in the process of facilitated communication. Unfortunately, the videotape is unclear as well because my position next to the client effectively blocks the camera's view of F2. But when I slow down the action of the videotape, all three of us seem to be rhythmically moving in the same direction at the same time as this message is typed. It would seem that unless F2 were part of the "facilitation," she would not be moving in the same rhythmic fashion as C2 and I.

In response to a question about whether C2 had ever evidenced the ability to type letters independently, F2 replied, "No, not yet. That's one of the things that I'd like to shoot for." She elaborated her answer, noting that C2 went from being "very floppy" to being "very stiff" depending on his mood. At that point I mentioned an impression that was very strong throughout my FC experience with this client. Positioning my right arm with my elbow pointing toward the floor, I stated, "It's almost like it's this vertical position." I was referring to the client's difficulty in keeping his arm in a horizontal position appropriate to typing and the concomitant tendency toward dropping his forearm, a position clearly incompatible with good typing form.

At that point I indicated to F2 that I'd like to give C2 an opportunity to ask me a question but that if he continued to have difficulty typing with me, perhaps she could facilitate with him so that he could answer it. I then said to the client, "Would you like to start again?" He nodded yes. I was surprised that he had responded affirmatively given the lack of success he was having with me. After what appeared to be open-ended, random movements, C2 began rhythmically jabbing at the keys. F2 said, "That's his trademark." I responded, "Oh, is that the perseveration they talk about, because I'm not doing that?" I then said, "Do you want to ask him that question?" I offered her my chair and was singularly relieved to take a backseat because I had performed so poorly. As F2 took her seat next to C2 she said, "You look kind of droopy." At the time, I wrote that "he looked completely out of it. He just sort of stared at me—almost through me, actually."

After a short break during which C2 had a cup of coffee, he and F2 began to type together. When he began, he was smiling to himself and generally seemed to be in another world. He continued to look down at the keys but, unlike during my facilitation with him, was typing in a variety of spots on the keyboard. Though C2 did have his head lowered toward the keyboard, I did not have the sense that either his head or his eyes were moving to accommodate his more expanded involvement with the keys. He seemed to be fixating on only one small part of the keyboard. There were even times when it was not clear whether he was focusing on the keyboard or staring at his lap.

The Tension Mounts

C2 did not appear to be paying attention to his typing. Rather, he was mumbling to himself and smiling, again as though in his own private world. F2 said to him, "What's happening is you're hitting between letters." She directed his attention to the screen and said, "I think you want to get rid of this." With continued manual support at the level of the wrist, he went to the delete key and methodically deleted a few letters. Prior to the last time C2 depressed the delete key, F2 said, "No. You want one *e*." He deleted it anyway and she said, "No. You want that *e*." My impression at the time was that he would have continued to jab at the delete key, as he had done previously with me, had his facilitator not intervened. Further, F2's comment clearly reveals that *she* had made a judgment regarding C2's "choice" of a particular word. Someone walked into the room, and C2 turned his attention to that person. Still not paying attention to the keyboard, he typed two more letters. Deleting a letter or two, F2 looked at me and said, "He wants to know if you're married." She gave a little laugh, as did I. Instead of waiting expectantly for my response, C2 stared off into space, past me, evidencing no reaction I could detect. There was nothing in his demeanor to suggest that he was even paying attention to us.

Next, I said to him, "Do you want to ask me something else?" He typed three or four letters while looking, out of the corner of his eye, toward his right side. At that time his attention did not appear to be on the keyboard. As the session went on, C2 began to exhibit a series of behaviors as he typed that I would classify as "interfering behaviors" (i.e., behaviors that distract from the task at hand). He began to make vocal noises interspersed with a few intelligible words. As this behavior continued, C2 began to evidence signs of agitation, clenching his jaw and grabbing at his shirt more frequently. At one point, he used his left hand to jab into space. This behavior contrasted sharply with his slow, rhythmic typing under wrist-level manual support. As the session progressed, C2 appeared to become more tense and agitated. At this time, F2 decreased support slightly so that it was at the level of the lower forearm with thumb support at the wrist. It appeared at one point that F2 was struggling with him to pull his hand back. At another time, he typed an entire series of letters while looking at me out of the corner of his eye. Judging from the positions of the facilitator and client on the videotape and the apparent degree of concentration on the part of the facilitator, C2's lack of attention to the keys was not obvious to F2.

C2 continued to type letter after letter while engaging in a kind of agitated vocalization that was increasing in intensity as the session progressed. Manual support at this point was at the *least* intrusive level—at the mid-forearm; however, use of the delete key indicated that accuracy was not always adequate. At this point, C2 was making a growling sound, each "growl" occurring as a key was jabbed. F2 appeared to be offering quite a bit of resistance during this time. At one point she said, "I'm not sure where you're going." She then pulled his hand back and put her head down on the side of her arm in a gesture that clearly dramatized her exhaustion, ostensibly resulting from the amount of exertion (and concentration?) required to pull the client's hand back. Given my earlier experience with respect to the client's inadequate muscle tone for typing, the apparent need for such exertion was indeed surprising. The client's increased tone and the effort required to manage it did, however, appear to be consistent with the heightened intensity that characterized his behavior at that point in the session. It may also have made possible less intrusive manual support. That may have been what F2 meant when she talked about the level of manual support being conditional on his mood. F2 shook his arm a bit saying, "Come on, loosen up." As she directed him back to the keyboard, he continued to make sounds and to utter some words. It was clear to me on a couple of occasions that his reaching over to the far right-hand side of the keyboard was out of sync with the *stationary* position of his head and eyes. My distinct impression was that C2 was not looking at the keyboard when he typed many of the letters; this is not to say that his attention to the keyboard was adequate at other times. In fact I found it disconcerting that this client was engaging in behavior that was clearly *incompatible* with attention to the task at hand. Still, I heard F2 say, "Good job." She sat back and said to me, "He wants to know if you're happy in life because you look happy." My follow-up notes indicate that I was completely taken aback by the question. I wrote, "Wow. Where did that come from? Even if I had felt as though C2's attention to task had been impeccable, his demeanor (i.e., his agitation and intensity) was clearly incongruous with the content of the question."

Interestingly, after typing the previous message, C2 *verbally* said, "Go back to work." I interpreted this as a request. His facilitator did not respond. They started to type again after F2 held her hand out for further facilitation. He repeated his verbal request to go back to work. Again, she ignored it. With wrist-level support, the typing continued. He was very agitated at this point, judging by the fact that he clenched his jaw with increasing frequency and intensity. My impression was that he was a captive audience. I also recorded the following observation a short time after this session: "Whereas his nonverbal/vocal behavior did not appear at all consistent with the typed message regarding whether I was happy in life, a case could easily be made that his agitation during typing was quite consistent with his clear verbal request, 'Go back to work,' particularly if the latter were construed as C2's way of indicating that he wanted to stop typing." In other words, it was eminently possible that he was reacting negatively to the blatant disregard of his verbal message. Nevertheless, the typing continued and produced the following message: *bacvkn to woriok*. His facilitator said, "Is this back to work?" He typed *yeesyes*. F2 responded that she was waiting for Steve to call. Thus, true to the tenets of FC, F2 acknowledged her client's request *only* when it was rendered via the medium of facilitated communication.

The pair continued to type despite the client's increasing agitation. At one point he actually raised himself from his seat in a gesture that punctuated his agitation. In contrast to C2's general level of agitation—in fact, seemingly oblivious to it—F2 calmly typed something else on the keyboard. C2 said with a questioning tone in his voice while nodding, "Go back to work?" I construed the accompanying nod as his way of adding behavioral emphasis to his request. Here, then, was a match between verbal and nonverbal behavior. This time his facilitator did respond to the verbal message and said, "Yes, as soon as Steve gets here." She then took his hand to continue typing. Although he did not appear to physically resist manual support, his reaction indicated that he was clearly agitated.

F2 excused herself for a moment to check on when Steve would pick up C2. The client sat placidly, in stark contrast to his high level of agitation a moment earlier. It was not until he and F2 began typing together again that he became tense and agitated once more. At this time his jaw was almost constantly clenched, and at one point he hit himself on the side of the neck. He made a gesture to get up, sitting down quickly in an agitated fashion. He began to vocalize under his breath in what seemed to be rhythmic hyperventilation with sound. At times he interspersed these sounds with words and phrases. At one point he said, "There she is." As with C1, C2's vocal and verbal behavior was clearly reminiscent of the "Who's on first?" routine uttered by Dustin Hoffman's character during times of stress in the movie *Rainman*.

A Lack of Synchrony

There were several remarkable aspects with respect to this situation, not the least of which was that C2's eyes seemed to be everywhere else but on the keyboard as he typed letter after letter in the same rhythmic, methodical fashion that contrasted so sharply with his overall level of agitation. This apparent disconnection between C2's overt behavior and his slow, even, rhythmic typing had a surreal quality about it that was underscored by his facilitator's complete, trancelike indifference to it. After several viewings of the videotape, I wrote the following description:

> He seemed to be clenching more and more at his shirt with his left hand. He certainly wasn't looking at the keyboard, and yet that same rhythmic typing continued. In no way did he seem to be paying attention to this exercise. In no way did he seem to be pleased with this exercise. As a matter of fact, he seemed highly anxious and tense, and this seemed to be escalating. His whole

body seemed tense and kind of stiff. Somebody walked in and captured his attention for a moment. He calmed down very briefly, and then as F2 continued to facilitate with him, holding his arm very close to the wrist, he started to again exhibit that hyperventilated type of breathing with vocalization attached to it. His teeth were clenched, his jaw was very, very tight, and he seemed clearly agitated. He began to move his head right and left while he sang through clenched teeth, though not happily, almost as though he was trying anything and everything to try to ameliorate his anxiety. This is my clear-cut impression. While he did that with his head, and while he was "singing" in that agitated manner, he was continuing to be facilitated, hardly skipping a beat and yet not seeming to pay attention at all. At one point he seemed to pull his arm back toward himself and become extraordinarily tense, almost trembling. I interpreted this as frustration. In summary, his body language, his vocalization/verbalization, with its agitated inflection, and his facial expression were all consistent with extreme frustration and anxiety. Only his slow, rhythmic typing seemed to stand separate and apart from the remarkable consistency of his overall behavioral reaction.

As the session progressed, C2's vocalizations took on more of a conversational quality. Phrases such as "Come on to my house," "Hi, Steve," and "Let's go see a movie" were clearly heard as C2 continued to type with wrist-level facilitation. Again, my impression was that the client was using this verbal routine as a coping mechanism to help ameliorate his stress. To my astonishment, F2 indicated that C2 had done a "great" job typing. Given the client's level of anxiety, I found this incomprehensible! That is, in response to the typed question *How is work?* this client typed *i5t is gooed 8i ol8 like st3eve iolk l8ikee you i like to work]*. Despite the obvious need to take some liberty in the translation, it would seem that the innocuousness of the typed message's content contrasts sharply with the emotionally charged context within which it was rendered.

As the session progressed, this client's level of "involvement" seemed to *lessen* even as his facilitator's seemed to *increase*. My notes from the review of the videotape follow:

> It seemed as though C2 was having some type of conversation with himself, but he seemed clearly agitated and frustrated. There were clearly times when he would type letter after letter and yet he was simply not looking in the direction of the keyboard. In fact, his gaze was averted to the right and he really didn't seem to be paying any attention to the typing. He was looking at the keyboard less and less as time progressed. He was grabbing at his shirt with his left hand more and more as time progressed. His vocalizations and verbalizations became even more frequent. It is very difficult to figure out how he is able to keep up this steady stream of vocalization and/or conversation and grab at his shirt with his left hand, and be looking around the room rather than at the keyboard, and yet be continuing to slowly and rhythmically type things out on the keyboard that are actual words.

Perhaps even more inexplicable than C2's behavior is the fact that his facilitator appeared completely oblivious to it, so great was her concentration and attention to the task at hand. In fact, at one point she turned to him and said serenely, "You're doing so well." I judged this comment to be distinctly out of sync with the behavior I observed at the time. Once again, I was struck by the surreal quality of the situation—the trancelike state of the facilitator and the agitated condition of the client. I was also struck by the fact that the act of typing seemed to be completely disconnected from everything else that was occurring during the session.

Unexplained Discordance

Although the F2-C2 dyad shared some similarities with the F1-C1 dyad, there were marked differences as well. The most striking area of commonality was the frequent *mismatch* between the client's verbal and nonverbal behavior and the typed message. C2, whose conventional communication was more limited, did communicate his frustration nonverbally, and the innocuousness his typed messages often stood in stark contrast to the intensity of his vocal/verbal and nonverbal behavior. I also observed the same type of verbal routine in C2 during times of stress that I had observed in C1 under the same conditions. Further, it is interesting that although C2 did not demonstrate the degree of functional use of language that C1 did, he was able to make a clear *verbal* request to go back to work. In keeping with the FC credo to ignore the verbal, his facilitator paid no heed to the request until C2 typed *bacvkn to woriok*. One can only speculate on the reason for discouraging attention to verbal behavior even when congruence between the typed and the verbal message has been clearly demonstrated by the client—unless, of course, the medium is more important than the message.

Another similarity between the two dyads concerns trust and emotional support. During much of this session, F2 and C2 demonstrated the same lack of synchrony that I observed between F1 and C1. Specifically, F2 either ignored C2's agitated nonverbal behavior or judged it to be indicative of the client's "doing so well." Again, it is difficult to reconcile how the facilitator's indifference to or misjudgment of the client's obvious, intentional communicative behavior (if rendered by any other means than FC) can be considered emblematic of an emotionally supportive relationship. Such behavior on the part of the facilitator seems instead to ride roughshod over it!

A major difference between this dyad and the F1-C1 team is the relative paucity of verbal language used by F2 in her interactions with her client. Whereas F1 interacted verbally with his client, F2 provided a minimum of verbal input for hers. In fact, FC sessions between F2 and C2 were eerily silent! In communicating with her client, F2 would characteristically type out a question or other message on the keyboard and then direct the client's attention to the computer screen by holding his hand up to it so that he could read what she had typed. She neither read the words aloud to him nor closely monitored his attention to the task. The significance of this cannot be overstated. Because of the lack of verbal input, C2 was left with only one method of comprehending his facilitator's messages: He had to independently read the computer screen. That said, on several occasions it was clear that F2 did not give C2 sufficient time or that C2 did not give sufficient attention to the screen to enable him to understand the written question. Incomprehensibly, even under these circumstances, C2 was never at a loss for facilitated words! Another difference between C1 and C2 was their disparate levels of literacy awareness. Unlike C1, C2 did not reference the computer screen, either to self-monitor or to self-correct, during the course of facilitated communication. Indeed, C2 showed a virtual lack of involvement (interest?) in viewing the computer screen, an observation that would seem consistent with a lack of literacy awareness. Notwithstanding, the typed transcript from this session is remarkable for its contextual relevance and for its demonstration of comprehension on the part of the client.

My personal experience in facilitating with C2 provided some valuable insights that could not have been gleaned in any other way. My unmistakable impression was that without *active* physical guidance on my part, message generation could not have occurred. Indeed, it was only after I was directed by the facilitator to "lead him to the letters" that some words began to emerge. As the transcript from that session clearly illustrates, this client was unable to generate the legible messages with me as his facilitator (and in some cases with *both* F2 and me providing manual support) that he was allegedly able to generate with F2 alone. (See Table A.10 in the appendix, transcript dated 5/27/93.) Given the amount of experience this client has had with facilitated communication, I am at a loss to understand such difficulty. Further, the frequently cited perception by FC proponents that problems in generating messages may be related to a lack of trust between facilitator and client does not seem to apply in this case either given the willingness of the client to interact with me and his level of cooperation during the time that I facilitated with him.

Undoubtedly, one of the more perplexing FC experiences with this client was his perceived knee-jerk reaction to typing as soon as manual support was rendered. Did he not need to know the question before he started to answer it? Finally, this interaction afforded me the opportunity to experience firsthand the feelings of inadequacy and the concomitant pressure to succeed that can accompany failure to perform in facilitated communication.

6

By Your Hand Alone:
The Messages of F3-C3

Behavior ultimately depends upon the way you conceive reality.
                                    —**Professor James Buchanan**

Observation of the F3-C3 dyad was particularly noteworthy, since this client's reportedly profound deficits in overall functioning and the apparent severity of his autistic disorder made him an unlikely candidate for literacy skills acquisition. There were notable differences between this dyad and the others as well as similarities among all three of them.

This dyad had been facilitating together since August 1991. At about the time I began my investigation of facilitated communication, a new facilitator was being trained to work with C3. I strongly felt, however, that this study would be better served by observing the F3-C3 dyad, since F3 was the more experienced facilitator and she and C3 already had a long-standing, established relationship. Table A.11 contains the transcript of the observed session; Tables A.4 through A.7 contain preexistent transcripts.

What You See: Outside the FC Experience

Differences between this client's level of functioning and overall environmental awareness and those of the other two clients in the study were immediately and profoundly obvious. Unlike C1 and C2, both of whom acknowledged my presence when introduced to me, C3 did not take note of my presence in any way. He was lying on an air mattress, engaging in self-stimulatory behavior, when I arrived. Almost immediately, he had a toileting accident that necessitated his leaving the room for a change of clothing. Surveying the room in his absence, I was struck by the fact that it was depressingly devoid of literacy artifacts or similar stimulating accoutrements.

When C3 reentered the room he went to a corner and sat on the floor. F3 spent quite a bit of time talking quietly to him to try to get him to come over to the table, where his letter board was set up. (Unlike the other clients in this study, F3 used a manual letter board instead of a computer for facilitated communication.) I was surprised to observe the extent to which cajolery was apparently needed to entice him to participate in facilitated communication given the length of time this dyad had been facilitating together and considering the centrality that communication usually plays in people's lives. After a while F3 got up and put chips and soda on the table where she and C3 were going to be sitting. C3 watched intently as she did this, though he made no move to get up until the facilitator walked away from the table to get something. At this point the client independently got up, went over to the table, and sat down, apparently enticed by the presence of food and beverage. C3 picked up the bag of chips and opened it with his teeth. He began to slowly eat them. After a few minutes, F3 sat down next to C3 and patiently waited for him to finish his chips. While he was eating, the facilitator explained the reason for my visit, paying homage to one of the signature aspects of the FC movement: "She's not here to test you to see if facilitated communication works," said F3. "She believes that it does work, and that you can type, and that other autistic people can type. She's just here to see what it's like. She's just learning about it." Throughout this explanation the client stared straight ahead and continued to eat his chips. He evidenced no behavior that would indicate that he was understanding or even paying attention to his facilitator; however, when F3 asked him if he wanted to wait until he finished his chips before typing, he gave a slight nod of the head. When it appeared that he had finished the chips, F3 reached for the empty bag, but the client resisted because he was still trying to finish the crumbs at the bottom. My distinct impression both at the time and upon review of the videotaped footage of the session was that F3 was being particularly careful to avoid a confrontation with her client. When C3 finally relinquished the empty bag, F3 left the table to get him a paper towel. Before she could return, the client reached over, picked up the bottle of juice, and opened it with his teeth. He began to drink it voraciously, finishing all of it all at once. As with the chips, C3 continued to try and drink from the bottle for quite a while after it was empty. Two things were immediately apparent. First, he wanted more juice. Second, he did nothing to directly communicate this to his facilitator despite the presence of his letter board.

What You Get: Inside the FC Experience

The FC activity began with the facilitator telling the client that she had been told he was having a difficult time lately. She then said, "So I just want to ask how you're feeling. How have you been feeling lately?" As a reference for his answer, she presented him with a variety of choices on a pad of paper. She guided his hand under each word as she read it aloud. The choices were *angry, depressed, happy, anxious, excited, stressed.* The facilitator looked up after she read the word *anxious* and saw that C3 was not looking at the board. She then redirected his attention to it. Because the client was generally looking down as the other words were read, it is impossible to state with any certainty that he was, in fact, actually attending to the written words. Index-finger isolation was nearly nonexistent. This was particularly surprising given the length of time this dyad had been facilitating together and the comments that F3 had made during the interview with respect to C3's "incredible fine motor ability." For the most part, it was not his index finger but rather his entire fist that made contact with the paper. This created a great deal of ambiguity with respect to letter selection, since his fingers spanned several letters. The level of manual support, both for pointing to the words and for letter selection, was at the wrist, extending to the palm. Despite this highly intrusive level of manual support, the facilitator gave little attention to index-finger isolation except to ask him to keep his finger out on a couple of occasions. Further, she did not appear to recognize the ambiguity that inadequate finger isolation caused in the selection of letters from the client's alphabet board. Consequently, although I describe this session according to the manner in which it was conducted— with F3 attributing the clear-cut selection of letters to her client—at no time did C3's imprecise contact with the letter board lend itself to the unambiguous selection of individual letters.

After the facilitator finished reciting the list of words on the pad, the client leaned very close to her. In response to the client's behavior, F3 said that it was really good to see him. She then directed his attention back to the pad of paper, turned the page, and began reading additional word choices to him. The list contained the words *mad, relaxed, sad, okay, tired,* and *sick.* Again, he looked up at one point and missed a word. This time the facilitator was unaware of his lapse and consequently did not redirect his attention. With the same manual support as before, the dyad began the process of facilitated communication. The facilitator read each letter as it was selected: "*a, b, b.*" The client hiccuped, got up from the table precipitously, and walked away. My notes from this session indicate that index-finger isolation was "very poor, making letter selection for the client, and recognition for the observer, a highly ambiguous process."

When the client returned to the table, his facilitator called out the following letters as C3 ostensibly pointed to them: "*a, b, a, b, a, d, o, n, e, d.*" After this configuration of letters was typed, the facilitator read it as the word *abandoned.* For selection of at least five of these letters, the client was *not* looking at the letter board. Analysis of the videotape later revealed that when the facilitator was aware of the client's lack of attention to the board, she always directed his attention back to it. This seems to indicate that she felt that attention to the board was indeed important. In fact, inattention to the board was "allowed" only when F3 was concentrating on the letter board herself and hence was unaware of the client's lack of visual attention to it.

Another important consideration with respect to the determination of letters by the facilitator relates to the problems caused by the client's inadequate index-finger isolation. F3 made judgments regarding letter selection even when the client's contact with the letter board was patently obscure (i.e., when his hand spanned more than one letter or when he came down between letters). Since finger isolation was, for the most part, virtually nonexistent, the client characteristically and at best either came down on the alphabet board with his whole hand or made contact with more than one finger. This made determination of letter selection highly ambiguous, if not impossible. Finally, and incomprehensibly, of all the words read to the client from which to select his response, *abandoned* was not one of them!

According to F3, C3 pointed to the letters *b* and *y*. It should be noted that he touched the letter board in the same area as the *b* prior to the facilitator calling out the two letters as noted; however, F3 saw that C3 wasn't looking the first time he touched the board and hence did not read that letter aloud. Even though manual support at this time was closer to the palm than the wrist, the facilitator still made no attempt to attend to the lack of adequate index-finger isolation or to the ambiguity it caused. Seemingly, it was not important to her. After the dyad had facilitated the word *by*, F3 said, "What's the next word?" Although the client hit the board twice, the facilitator read nothing. She then repeated her question. At this point the client, with the same level of support as before, "pointed" to the following letters: *d, d, a, a*. At this point C3 looked at F3. The facilitator said, "What comes after *a*?" C3 touched the letter board three times, all in the same general vicinity. After this, he leaned toward the facilitator and tried to put his arm around her neck. She took his arm and redirected him to the board. He put his face very close to hers; they were nose-to-nose at one point. The facilitator responded to this by saying, "I know, it's really good to see you." He leaned toward her again while she continued to gingerly redirect his attention to the letter board. He then, according to what she read, hit an additional letter, after which she read the message that he had allegedly spelled out: *abandoned by [F3]*. In the interest of confidentiality the additional letters allegedly selected have not been named, but in my opinion, the facilitator's judgment that the client had typed her name is certainly open to conjecture given all of the circumstances surrounding this interaction. This aspect of the message will be elaborated elsewhere.

Once again the client reached out for F3, this time with both hands. At one point he appeared to sniff her hair. She seemed a bit uneasy, though not overtly fearful. The next series of letters were *bbad*. The facilitator read this as the word *bad*. Next, the letters were *can*. F3 read, "can." The next series of letters were *dad*. C3 *was not looking at the keyboard during the selection of these letters*. The facilitator said, "It looks like you're typing dad's bad or dad bad." This judgment seemed precipitous given the information available at the time. Next, she asked him to explain the message. The series of letters that followed formed the word *abandoned*. The client gave a slight smile and began to hit the same area of the letter board. F3 said, "Do you want to stop talking about that?" She then said that they would talk about something else; however, the client got up and walked away. He walked across the floor twice and then went over to the corner of the room and sat on the floor.

F3 said that she knew it was hard for him to type about those things because he felt abandoned by a lot of people. She went over to where he was sitting and explained that his dad had not abandoned him, as he came to see him every week. She tried placating him and cajoling him into typing. She promised him frequent breaks. He did not make a move to continue the interaction. Finally she asked him to type that he was done. She brought the board to C3.

He "typed" the word *abandoned,* according to F3. He then selected the word *mad*. He then typed many letters that his facilitator had difficulty interpreting. She said, "I know this is frustrating, especially when I can't figure out what you're typing." The client looked down at his lap at that point.

I found one of the last FC interactions to be of profound significance from the perspective of possible unconscious facilitator influence. F3 read each of the following letters as the client made his selection: "*b, a, d.*" After extensive review of this segment on the videotape and input from a peer reviewer, it is apparent that the facilitator actually read the letter *d* a split second *before* the client had "selected" it (i.e., made contact with the letter board). She then said, "Bad because what?" At that point, C3 looked at her quite deliberately and moaned. F3 ignored this and said, "I feel bad because what?" He continued to deliberately look at her—an action that was not in his customary repertoire—as he placed his left arm in his mouth. The facilitator ignored this as well, saying, "I'm not sure what you're typing. I'm not sure what this word means." The client's moaning became more intense. F3 now tried to verbally and physically get him to stop biting his arm. She struggled with him for a time, saying, "It's tough. It's not as easy as talking is it?" F3's remark made no sense; he is, after all, *nonverbal!* F3 was unsuccessful in getting C3 to remove his arm from his mouth until she said, "Do you want a break?" Only then did he stop biting his arm. At that point F3 put the board in front of C3 once again and took his right hand in order to begin facilitation. Although the client did not resist giving her his hand, he *immediately* put his right arm back in his mouth as he moaned and stared intently at F3's face. This time it almost appeared that the client was moaning no. F3 said, "You know that if you're getting upset you can type that you're done. It's as easy as that, *but you have to type it*" (italics added). Was his communicative intent not clear enough without the typing? He took his arm out of his mouth as she said this; however, he kept it in the "ready position." She then said something that I couldn't understand, but the last word was *finished*. C3 then put his arm down and took her hand. He hit the letter board three times on the far right-hand side. F3 said, "Okay. That's great. That's good that you could type that *no*." My notes indicate that C3's selection of the "word" was far too ambiguous to call.

An Unlikely Candidate

Even by FC standards, this client's candidacy for facilitated communication seems shaky at best and suspect at worst. For one thing, by report and by observation, C3 evidences the most severe impairment in intellectual functioning, adaptive behavior, and autistic disorder of all three clients in this study. For another, nothing in his educational or environmental background leads one to believe that his exposure to literacy events would have been sufficient to allow him to develop, on his own, the ability to read or to put letters together to form words. Remember that according to C3's father, his son's special education program at the state hospital afforded him "no exposure to academic information." In elaborating the point, he stated, "Before facilitated communication [C3] was totally unaware of letters or words." C3's placement in an intermediate care facility—and in residential settings before that—could hardly be considered an ideal environment in terms of enrichment and exposure to literacy artifacts. Further, the sterile environment in which I observed him offered virtually no opportunity to foster literacy awareness.

Even more significant from the perspective of his candidacy for facilitated communication, C3 did not at any time demonstrate in my presence the use of a conventional, reliable, functional communication system; nor did he demonstrate behaviors that are associated with literacy awareness. Contrarily, by report of his facilitator and by my own observation, C3 utilized a variety of primitive, nonconventional communicative behaviors to satisfy his needs (i.e., the use of contact gestures and a few idiosyncratic manual "signs"). In many cases he used aberrant behavior to communicate his intentions. Pragmatically, apart from facilitated communication, the only function this client utilized in my presence was the protest function, and even this was nonconventional: He either left the situation or demonstrated self-injurious behavior (i.e., biting his arm). In addition, C3 reportedly also used aggression to extricate himself from situations that he found troublesome.

Even from the perspective of receptive language ability, there is considerable doubt that C3 is able to comprehend language input to the extent to which his facilitator gives him credit. For example, during the interview F3 described her client as understanding "a lot," but this judgment did not square with her concomitant description of him (supported by examples) as evidencing difficulty following her verbal directives. Neither did it reflect the descriptions of him in his record.

All of these factors taken together would seem to at least provoke speculation with respect to this client's alleged ability to express complex feelings and emotions and to use vocabulary of some sophistication (i.e., *abandoned*) to code those thoughts. Not only is there no attempt by anyone to come to terms with the numerous disparities one finds, there is actually face-value acceptance of facilitated communication with accompanying rationales (rationalization?) to explain away the discrepancies that exist. All the while, C3 remains in a day program setting that is even less stimulating and far more isolated than a standard sheltered workshop.

When one juxtaposes all of these factors with C3's alleged ability to utilize facilitated communication as a means of expression, one is left with the unmistakable conclusion that FC stands alone, as an island unto itself. There is neither supportive documentation for this client's alleged level of literacy development nor anything about his overt behavior outside the confines of facilitated communication to suggest the existence of high-level literacy and pragmatic communication development. Even within the FC session, C3's "selection" of letters was highly suspect given his imprecise contact with the letter board. Further, given the emotionally charged messages that are attributed to this client, one can't help but call to mind his father's fears about facilitated communication and the possible "injustice" that could be done in its name.

Notwithstanding the obvious differences between this dyad and the other two in this study, there were noteworthy similarities. Here, as in the cases of F1 and F2, there is the practice of ignoring the client's obvious, intentional communicative behavior (e.g., C3's biting his arm while intently making eye contact with F3 and eventually adding vocalization as a means of extricating himself from the situation). Further, in keeping with the primacy of the "typed" message, even though F3 infers from the client's behavior that he wants to stop facilitating, she nonetheless still insists that he *type* his message. As with the others, this facilitator's disregard for C3's communicative intent causes him obvious frustration, as judged by the escalation of inappropriate behavior that serves to punctuate it. Finally, and to my way of thinking most disturbing, are the missed opportunities in all three dyads to honor the clients' communicative efforts when the latter run contrary to the content and conduct of facilitated communication or to the expectations and agendas of the facilitators.

7

Getting the Message Loud and Clear

The medium matters because it defines the arena of sentience. The screen not only carries the words, it also says that communication is nothing more than the transfer of evanescent bits across a glowing panel.

—Sven Birkerts

In all cases, the messages that clients generated via facilitated communication were at a significantly higher level of pragmatic and semantic sophistication than their observed and reported abilities in speech, language, and communication. Utterance length and sentence structure were also more sophisticated than one would expect given the clients' diagnoses and their institutional backgrounds. My own observations of these clients' abilities were quite consistent with what was reported in their records. The sophistication of their messages, however, stood in stark contrast to both.

One would not expect to find adult clients who manifest the dual disability of autism and mental retardation to be capable of using such abstract, high-level vocabulary as *abandoned* and *facade*. Yet both words were allegedly generated by the client who manifested the severest disability overall. Likewise, one would not expect such clients to be proficient at maintaining appropriate use of deictic forms (i.e., words used to specify place, time, or person) or to be able to use idiomatic expressions with ease. Nevertheless, C2 evidenced surprising facility with the former and clear evidence of the latter (e.g., *i red in the face*). Conventional wisdom also mitigates against these clients manifesting the degree of sophistication in the use of the pragmatic functions of communication that their messages reveal, especially since pragmatic ability (i.e., the social use of language) is considered by people in the field of autism to constitute one of the primary

116

areas of deficit in the disorder. Before I discuss my findings in greater detail, a brief review of the pertinent literature related to pragmatics is in order if the reader is to appreciate the nature and extent of the pragmatic deficits in autism and their implications for message generation in facilitated communication.

Disordered Pragmatic Development

Empirical support for conventional wisdom may be found in the autism and communication literature. For example, in a study conducted by Wetherby and Prutting (1984), two of the most well respected researchers in the area of pragmatics, children with autism "displayed a relatively homogeneous profile of communicative functions that was both *quantitatively* and *qualitatively* [italics added] different from that of normal children" (p. 373). These investigators went on to characterize this finding as particularly striking given the "variability in mode and linguistic complexity of communicative means" (p. 373). Thus the more limited repertoire of communicative functions found in children with autism was deemed to reflect *disordered*, as opposed to merely *delayed*, development. This is an important distinction, for this finding would mitigate against the view that children with autism simply "catch up" to their normally developing peers at some later time. Fay (1980) lends support to this claim by noting that early difficulty with pragmatic functions may later evolve into higher-level pragmatic deficits in conversational discourse instead of simply abating. Thus given the weight and quality of research evidence, I consider the argument that pragmatic deficits may be outgrown to be spurious and hence inappropriate to explain the level of pragmatic sophistication found in clients' facilitated messages.

Wetherby and Prutting (1984) also found a distinctive pattern among children with autism with respect to the way they *acquire* the pragmatic functions of communication. Whereas typical children develop these functions synchronistically (i.e., at the same relative time), those with autism acquire them one at a time. Basing their assessment of the cognitive-social abilities of children with autism on the pioneering work of Bates and her colleagues (1979) with typical children, Wetherby and Prutting (1984) found that the heterochronous development of the communicative functions in autism was also associated with lower-level skill development in symbolic play, a finding that lends support to Piaget's (1967) assertion that a common semiotic function underlies both child's play and language development. This finding too has implications for the clients in this study, for it should be obvious that they neither carried diagnoses nor came from educational and environmental backgrounds that would lead one to believe they had had either the inclination or the opportunity to participate in the high-quality play interactions that provide fertile ground for the development of symbolic language.

Building on the work of Curcio (1978) and Wetherby and Prutting (1984), Wetherby (1986) presented an ontogeny of communicative functions for children with autism that evolved from communication for nonsocial purposes (e.g., behavioral regulation) to communication for quasi-social purposes (e.g., attracting attention to oneself) and finally to communication for social purposes (e.g., directing the attention of another individual to an item or event). She also made it clear that this profile was *specific to children with autism* as opposed to characteristic of an earlier stage of normal development, stating that "some autistic children may never develop certain 'later-emerging' functions (i.e., later for autistic children)" (pp. 307–308).

Support for this contention may be found in Seibert and Hogan's (1982) analysis of the social domain in typical children. The three dimensions they studied were social interaction, joint attention, and behavioral regulation. These dimensions correspond to the category of broad pragmatic functions in my study. Seibert and Hogan (1982) acknowledge that from a macroperspective, skill development in all three dimensions occurs concurrently in typical children, but they nevertheless analyze the relationship of each to the other from a microperspective in order to identify the componential behaviors that underlie them and to gain greater insight into the manner in which skill development progresses over time. As such, their analysis contrasts sharply with the analysis Wetherby (1986) sets forth for children with autism. Specifically, their findings suggest that typical children develop the behavioral regulation function *after* the two more social functions. In contrast, Wetherby (1986) found that children with autism develop the nonsocial (i.e., behavioral regulation) function *prior* to the more social functions (i.e., social interaction and joint attention). This finding clearly underscores the distinct difficulty that children with autism have with social information.

Marked Discordance

Given these research findings and the institutional backgrounds of the adult clients in this study during their formative years, it is difficult to understand how their facilitated messages could demonstrate such an impressive degree of proficiency in using pragmatic functions and linguistic devices to convey their intents. Such skills seem all the more implausible when one considers that these clients were institutionalized at a time when little was known about the importance of early intervention, language and environmental stimulation, and the significance of play in the development of symbolic behavior. Discordance is particularly marked for C2, as his typed transcripts demonstrate impressive pragmatic ability at the level of conversational discourse despite the fact that his verbal expression and his general behavior are, while commensurate with each other, nowhere near this level of sophistication.

With respect to C1, even though her verbal pragmatic ability and the written pragmatic ability observed in her typing more closely approximate each other during facilitated typing and are basically commensurate with her independent typing, it is indeed possible, given her repetitious use of several "stock" social phrases, that certain of these communicative functions may have developed as part of a social routine. If so, they may be more reflective of a ritualized use of language rather than of language that is employed in the service of a truly social act (Wetherby 1986). Consequently, C1 may be less competent pragmatically than her superficial use of language indicates. Likewise, it is difficult to reconcile C3's use of high-level abstract terms (e.g., *facade, abandoned*) with his continual and customary use of nonsocial, primitive contact gestures and other nonconventional and aberrant behaviors to express his intents outside of facilitated communication.

Further, despite the rich research base documenting atypical language use in children with autism (e.g., pronominal reversal, word retrieval difficulty, metaphoric language, immediate and delayed echolalia, and stereotypic language use) (Cantwell, Baker, and Rutter 1978; Caparulo and Cohen 1977; Fay and Schuler 1980), virtually *none* of these atypicalities show up in the FC transcripts. C2 offers a particularly interesting contrast between his transcripts and his reported and observed verbal expression. Typed transcripts reveal excellent use of pronouns, conjunctions, and other parts of speech that characterize fluent discourse. In contrast, by report and by observation, C2's speech is telegraphic in nature, that is, marked by the omission of pronouns and connecting words that add fluency to verbal utterances.

With respect to C1, her preexistent typed messages contain repetitions of portions of the typed questions to which she was exposed, giving them an echoic quality. (See Table A.2 in the appendix, transcript dated 8/20/92.) This leads one to question whether C1 may have developed a strategy for answering complex questions based on repetition of the basic elements within them. If she had developed the ability to do this, it is conceivable that some of her typed utterances may appear to reflect greater sophistication than she might actually be capable of. For example, in response to F1's question, "Would you be willing to explore new possibilities?" C1 responded, "I would like to explore new possibilities." Or were the basic sentence elements seen in the preexistent transcripts carrier phrases typed by her facilitator for the purpose of eliciting an automatic response? F1 did, after all, type out "I like to say" when I observed this dyad during one of the FC sessions. Finally, all of these observations should be considered in light of the unusual and often asynchronous interactional elements governing facilitated communication that were discussed in the earlier chapters.

The degree of pragmatic and semantic sophistication of clients' facilitated messages is also difficult to reconcile with the fact that deficits in social behavior and communication constitute *stable* and highly *consistent* findings in autism. Further, these findings hold true for individuals who are considered "high-functioning" (Tsai 1992; Wing 1992) as well as for those who are described as less capable. In fact, deficits in social behavior and communication are considered by many experts to be core features of the autistic disorder. Indeed, even when high-functioning individuals with autism do possess sophisticated language skills, they nevertheless manifest problems in the area of pragmatics, that is, in the *use* of their language for social communication purposes (Twachtman-Cullen, in press; Wing 1992). The centrality of the social communication deficit in autism led Tanguay (1990) to refer to it as the defining feature that "distinguishes retarded autistic persons from nonautistic retarded persons, or normal-IQ autistic persons from normal persons in general" (p. 201). Likewise, Frith (1989) cites difficulty in the social use of language for communication purposes as a "universal feature of autism" (p. 120).

I found other difficult-to-reconcile disparities in this study. For example, despite C1's more highly developed communication skills and her significantly richer environmental background, her transcribed messages were generally *less sophisticated* than those of the other two clients with respect to content, vocabulary, and the expression of feelings. C2's messages were remarkable for their social overtones. Not only was he able to use idiomatic expressions, he was also able to give compliments and engage in lighthearted social banter. In addition, his messages were marked by many more conversational initiations and elaborations than either of the other two clients in this study. And C3, despite the paucity of utterances available for him, allegedly produced abstract, philosophical information (e.g., referring to typing as a facade, expressing the opinion that people fear him, and discussing his feelings of abandonment) not found in the FC messages of even the highest-functioning client in this study.

It should be noted that during the course of the interviews, F1 did quote messages allegedly generated by C1 that were both at a higher level of sophistication and remarkable for their stylized use of language. Their lack of inclusion here was in direct response to the facilitator's concern that those messages contained identifying features that could infringe on his client's right to confidentiality. The messages I did select for analysis were representative of this client's more current FC performance and reflect the following statement by F1: "With her [C1] it's really interesting because over time what we've seen is that her typing and her speech have become more consistent."

"Perfect" Asynchrony

Although the level of semantic and pragmatic sophistication evident in clients' transcripts was distinctly out of sync with their reported and observed functioning levels, it did reflect concordance with facilitators' judgments regarding their clients' abilities. Thus it is fair to say that the analysis of facilitated messages gives rise to more questions than it answers, for here too one sees the derailment of conventional wisdom. Specifically, instead of the more capable client evidencing greater sophistication in message generation, the *less* capable clients demonstrate this quality. This lack of conventionality, inexplicable though it may be, is very much a part of the FC landscape, as the following statement by Biklen (1993) clearly illustrates: "Nevertheless, it is especially noteworthy and encouraging that among those who are able to demonstrate high levels of literacy and numeracy through facilitated communication are people who were previously *presumed* [italics added] to be among the 'lowest' intellectually functioning persons labeled 'autistic'" (p. 29). Given the concordance among research findings across several fields with respect to these issues, Biklen's use of the word *presumed* seems more than a little presumptuous!

The findings of this study also contradict, or at least cast doubt upon, a "caught not taught" view of literacy development, an argument used by FC proponents to explain (rationalize?) the acquisition of literacy skills in the absence of specific attention to them. Here again, the individual with the more enriched environment (and hence ostensibly greater exposure to literacy materials) demonstrates a level of pragmatic and semantic skill development in facilitated communication that is *lower* than that of clients with more impoverished backgrounds (and hence less exposure to literacy materials). Surely even FC proponents would agree that the institutions of fifteen or twenty years ago could hardly be described as either stimulating or enriching, particularly regarding literacy skills acquisition.

Conveniently, facilitators deal with the disparities between their judgments of their clients' abilities and the weight and consistency of information to the contrary by calling for a reconceptualization of the autistic disorder. The rationale for this should be obvious given our current, research-based understanding of autism. Absent a redefinition, facilitators would be hard pressed to explain the presence of sophisticated literacy and pragmatic ability in adult clients whose early lives were mainly spent in highly restrictive, and more than likely sterile, institutional settings. This would seem to be a particularly thorny issue for facilitators to grapple with given their universal lack of esteem for such settings and their recognition of the detrimental effects of institutionalization in general. Likewise, without a reconceptualization of the autistic disorder, facilitators would undoubtedly have grave difficulty explaining the apparent "disappearance" of the social and communication deficits that inevitably seems to occur quite literally at the hands of facilitators.

A Matter of Confusion

Importantly, facilitators seem to have confused *literacy* with *pragmatics*. That is, facilitators accept their clients' pragmatically competent messages as manifestations of their exposure to literacy artifacts within their environments. However, *literacy* and *pragmatics* are not identical constructs: nor is development in one area necessarily contingent on development in the other. Many people who do not possess functional literacy skills are nonetheless able to express themselves quite well pragmatically. Moreover, even high-functioning individuals with autism who do demonstrate the ability to read and write inevitably evidence difficulty with the pragmatics of communication, as the latter is a *universal* feature of the disorder.

Generically speaking, *literacy* refers to the ability to read and write. Even if one were to adopt a more encompassing, interactional view of literacy, clients in this study would, according to their diagnoses and their environmental and educational histories, still be compromised. This judgment is based on the work of Linda Miller, an expert in the area of literacy development. According to Miller (1990), "Literacy arises out of the context of shared events and experiences and out of the communicative interactions emerging from those activities" (p. 2). Again, the institutional backgrounds of these clients would not have served them well in this regard.

According to *Random House Webster's College Dictionary* (1991), *pragmatics* refers to "a branch of linguistics dealing with language in its situational context, including the knowledge and beliefs of the speaker and the relationship and interaction between speaker and listener" (p. 1059). Thus even if the clients in this study had been able to amass a good deal of information about the words they may have been exposed to in their environments (which is difficult to accept on face value given the customary sterility of residential settings of that era), this would still not account for the pragmatic sophistication of some of their facilitated messages. To summarize, notwithstanding some shared developmental features, *pragmatic communication* constitutes a different dimension than does *literacy*, a fact that facilitators in this study and in general seem consummately unaware of.

If one relies on empirical evidence available in the literature bases across several fields (rather than on the *suppositions* that facilitators generate to justify the discrepancies that contrast sharply with that evidence), one may extrapolate from what is known about infant development in general and autism in particular that the clients in this study were undoubtedly also compromised in their abilities to participate in the synchronous and reciprocal interaction patterns that are associated with the development of sociocommunicative (i.e., pragmatic) ability in normal infants (Brazelton and Cramer 1990; Kaye 1982; Schaffer 1977; Stern 1977). One may also infer that these clients were similarly impoverished in the development of symbolic play, a factor that would further negatively impact their development of language (Nicholich 1977; Piaget 1967). Finally, given the complexities involved in the construct of pragmatics—its relationship to semiotics (i.e., the ability to use symbols)—and an understanding of how the use of signs affects the attitudes, behaviors, and beliefs of communicative partners (Arwood 1983; Watzlawick, Beavin, and Jackson 1967) and given the multi-faceted nature of this construct vis-à-vis its nonverbal and semantic elements, postulation of a "caught not taught" theory of pragmatic communication development seems ludicrous at best and irresponsible at worst.

Lost in the Translation

Perhaps the most striking finding of this investigation with respect to message generation is the fact that a great deal of information gets lost when transcripts are viewed apart from the dyadic interactions that produce them. The dynamics of the interactions between facilitator and client provide a context that is essential to understanding the meaning of these messages and how they are produced.

Analysis of videotaped FC sessions gave me an appreciation for the contextual elements governing the generation of messages and clearly revealed the conspicuous and inevitable deficiencies of any analysis conducted apart from these contextual elements. This finding has important implications not only for reviewing the printed transcripts out of context in the present study but also for using transcripts in other situations involving facilitated communication, for example, as *proof* of clients' intent in important matters governing their lives and as prima facie evidence of FC ability. The following observations illustrate the extent to which valuable information can get lost in the translation if transcripts are analyzed apart from the contexts in which they are generated:

1. Printed transcripts do not reflect the fact that facilitated communication can be a laborious and cumbersome task, as judged by the length of time and amount of effort involved in typing out many of the words.
2. Printed transcripts do not reflect the number of mistakes, "false starts," and deletions that characteristically occur.
3. Printed transcripts do not reflect the type or amount of either verbal or physical prompting by facilitators (e.g., saying "push it," or pointing out the correct letter, respectively).
4. Printed transcripts do not reflect the degree of manual support provided.
5. Printed transcripts do not reflect the emotional reaction of the client or the response of the facilitator.
6. Printed transcripts do not contain information related to the match or mismatch between verbal and nonverbal behavior; nor do they reflect discrepancies between either of the latter behaviors and the typed message.

7. Printed transcripts do not usually include any information with respect to the client's verbal behavior because typing has primacy over talking.
8. Printed transcripts do not indicate whether the client was looking at the keyboard; nor do they provide any information with respect to literacy awareness activities (e.g., reciprocal referencing of the keyboard and screen).
9. Printed transcripts do not provide information with regard to any of the contextual elements governing the communicative situation.
10. Printed transcripts are "silent" on the issue of possible facilitator influence.

Given these observations, one has to wonder what might have been lost in the decontextualized transcriptions that are inevitably included in publications and conferences extolling the virtues of facilitated communication (Biklen 1990, 1993; Haskew and Donnellan 1992). It should be obvious that when contextual variables are set aside, a large and crucial portion of the communicative message is eradicated and interpretation of the message becomes sketchy at best and largely at the mercy of the facilitator at worst. The reader should take these issues into account in reviewing the semantic and pragmatic analyses of the *preexisting* transcripts in this study. Even with the best of intentions, printed transcripts ignore a multitude of contextual variables.

PART THREE

Unsettling Reviews

I undertook the present study for the express purpose of exploring the factors involved in facilitated communication, particularly with respect to the role of the facilitator, in order to tease out those quintessential elements foundational to an understanding of the method. As noted previously, the selection of a qualitative research design reflected both my recognition of the complexities involved in the phenomenon of FC and my commitment to honoring proponents' lack of comfort with quantitative procedures. Thus I both observed and experienced facilitated communication within the natural environment as part of the context of clients' and facilitators' daily lives.

Acknowledging the cautions I raised earlier concerning the inherent limitations in qualitative research, I believe the validity of the findings in the present investigation was enhanced by the overall consistency that emerged from the triangulation of information sources and by the confirmation of my own judgments by the peer debriefers consulted. Further, my interactions with clients and facilitators and my actual participation in the process of facilitated communication afforded me intimate exposure to the methodology and provided valuable insights that would have been otherwise unavailable. Finally, by seeking out discomfirmatory information from FC advocates, I was able to generate alternative explanations for some of the phenomena I observed in this study. This enabled me to witness the tenacity with which proponents hold to their beliefs even in the face of obvious contradictory information.

Overall, the findings of this investigation reveal a good deal of internal consistency in each client's record with respect to reported degree of intellectual impairment, demonstrated skill development, and extent of behavioral disturbance. Specifically, *higher* reported intelligence was associated with a more *advanced* level of skill development and a *lower* incidence of maladaptive behavior. Conversely, *lower* reported intelligence was associated with a *lower* level of skill development and a *higher* incidence of maladaptive behavior. Despite the fact that this pattern is not quite as definitive with respect to the environmental and educational backgrounds of the clients, it does seem to follow the same general trend *if FC is set aside*; that is, the more stimulating the background of the client, the greater the evidence for both literacy awareness and increased use of the pragmatic functions of communication.

Before I discuss the ramifications of my findings regarding the suitability of facilitated communication as a tool for self-expression in persons with autism and mental retardation, a final word of caution is in order. Given the subjective nature of this study and the absence of some of the standard safeguards with respect to reliability and validity (i.e., control groups and objective instrumentation), replication of findings, in the tradition of quantitative research, is not to be expected on a point-for-point basis. However, the broad themes that emerged from this study should certainly be discoverable in other similar settings and situations. Support for this contention is found in Biklen (1993): "It is assumed that if researchers have a shared perspective and can establish similar levels of rapport with their subjects, *they can observe the same things similarly*" (italics added; p. 4).

With this in mind, in Chapter 8 I endeavor to make sense of the numerous contradictions that surface in facilitated communication. In Chapter 9 I meet the issue of facilitator influence head on, suggesting possible reasons for its occurrence in facilitated communication. Chapter 10 deals more expansively with the controversial issue of facilitator influence before summarizing the findings of this investigation. In Chapter 11 I take a hard look at the FC culture in an attempt to make sense of the methodology, the forces that shaped it, and the mystique that surrounds it.

Clearly, the findings of this study raise critical questions on ethics and responsibility. In addition, they contain important implications for future research, particularly with regard to the complex nature of unconscious facilitator influence and the possible detrimental effect this may have on the client in general and on communication in particular. Ultimately, the findings of this investigation underscore the critical need for responsible research into the validity and efficacy of facilitated communication *prior* to rendering judgments and delivering pronouncements in its name.

8

From Discordance
to Disconnection

No point in asking Greenfield what he was up to; he had pulled up his
mental drawbridge and there was no way over the moat.

—Lucille Kallen

The World of the Clients

Clearly, C1's environmental background was more stimulating than either
C2's or C3's. Both her mother and her facilitator confirm the information
in her record. However, her early background is enhanced simply by virtue
of comparing it to the barren environments of the other two clients in this
study. And much of the environmental stimulation she received was *supple-*
mental in nature (i.e., provided by her mother and significant others in her
life), not provided in her residential setting. According to their records, the
other two clients in this study did not receive the quality of environmental
stimulation that C1 experienced. C1's preschool history reveals that she did
have some exposure to typical peers, and her later educational history contains references to a preacademic component. These experiences were reportedly not available to either C2 or C3. It is not surprising, therefore,
that C1 was the only client in this study whose record indicated that she
possessed functional, albeit rudimentary, literacy skills in the form of reading and writing prior to the initiation of facilitated communication. This
factor is highly significant vis-à-vis the results of this study and will be further elaborated elsewhere. I found additional consistency with respect to
C1's reported speech and language development. Of the three clients in this

127

study, C1 was reported to be the most competent communicator; my own observations confirmed this.

Neither C2 nor C3 had educational or environmental backgrounds that were hospitable to the development of literacy skills. In C3's case, the record was confirmed by his father. The records of both clients indicated that, unlike C1, their educational programs were strictly *functional* as opposed to preacademic. C3 had spent a considerable part of his life in intermediate care facilities, which are ordinarily reserved for clients with more severe disabilities. C2's record cited maternal deprivation and environmental impoverishment in addition to placement in segregated, institutional settings. The lack of ongoing parental presence in C2's life lends credence to the claims of environmental as well as emotional impoverishment.

Regarding communication development, C3's record documents his lack of competence. Based on a fairly detailed account in C2's record, it appears that he utilized speech as a means of communication with greater frequency than was seen during the course of this study. Although it is possible that C2's record overestimated his speech and language ability, the specificity of the information and the number of references to this ability seem to mitigate against this interpretation. This disparity may well be a by-product of this client's experience with facilitated communication, since verbal communication was *actively discouraged* by the facilitator's ongoing lack of attention to C2's verbal utterances regardless of whether they were contextually appropriate. Underscoring this lack of esteem for verbal communication is the fact that his FC sessions were conducted in virtual silence. Thus it is certainly reasonable to infer that the facilitator's continual lack of reinforcement of C2's verbal behavior discouraged—or even extinguished—this behavior within the FC context. Whether this effect generalized to other situations is beyond the scope of this study; however, it is an area well worth pursuing in the future.

If we put aside FC for the moment, each client's demonstrated functioning level appears to agree with the record (with the exception of the disparity between C2's reported and observed speech and language output). Information in the records regarding the clients' day-to-day vocational activities, self-care ability, strengths and weaknesses, and educational and environmental backgrounds were all consistent with my observations as well. Once facilitated communication enters the picture, consistency among several cogent factors takes a backseat. Facilitators are all too willing to disregard contradictory information and to resolve all issues of discordance in favor of facilitated communication, setting in motion a pattern of disconnection that permeates their judgments. The results of this study raise the possibility that the roots of this disconnection are implanted in the fertile belief systems of the facilitators.

The World According to the Facilitators

My interviews with facilitators revealed a great deal of consistency among them with respect to their views on facilitated communication and autism. Perhaps most significant, however, was their impressive knowledge of facilitated communication in contrast to their meager knowledge, and in some cases inaccurate views, of autism. For example, not one of the facilitators acknowledged the hallmark features of autism (the social and communicative impairments) or seemed to understand the concept of pragmatics. They also did not seem to have more than a rudimentary understanding of the sensory deficits that inevitably accompany the disorder or of the myriad ways such deficits affect clients' understanding of and responses to their environments. In some cases facilitators' lack of understanding of the autistic disorder and their corresponding commitment to facilitated communication led them to make attributions that were in direct contradiction to the autism research literature. For example, F1's comment that people with autism have a lot of empathy runs counter to the research-based claim of Meltzoff and Gopnik (1993) that "children with autism show a relative lack of empathy—little indication that another's sadness touches them, that another's joy makes them feel happy" (p. 358). One may speculate that facilitators would react to this statement with the same assumption they make about literacy, that is, that empathy develops in a "caught not taught" manner. This is an argument, however, that has no more empirical support than the "catch-as-catch-can" view of literacy. Furthermore, any argument for empathy appears to be a circular one; that is, because clients are allegedly able to express powerful thoughts and emotions they must be empathetic, and because they are empathetic they are able to express powerful thoughts and emotions. Finally, at least within the confines of this study, there was *never* an attempt by facilitators to even question the veracity of the basic premises on which their arguments for FC were based. Rather, as in the case of empathy, premises were *always* accepted on face value even in the midst of significant information to the contrary.

I also found consistency among facilitators with respect to their views regarding the pragmatic competency and the literacy development of their clients. In all cases, facilitators not only failed to distinguish between the two concepts, lumping them together as a single construct, but also admitted to having little understanding of the concept of pragmatics in general. None of these factors, however, constrained facilitators from rendering opinions on the subject! Not surprisingly, all of them reported a much higher level of overall competency than was apparent in either the clients' records or their day-to-day functioning. Moreover, they based their opinions solely on their clients' performance with respect to FC and clung tenaciously to their beliefs. The propensity to hold fast to the tenets of facilitated communication, even in the face of circumstances that would contraindicate its use, is a recurring theme among facilitators in general, as judged by their attempts to explain away behavior that would typically serve as evidence against FC. An example of this is the use of arguments such as channeling (Calculator 1992) and telepathy (Haskew and Donnellan 1992) to justify the typing of information to which *only* the facilitators have access. That I found the same propensity to stand by FC among the facilitators in this study only serves to underscore the stability of this finding as a central factor in the belief systems of FC proponents.

At the risk of oversimplification, belief in the client's competence may be the cornerstone of the FC culture and a prime mover in the advancement of the cause. Armed with such a belief, facilitators expect success. It should come as no surprise, then, that in spite of these client's reported and observed lower levels of functioning, they lived up to their facilitators' expectations with respect to generating sophisticated facilitated messages.

The Domain of Relationship

Observation of the process of facilitated communication was particularly illuminating with respect to the dimension of relationship. Facilitators' claims in this study that trust and emotional support are crucial to the conduct of facilitated communication were not supported by my own observations of the dyadic interactions. I was struck by the frequent lack of synchrony between facilitator and client in all three of the dyads. This was particularly evident when there was a mismatch between the client's verbal and nonverbal behavior and the typed message. At such times facilitators steadfastly honored the tenet of facilitated communication that directs them to ignore behavior (both verbal and nonverbal) and pay attention only to the typing. Thus facilitators' belief in the primacy of typing over all other forms of communication creates a built-in barrier to relevant and important aspects of the communicative message. In addition, it violates the pragmatics of human communication. According to Arwood (1983), a prime mover in the advancement of pragmatic theory, an important aspect of pragmatics consists of "the need to consider the action or behavior as part of the linguistic moment" (p. 22). According to pragmatic communication theorists Watzlawick, Beavin, and Jackson (1967), all behavior has communicative value. Finally, a belief in the primacy of typing requires a corresponding *disregard* for the rich literature base that addresses the interconnectedness of behavior and communication (Donnellan et al. 1984; Durand, Berotti, and Weiner 1993; Prizant and Schuler 1987; Watzlawick, Beavin, and Jackson 1967).

The implications of facilitators' tenacious adherence to their beliefs even in the face of significant evidence to the contrary are singularly alarming.

Facilitators' disparagement of what they characterize as "interfering" verbal and nonverbal behaviors during typing removes an important safeguard (against facilitator influence) by not allowing clients the right to use such behavior to react either to the facilitated messages or to the interactive situation. Further, it is difficult to conceive how such disparagement would be consistent with the establishment of an emotionally supportive relationship with the client. I observed this practice in all three dyadic relationships, but I found it particularly distressing in the F1-C1 dyad in view of the readability of the client's communicative intent, the strength of her *persistent* efforts to repair messages, and the degree of frustration she exhibited when those efforts were disregarded.

Communication Denied

Of the three clients in this study, only C1 was reported to have possessed functional literacy skills in the form of reading and writing *prior* to the initiation of facilitated communication. Further, she not only demonstrated actual use of those skills during FC sessions but also demonstrated literacy awareness in the form of reciprocal referencing of the keyboard and computer screen, ostensibly to monitor her typing. She was by report and by observation the most competent communicator overall. Concomitant with her ability to utilize a variety of pragmatic functions and linguistic devices to get her messages across, I observed her successfully employing readable (i.e., conventional) nonverbal behavior in the form of gestures and manual signs. She used this behavior to supplement, repair, and add force to her verbal messages. Most significant, however, given its importance vis-à-vis the concept of communicative intent, was her ability to persist in her attempts to express herself. This latter skill poignantly underscored many of the other judgments I made with respect to the intentionality of C1's communicative attempts.

Consistent with the previously noted information, C1 functioned with the least intrusive amount of manual support and also demonstrated the ability to type *independently*. She did, however, also manifest difficulty with sentence generation, spelling, and word selection and retrieval. In addition, receptive language ability and auditory processing were at times problematic. In summary, my observations reveal that C1 possessed a functional, albeit somewhat rudimentary, communication system. And it was clear to me that she expressed herself far more successfully when she utilized a *variety* of communicative behaviors to convey her intent rather than when she was limited to only one means. Thus F1's insistence that C1 convey her thoughts *only* through the medium of facilitated communication and his disregard for both her verbal and nonverbal behavior not only *decreased* the effectiveness of her communication but also caused her a great deal of frustration as well.

Denying C1 the right to utilize a variety of communicative means, including speech, in addition to augmentative components (e.g., FC) is in direct contradiction to the augmentative communication literature. According to Vanderheiden and Yoder (1986), experts in the area of augmentative communication, "Emphasis should not be placed on the development of an augmentative communication system, but on the development of an *effective overall communication system*, one that includes speech and standard and special augmentative techniques as components of the system" (p. 6). Further, J. L. Twachtman (1996) underscores the importance of honoring *client* as opposed to *caregiver* preferences in determining communicative means if true functionality is to be established.

The unmistakable impression one derives not only from the F1-C1 dyad but also from the other two dyads in this study is that the opposite priority holds true in the case of facilitated communication. That is, not only are other means of communication deemphasized, they are actually sacrificed to FC. Thus the goal is not the development of an *effective* communication system but rather the glorification and advancement of facilitated communication. Indeed, one must question the value of a methodology ostensibly designed to *facilitate* communication that, by its very nature, abrogates the client's right to express herself or himself in the manner that most effectively gets the intended message across.

Coming Full Circle

C1 added an important, if confusing, dimension to this study both because of her prefacilitation literacy skills and because of the unanticipated discrepancy between her earlier *facilitated* output and her more recent *independent* typing. Specifically, her earlier facilitated messages were quite sophisticated with respect to content and vocabulary; her later, independent messages, by report and by observation, were not only less sophisticated but were generally commensurate with the prefacilitation language and literacy ability reported in her record. I feel that this observation is enormously significant because it is consistent with what Smith and Belcher (1993) found in their study of facilitated communication. They demonstrated that their subjects' verbal literacy skills "did not surpass their nonfacilitated literacy output" (p. 180). This finding argues against attributing literacy skills to the phenomenon of FC alone. Interestingly, this client's prefacilitation literacy development dovetails nicely with the lower level of sophistication in her independent typing, but it doesn't come close to accounting for the higher-level sophistication of her facilitated messages. It is indisputable that as C1 has moved toward greater independence in her typing, the similarity (consistency) between her speech and her typing has increased. In addition, her independently typed messages have become *less* sophisticated than those earlier messages typed under highly intrusive manual support. Thus, there seems to be an inverse correlation here between sophistication and physical support. In the acquisition of most other skills, the opposite would be true; as skill level increases, one would expect greater sophistication as well. Could it be that C1 has come full circle, that she is back where she was prior to FC? Her record and history seem to suggest this.

These observations lead to two questions: Why is the level of sophistication higher with facilitation than without it? Why has facilitated communication achieved such a level of prominence in this client's communicative repertoire that it has virtually eclipsed all other forms of communication available to her? The latter question is particularly important because, based on the findings of this investigation, facilitated communication provides C1 with a *less* effective form of communication. It also trivializes her *functional* verbal and nonverbal behavior, deprives her of her right to use these two means to react to the typed messages, and as noted previously, causes her a great deal of frustration.

An Entity unto Itself

The same pattern of disparagement for accompanying verbal and nonverbal behavior that I saw in the F1-C1 dyad was present in the other two dyads in this study. Mention has already been made of the possible negative effect FC may have had on C2's verbal behavior. Thus the findings of this study suggest the possibility that verbal clients may be affected differently than nonverbal clients. Specifically, inattention to an FC client's verbal behavior may cause it to decrease and may cause the client anxiety and frustration.

Of the three dyads in this study, F1-C1 gave me the best opportunity to view the effects of facilitated communication on a client with clear evidence, apart from FC, of functional literacy and pragmatic skills. What emerged from this experience was both unexpected and very disturbing. I observed that C1's knowledge and use of verbal and nonverbal communication clashed with her use of facilitated communication. For example, in almost all instances in which this client evidenced agitation and frustration, the cause was the lack of concordance between the message the client was seemingly trying to convey through a combination of verbal and nonverbal means and the message that was emerging through facilitated communication.

Even more disturbing, facilitated communication appears to contain a built-in assumption that is particularly detrimental to the more literate and pragmatically sophisticated client: Verbal utterances that do not appear to support the typed message are meaningless echoes. This is not an accurate view of echolalia and the functions it serves (Prizant and Duchan 1981; Prizant and Rydell 1984). This mental set against *unwanted* verbal utterances during the act of typing creates a barrier between the verbal client and the facilitator such that *only* the typed message is honored. This leaves a literate and pragmatically competent client "incapable" of modifying or protesting against messages that may not be his or her own. In such cases, the client is left with little recourse other than to engage in aberrant behavior (i.e., self-injurious or aggressive behavior) to communicate his or her intent, for *in the absence of being able to speak out, the client will most probably act out.* Such aberrant behavior was demonstrated by all three clients in this study regardless of whether they were verbal. Even C3, who was nonverbal, displayed intentional, albeit aberrant, communicative behavior during facilitated communication that was ignored in deference to the primacy of typing over all other forms of communication.

An Unsettling Experience

As noted previously, my interactions with two of the clients in this study allowed intimate exposure to aspects of facilitated communication that would not have been available otherwise. The startling observation drawn from both of these experiences is the extent to which my attitude and my performance were affected by factors that had more to do with the conduct of facilitated communication than with the actual participation of the client.

In the case of C1, my desire to have her be successful led me not only to ignore obvious, intentional communicative behavior but also to bend the rules of interpretation to accommodate the letters she had already typed. Even more disturbing, however, is the fact that I was completely unaware at the time I was interacting with the client of the effect my attitude had on my consequent behavior. Worse yet, my impression of that interaction at the time I was involved in it was positive! It was only after careful scrutiny during multiple viewings of the videotaped footage and input from the peer reviewer that my approach and attitude were apparent to me. Facilitators also, given their inexorable commitment to the technique and their concomitant desire and expectation for success, may be unlikely to make objective decisions during facilitation.

In the case of C2, I was specifically struck by the intense pressure that my incompetence with respect to message generation had on my willingness to follow the facilitator's directive to "lead him to the letters." I was also unsettled by what appeared to be the client's complete motor passivity and apparent purposelessness as I facilitated with him. Equally disturbing was the fact that on several occasions C2 began to type even before I had begun to ask a question or before I had finished asking one. Interestingly, the latter phenomenon is similar to that observed in the case of Clever Hans, the famous "talking" horse that was discovered in Germany around the turn of the century.

In describing Oskar Pfungst's series of classic experiments on Hans's alleged ability to answer questions posed to him in German, perform arithmetical computations, and engage in other remarkable acts of verbal and abstract reasoning, Candland (1993) gave the experiments *paragon status*. In other words, they were typical of "the tenets and powers of the experimental method when applied to behavior" (p. 111). Pfungst observed that "if the questioner [of Hans] retained the erect position he elicited no response from the horse. . . . If, however, he stooped over slightly, Hans would immediately begin to tap, *whether or not he had been asked a question*" (italics added; cited in Candland 1993, pp. 127–128). Unconscious cueing was determined to be the source of Hans's cleverness. Given that a similar phenomenon was observed in C2 (i.e., beginning to type at the touch of my hand) and given the many disparities that exist with respect to FC in general, the concept of unconscious cueing is well worth pursuing in an attempt to understand the phenomenon of facilitated communication and its ramifications for the clients whose thoughts it purports to "unlock." Interestingly, the Clever Hans phenomenon has been continually invoked by skeptics of FC as a sobering reminder of the power and insidiousness of unconscious influence.

9

Behind the Mystique

Every man, wherever he goes, is encompassed by a cloud of comforting convictions, which move with him like flies on a summer day.

—Bertrand Russell

There are many reasons for the occurrence of facilitator influence, not all of which should be considered unwholesome or, worse yet, sinister. In fact, many of these forms of influence are normal by-products of human communication and hence are naturally embedded in that process. The phenomenon of co-construction, a way of influencing message generation by capitalizing on the redundancy that characterizes our language, has already been mentioned. An example of co-construction is the common practice of finishing someone's sentence during conversational discourse. Even more basic than this, however, are the reciprocal (i.e., transactional) influences that are an intrinsic part of the communication process. Communication by necessity involves both a sender and a receiver, both of whom shape and in turn are shaped by the messages they generate. Thus, influence per se is neither good nor bad. It is simply part of the process of human communication.

In normal communication, if misinterpretations occur in the transmission of messages, communicative partners are free to inform their listeners and to clarify their intents. In facilitated communication, however, unless protestations and clarifications regarding message generation are rendered through the medium of FC itself, they are discounted. It is at this point that influence begins to take on a more ominous countenance.

The findings of this study shed light on the controversial issue of facilitator influence with respect to message generation by teasing out the complexities and subtleties inherent in the concept itself. Before we proceed, it is important to consider what is meant by the term *influence*.

Latitude or License?

It is often assumed, particularly by those who have concerns about the validity of facilitated communication, that when influence does occur, it does so on a conscious or volitional level. Such a unidimensional view not only "demonizes" the facilitator in Machiavellian fashion but also leads one to disregard the many ways in which facilitators may influence the messages of their clients unconsciously, that is, without the intention or desire to do so and without the awareness that they are doing so. The findings of this investigation, however, lead one to conclude that it is precisely these unconscious forms of facilitator influence that are the most insidious and the most resistant to remediation. Quite simply, if facilitators aren't even aware of the ways in which they are inadvertently influencing message generation, why would they seek to take steps to alter their behavior? Further, absent such awareness, would it not be natural for them to attribute any and all typed messages solely to their clients, vehemently denying that they had played any role in message generation other than to *facilitate* the client's communicative intent?

In fact, the matter of facilitator influence turned out to be a multidimensional construct that was not only directly linked to but actually intertwined with facilitators' belief systems, their mind-sets, and their overriding commitment to facilitated communication. All of these factors, operating together, created a subjective—even symbiotic—environment in which *influence* was seen as *help* and *latitude* gave way to *license*. Consequently, facilitators did not recognize or acknowledge specific types of decisions on their part as influential, ostensibly because they did not reflect either their own conscious communicative intent or deliberate attempts to lead their clients to specific keys. Not only did I clearly see influence of both a subtle and overt nature in the decisions that facilitators made, I also witnessed the impact that their influence had on both the messages that were generated and the behavior of their clients.

In some cases facilitators talked about providing *correction* to clients without acknowledging or even recognizing the implied judgment inherent in deciding what is correct versus what is incorrect. The reader is reminded of the "correction" that F1 applied in the word-association task for the word *work*. C1 had typed *mo* and was reaching for the letter *p*. Even though the word *mop* would have been a perfectly acceptable association for the word *work* (and one that would have reflected this client's actual work experience), her facilitator applied the correction necessary to "allow" the word *money* to be generated instead. The correction was justified by F1 on the following basis: "You typed *mo* and then you had a tendency to type *p*." That his decision obviously influenced the typed output needs no further elaboration.

Facilitators also talked about the importance of pulling back on the client's hand, ostensibly to prevent perseveration. At the same time, they sanctioned the practice of allowing themselves the leeway of deciding when it would be appropriate to pull back and when it would be appropriate to let go. Again, there appeared to be no awareness that such decisions not only require judgments with respect to letter selection but also reflect facilitator mind-set. Directives to delete and statements such as, "I'm going to pull your hand back unless I think that's what you're really trying to go for"—uttered by F1—illustrate that there are many decisions taking place in the minds of facilitators with respect to the letters and the words that are eventually chosen. Remarkably, facilitators view such obvious forms of influence from the benign perspective of simple "help."

Reading Between the Lines and Beyond

Overinterpretation of messages was another area fraught with the danger of facilitator influence. This tended to take many forms, from exercising great liberty with the interpretation of the typed message (e.g., *ukkghkj* as the word *yucky*) to guessing the word that the client was ostensibly attempting to type. Again the reader is reminded of another word-association task described for the F1-C1 dyad. In this particular case the target word was *summer*. After C1 had typed *swi*, she pointed to the screen, shook her head, and said, "*i*, nope no *i*." In spite of the client's *clear verbal and nonverbal message*, F1 responded, "That letter belongs there." The reader does not have to guess that the facilitator had assumed C1 was typing *swim*, for a short time later, he actually said, "What's the next letter in *swim*?" This interaction also clearly underscores facilitators' lack of esteem for verbal utterances and their complete disregard for messages delivered in that form.

At times, especially when facilitators did have specific letters or words in mind, even their sincere attempts to guard against influencing their clients were in themselves influential. For example, machinations to avoid influencing the message—such as F1's counseling a facilitator to "come down on [a letter] above" the one he or she anticipated—are clear evidence of leading the client to a particular letter. Granted, the letter is not the one anticipated by the facilitator, but it is not necessarily the one desired by the client either!

Ineffective "Safeguards"

Despite facilitators' verbal acknowledgments that unconscious facilitator influence is indeed possible and despite their professed and apparently sincere interest in providing safeguards against it, in this area I also saw significant shortcomings. The safeguards I observed were nothing short of anemic—if not inane—when compared to the momentous consequences that can and often do occur because of undue influence. At times, these safeguards consisted of little more than simple *awareness* of the possibility that facilitator influence could occur, as though simple sentience could somehow guard against it. At other times, corroboration by an independent facilitator was taken as proof of validity and hence as freedom from influence. There seemed to be no recognition that if the second facilitator had access to the same information on the client as the original facilitator, contamination could easily occur and throw the findings into question. Stated differently, the new facilitator might be just as subject to unconscious influence as was the facilitator whose work was being "validated." Under such circumstances, one has to ask just how independent the validator really is!

Two additional points need to be made with respect to the argument for an independent facilitator as a check on validity. The first concerns the matter of facilitated output. Specifically, if *like* output from an independent facilitator is taken as proof of validity, why isn't dissimilar output, generated under the same set of conditions, considered a marker for lack of validity? In fact, facilitators either discount completely or explain away the dissimilar output in the same inane, unidimensional fashion that marks so many of the explanations used to justify FC. Witness the argument used by Biklen (1993) to gloss over the well-known comprehension problems that accompany the phenomenon of hyperlexia: "Labeling such skills as 'decoding' and 'word calling' seems little more than an elaborate and not so subtle way of denying the students' competence, saying in effect: They are not reading" (p. 59). Presumptive arguments that confer imprimatur status on facilitated output when it represents the desired outcome but that discount it when it doesn't are self-serving at best.

The second point concerns the Australian case, cited earlier, in which *nine separate facilitators—including Rosemary Crossley herself*—reported allegations of sexual abuse by a woman with autism only to have the charges dismissed when the likelihood of facilitator influence was revealed. That case alone ought to have dealt if not a deathblow, at least a knockout punch to the credibility of the validation-by-independent-facilitator argument. That it did not testifies to the detrimental effect that a passion to believe exerts on common sense and good judgment.

The Consequences of a Mind-Set

Undoubtedly, the most subtle and insidious form of facilitator influence stemmed from facilitators' intense commitment to FC. So powerful was this commitment that it exerted a domino reaction with respect to resolving *all* matters of controversy and inconsistency in favor of facilitated communication, regardless of the "stretch" required to do so. For example, rather than considering C2's *inaccurate* messages as examples of possible invalidity, F2, in direct contradiction to the autism research literature on deception (Sodian and Frith 1992, 1993), decided the issue in favor of facilitated communication. She attributed the inconsistencies to *lying* on the part of the client. By so doing she effectively removed yet another safeguard to possible facilitator influence, that is, consideration of alternative, more plausible explanations for these frank discrepancies.

In summarizing this highly contentious matter of facilitator influence, I believe it is fair to state that the issue is both multifaceted and complex. Heretofore the matter of authorship with respect to typing has been considered mainly from the unilateral perspective of manual support. The findings of this investigation not only indicate that there are a variety of ways in which message generation may be influenced by facilitators but also reveal that some of these forms of influence are actually considered a means of helping clients to become more proficient in their typing. As such, they are specifically sanctioned by facilitators. Unfortunately, the boundaries between *help* and *influence* are often indistinguishable. Finally, these findings also reveal that the most insidious form of influence is that which occurs below the level of facilitators' consciousness.

Blind Faith Acceptance

Another complicating factor in facilitator influence, and one that is undoubtedly born of the passionate commitment to the methodology itself, concerns facilitators' blind faith acceptance of FC regardless of evidence to the contrary. The facilitators in this study appeared not so much to be looking for explanations for discrepancies as looking for ways to justify such occurrences within the framework of facilitated communication. Blind faith acceptance was furthered by facilitators' inadequate knowledge base with respect to autism and sociocommunicative development. A stronger knowledge base might have provided these individuals with checks and balances on their judgments—a standard by which to responsibly evaluate disparate information. Insufficient knowledge often caused them to make judgments that were inconsistent not only with what is known about autism but also with what is known about both language and communication development. Many times their judgments actually flew in the face of well-researched principles across both fields. What they didn't know, however, couldn't really bother them!

Facilitators also seemed singularly unfamiliar with other developmental areas affected by the autistic disorder (i.e., infant development, play skills development, and emotional development). Consequently, much of the information they gave with respect to their clients was contradictory to the literature bases across several fields—not just the field of autism, as proponents of facilitated communication would have one believe. It seems, then, that in order to believe in the principles of facilitated communication as they were discussed and practiced by facilitators in this study, one has to discount much of the seminal research across several fields.

In the final analysis, facilitators' intense commitment to FC and their belief in its power to unveil the stores of knowledge, hidden literacy, and language skills they claimed their clients possessed created a fertile climate for the seeds of unconscious facilitator influence to take root and flourish. The intensity of their commitment and the subliminal mind-set in favor of FC that it created also effectively insulated them from considering *any* explanations for phenomena that might run counter to claims made for facilitated communication. Thus their expectations for success helped to generate the very successes they reported.

A Common Heritage

Meeting the issue of facilitator influence head on, Sheehan (1994) states, "Unintentional or unconscious facilitator cueing may actually be at the heart of that which is occurring in facilitated communication." In building his case, he relates the FC phenomenon to other pseudoscientific phenomena for which unsupported claims have also been made. In addition to the case of Clever Hans, these include the following: the Ouija board phenomenon, table turning, and water witching. Curiously, the introduction of all of these phenomena was accompanied by the same evangelistic fervor, degree of controversy, and polarization that has occurred in the facilitated communication saga. What is even more remarkable, however, is the similarity of the reactions and arguments on either side of the resulting debates.

On one side of the issue stand the true believers. These individuals not only adopt a seeing-is-believing stance but also see no need to validate what they have already accepted as fact. On the other side of the issue stand the skeptics. These individuals see scientific scrutiny as the best means of validating extraordinary claims for inexplicable events.

The phenomenon of water witching (use of a divining rod to locate underground water) is viewed as prototypic of the genre of "inexplicable" phenomena (Sheehan 1994). Like its counterparts, it carries many of the trappings associated with the phenomenon of facilitated communication. As such, it serves to further illuminate many of FC's most prevalent and contentious explanations.

As with facilitated communication, predominant support for water witching comes from eyewitness accounts. These testimonials are, by their very nature, subjective. Further, the lack of available objective verification seems to set the stage for discord, causing those testifying to the phenomenon to become defensive even in the face of legitimate questions and concerns. In addressing the matter of testimonials, Vogt and Hyman (1979) state, "One reason why testimony is so unreliable is that at the time of original perception, there is too much to observe. A person can only attend to a finite number of things at one time" (p. 43). The relevance of these comments with respect to FC is clear from the following description of the FC process by Biklen (1993):

> Facilitated communication often requires the facilitator to do several tasks at once, for example, carrying on a verbal conversation with the person being assisted or with others in the room, watching the person's eyes, looking at the printed output, thinking of the next question or activity and at the same time keeping your mind on the present activity, and so forth, in addition to providing physical support and encouragement. (p. 22)

In addition to specifying all of these tasks, Biklen (1993) directs facilitators to "keep your eyes on both the person's eyes and on the target" (e.g., letter keys) (p. 22). Given the sheer volume of items to which the facilitator must attend, it is easy to see how important information might get lost in the imprecision of the moment. My own experience during my interaction with C1 may well be partially explained on the basis of the "too much all at once" phenomenon. I viewed the interaction as positive when it was happening only to revise that judgment after intensive viewing of the videotape. Clearly, the flood of on-the-spot impressions, combined with a mindset primed for success, does little for objective decisionmaking.

Vogt and Hyman (1979) underscore this judgment by pointing out that expectations can also operate to alter the perception of the original experience. There can be no question that facilitated communication operationalizes the doctrine of expectation. Specifically, having high expectations for clients is an integral part of the FC phenomenon and a theme that was echoed by each of the facilitators in this study. Ordinarily viewed as one of FC's most positive components, expectation may well have serious, previously overlooked risks. Indeed, it is distinctly possible that expectation may have tipped the FC scales in favor of unconscious influence by creating a mind-set for success even in the face of overwhelming evidence to the contrary. My own involvement with two of the clients in this study clearly underscores the perception-shaping power of expectation.

Water witching and facilitated communication share additional parallels with respect to validity concerns and the arguments generated by supporters of the respective techniques to justify their positions. According to Vogt and Hyman (1979), there is a lack of scientific evidence for water witching:

> The evidence for it, when assembled and examined, is not merely insufficient; according to current scientific standards . . . it is appallingly negative. We know of few other hypotheses that have been put forth so persistently over

such a long span of years with such consistently negative experimental findings as the hypothesis that water witching "works." (p. 82)

Facilitated communication, though a much newer phenomenon than the age-old "art" of water witching, is undeniably marked by the same lack of scientific validation. In summarizing the results of experimental research studies on FC through April 1994 as preparation for its position paper on facilitated communication, the American Speech-Language-Hearing Association had this to say:

> Experimental research has provided minimal support for the efficacy of facilitated communication when it is defined in terms of demonstrations, under controlled conditions, of users authoring messages independent of facilitator influence. To the contrary, *with few exceptions, communicators have generally been unable to convey accurate messages when their facilitators lacked information necessary to respond correctly* [italics added]. (pp. 25–26)

Jacobson, Mulick, and Schwartz (1995) addressed controlled studies of facilitated communication, stating,

> Relevant controlled, peer-reviewed, published studies repeatedly show that, under circumstances when access to information by facilitators is systematically and tightly manipulated, the ability to produce communication through FC varies predictably *and in a manner that demonstrates that the content of the communication is being determined by the facilitator* [italics added]. (p. 754)

Overall, there is remarkable correspondence between the arguments used to support water witching and those used to support facilitated communication. Evidence of this is clearly seen in the water-witching arguments listed by Vogt and Hyman (1979):

1. The "one good case" argument (p. 82). Here supporters of the water-witching phenomenon dismiss the lack of scientific evidence based on the idea that reported successes in the field may be used to negate the weight of objective data. The "one good case" differs from those that have been scientifically investigated in that it is usually based on anecdotal evidence and testimonials, both of which are highly subjective and hence open to different interpretations. The parallels to FC need no elaboration here, since most of the claims for its success are based on just such anecdotal evidence.

2. The "core of truth" argument (p. 83). This argument holds fast to the principle that there must be some validity to the phenomenon if so many people believe in it. With tongue in cheek, Vogt and Hyman (1979) respond to this argument by quoting an old Chinese proverb, "If a thousand people say a foolish thing, it is still a foolish thing" (p. 83).

3. The "It would be a good thing for mankind" argument (p. 84). This argument seems particularly pertinent to the facilitators' position that FC

opens up a world of opportunity for clients to participate in important decisions governing their lives. Unfortunately, without first determining the validity of the technique under consideration—be it water witching or facilitated communication—the veracity of such claims is highly suspect. In elaborating this point, Vogt and Hyman (1979) state, "Almost every major scientific boner—and there have been many of them—can be traced to a zealous desire to see the world as we would like it to be rather than as it actually is" (p. 84). This argument is particularly relevant with respect to FC. Green (1994b), an outspoken opponent of FC, cautions, "The zealous promotion of facilitated communication without evidence to back it up is reason enough to be skeptical."

4. The "unfairness of the artificiality of laboratory conditions" argument (p. 85). Nowhere are the parallels to facilitated communication seen more dramatically than in this argument. A variety of rationales has been set forth by facilitators to discredit experimental (i.e., laboratory) investigation of the technique. According to Jacobson, Mulick, and Schwartz (1995), "Controlled research that disconfirms the phenomenon [FC] is criticized on the grounds of rigor and procedure not even remotely addressed by studies that purport to demonstrate the effectiveness of the technique" (p. 757).

In summary, FC criticism with respect to testing for validity may be subsumed under the general rubric that scientific testing somehow violates the bond of trust considered integral to the process of facilitated communication. Facilitators imply that something about scientific validation is decidedly unwholesome when applied to FC. For example, in referring to a specific type of validation procedure suggested by some researchers, Biklen (1993) states, "A test with blindfolds would convey to students that the facilitators are questioning their competence. This could undermine students' confidence in themselves and in their facilitators" (p. 124). Not only is this argument based on groundless assumptions but it seems specious as well. On its face it appears to have some merit—after all, no one wants to be found guilty of undermining a person's confidence. A closer look, however, reveals that Biklen confuses the validity of the *method* with the validity of the *person*. Quite simply, putting the method to the test is not the same thing as putting the person to the test, especially if validation procedures are sensitively rendered by individuals whose motives are honorable, that is, who want to be certain that people with disabilities have available to them treatments with *demonstrated* validity.

The Case for Unconscious Influence

In addressing the subtleties involved in the process of facilitated communication vis-à-vis the practice of water witching and similar paranormal phenomena, Sheehan (1994), in a thought-provoking presentation at the National Conference of the Autism Society of America, made a powerful case for unconscious facilitator influence. Citing the "overwhelming number of research studies that are not showing any good results," Sheehan (1994) stated that facilitator influence, at least in many of the studies, is "an undeniable fact." In building his case with respect to the basic cause of such influence, he implicated the way in which facilitated communication has been packaged here in the United States. According to Sheehan (1994), "The basic problem is that facilitated communication training was introduced as facilitated communication—that the *training* was left off." In terms of facilitated communication training, FC is considered a *means* to an end—a teaching strategy. This orientation, according to Sheehan, is reflective of the Crossley approach to facilitated communication and is one he supports as a "tool to help us assess and develop teaching programs to help the individuals." It is an orientation that underscores the importance of good technique and attention to the technical aspects of FC. Facilitated communication per se is an *end* in itself. This approach emphasizes the importance of FC output even if it is generated under conditions that would ordinarily be considered highly suspect (e.g., when the client is not even looking at the keyboard). Sheehan identifies this latter perspective as the "Syracuse approach." The chief proponent of this approach is Douglas Biklen. It is the Biklen orientation that has set the tone for facilitated communication in the United States.

Sheehan lists as fundamental to the Syracuse perspective the assumption that "we're dealing with a highly intelligent person. The impression we're left with is that we're dealing with somebody who is trapped in a body that doesn't work, and all we have is a neurological problem." It will be remembered that all of the facilitators in the present study, to one degree or another, subscribed to this theory. Thus, according to Sheehan (1994), FC as it has been promulgated in the United States trains facilitators to "sit and wait and have a high expectation that something is going to happen." Trained in this manner (i.e., to expect high-level thoughts to be revealed) and given the basic assumption of the approach that has been fostered in this country (i.e., that the client possesses a high degree of competence), facilitators may have been preset "to listen to those whose bodies have prevented them from speaking" (Sheehan 1994) in order to "hear" their innermost thoughts. The veracity of Sheehan's claims is poignantly underscored by Biklen's (1993) own words: "One of the most personally disappointing aspects of our using facilitated communication or of seeing it used by other people is that for many professionals it *is* merely a new teaching or communication technique" (p. 187). The obvious implication is that FC is far more, at least in the mind of Douglas Biklen.

Given this apparent predisposition and based on the work of Vogt and Hyman, Sheehan (1994) sets forth the view that unconscious facilitator influence in FC occurs as a result of *ideomotor action*. This term was first coined by William B. Carpenter to explain behavior that could not be accounted for on the basis of conscious volition. According to Carpenter (as cited in Vogt and Hyman 1979), "Ideas may become the sources of muscular movement, independently either of volitions or of emotions" (p. 132). Vogt and Hyman (1979) go on to state, "This is especially true when the ideas are *suggested* to the subject or are the result of *expectant attention* such as is the case in hypnosis, table turning, and water witching" (italics added; p. 132). It should be obvious that the same set of conditions holds true for facilitated communication.

The notion of ideomotor action was further elaborated by William James in the late 1800s. He described the principle as predominantly operative when other ideas are not present in the mind to conflict with it (Vogt and Hyman 1979). Still, he did not rule out "incipient action" even when opposing ideas were also present. In the 1930s, Edmund Jacobson, employing electrophysiological techniques, carried out a series of classic experiments revealing that the act of thinking was indeed accompanied by "implicit muscular responses" (Vogt and Hyman 1979, p. 137). Thus the technology needed to determine the presence of ideomotor action has been available for more than sixty years. Given the nature of the controversy in facilitated communication, definitive answers to the question of ideomotor action would seem to be a reachable and important goal.

In elaborating the concept of ideomotor action as it applies to FC, Sheehan (1994) distinguished between two different types: inadvertent cueing (characterized by the Clever Hans phenomenon) and unconscious facilitator responding. The latter is seen in such paranormal activities as table turning and water witching and in the Ouija board phenomenon. Sheehan feels that both aspects of ideomotor action are probably operative in facilitated communication but that unconscious facilitator responding is predominant.

A Revealing "Training Program"

Tying ideomotor action to the concept of suggestibility, Sheehan (1994) outlines a tongue-in-cheek "training program" based on Vogt and Hyman's (1979) training program for water witching. The goal: to teach unconscious responding to potential "pseudofacilitators." In so doing he applies the mechanisms at work in water witching to facilitated communication and makes a very convincing case for the power of suggestion with respect to the conduct of FC. According to Sheehan (1994), the following elements are necessary:

1. Verbal suggestion. The idea is planted in the facilitator's mind that he or she can do it. All that is necessary is to *wait* for the client to bring forth his or her ideas.

2. Intense concentration. The facilitator must be very focused on the task at hand.
3. A trancelike state. All competing stimuli are blocked out. Often there is accompanying physical exhaustion.
4. A state of tension. The muscles are under a high degree of stress.
5. Intense emotional experience. There is also emotional exhaustion.
6. Receptivity to cues. The facilitator is unaware of the presence of such cues.
7. Practice. The skill of facilitating improves with practice.
8. Absence of feedback. The facilitator receives no information from his or her muscles that he or she is in any way responsible for the movements.
9. Defensiveness. There is a need to defensively assert, even in the absence of questions regarding authorship, that the communication is coming from the client.

In summarizing his views, Sheehan (1994) states, "I believe we probably have thousands of well-intentioned, poorly trained, pseudo-facilitators who are unconscious victims of ideomotor action and suggestibility."

Sheehan's foray into the paranormal despite the science-resistant nature of the subject matter is respectful and objective. A proponent of facilitated communication training as a teaching strategy, he endeavors to examine the unconscious processes that may underlie FC's most controversial issue (i.e., facilitator influence), which if not fully examined may ultimately sound FC's death knell. Sheehan's fundamental message is, "Put the training back into facilitated communication, and make validity testing a primary concern" (Sheehan 1994).

Sheehan's proposition that ideomotor action and suggestibility are factors in such phenomena as table turning, water witching, and, by implication, facilitated communication is supported by experimental evidence. According to Vogt and Hyman (1979), "Primary suggestibility and its manifestation in ideomotor action has a firm empirical basis. The kinds of similarities that we saw in water witching, pendulum swinging, table turning, muscle reading, Ouija boards, and the rest result from a common principle" (p. 149).

Viewpoints from the Edge

The respectful and responsible manner in which issues related to the paranormal were raised by Sheehan, a proponent of FC training, stands in stark contrast to the reports of mind reading that have surfaced in the FC literature. These are often characterized by such anecdotes as the following:

A young man we know told his facilitator what her high school nickname was, and that she had a deceased relative who had been a musician. He was correct in every detail, including her feelings about her uncle. A mother told us about the adjustments she has made knowing that she can have no secrets from her teenage daughter. And another mother told us that her adult son has no need to hear what she and his other two facilitators want him to know: he simply types his responses to their unspoken comments. (Haskew and Donnellan 1992, p. 9)

Unlike the "firm empirical basis" on which Sheehan rests his case, Haskew and Donnellan (1992) rest theirs on the following:

It may be that a sixth sense is present in all of us at birth, but as speech and locomotion develop the need for it fades. Still, many people seem to retain vestigial psychic abilities, especially at times of accident or trauma, and there is much anecdotal and scientific literature describing these. For people with impaired communication capacities the sixth sense may remain active and utilized. The speaking world is simply rediscovering it. (p. 9)

Such anecdotes and rationales have done little to quell the genuine fears of those who seek to guard against facilitator influence and the havoc it has wrought in some lives. Neither have such anecdotes improved the credibility of FC in the scientific community.

In commenting on the matter of telepathy and paranormal abilities in general, Crossley (1994) herself related the issue to unconscious cueing:

In any instance where paranormal abilities are suggested for or by a communication aid user the first step should be to examine the facilitation process closely, both to see if a mechanism for transmission of information can be discerned and to see if the level of facilitation can be reduced. All facilitators involved should review their practices, referring back to the basic principles of facilitation, especially monitoring eye contact, pulling back, and reducing support. *It is also important that new facilitators are not told to expect "telepathic" communication, because this expectation may lead them . . . to create it unconsciously* [italics added]. (p. 111)

Thus Crossley acknowledges that expectation may well set the stage for unconscious facilitator influence. The marked similarity to Sheehan's point of view should be obvious. Something else should be obvious as well. Arguments in support of mind reading and channeling send a clear message that *all* things are possible under facilitated communication as long as one is willing to set aside common sense and reason to accommodate the preferred "reality."

10

If I Hadn't *Believed* It, I Wouldn't Have *Seen* It

Beware the people who moralize about great issues; moralizing is easier than facing hard facts.

—John Corry

In reviewing the findings of this study, one is struck by the fact that facilitated communication stands as an island unto itself, not only curiously disconnected from most other aspects of clients' daily lives but oddly out of sync with records and reports from significant others with respect to clients' cognitive functioning, literacy development, and language and communication ability. However, if one sets aside information based upon facilitated communication, there is remarkable consistency with regard to *all* of these parameters for each of these clients.

Curious Complacence

A further indication of the way in which FC seems oddly disconnected from many other aspects of clients' lives relates to the fact that there does not seem to be any attempt to deal with the marked discrepancies (and in some cases, marked incompatibilities) between the facilitators' judgments of their clients' competence and the clients' actual circumstances. For example, even though their facilitators judge them to be intelligent and competent individuals, these clients continue to be served by an agency that accommodates only individuals with mental retardation. Further, there is no attempt on the part of facilitators to alter their clients' situations based on newly discovered information regarding their alleged high levels of competence. In fact, as zealous as they are in their proselytization of facilitated communication, these facilitators remain curiously complacent and strangely silent with respect to advocating for such things as the undoing of state-authorized guardianships, which put control of major life decisions concerning the client into the hands of an anonymous bureaucracy. The facilitators' level of commitment to FC, as reflected in clients' reportedly greater involvement in some decisions affecting their lives (i.e., participation at in-house meetings), does not appear to extend to attempting to "rectify" the judgments and information in client records that allegedly underestimate their intelligence and usurp their exercise of control over their lives. Given facilitators' unanimous belief in the validity and veracity of the claims made through facilitated communication, one would have to ask why. One would also have to question why such allegedly competent clients would not exercise their newfound "voices" by attempting to wrestle control over their lives from the state. Inexplicably, both clients and facilitators are curiously silent on these crucial issues.

Worlds Apart

Given these discrepancies, one is left with the overwhelming impression that the clients in this study live in two very different worlds. One is the *actual world*—the one in the diagnostic reports and narratives that describe their lives and functioning levels over a long period of time and the one punctuated by the actual circumstances of their day-to-day existence. The ways these clients go about the business of their daily lives in this world appears to have changed very little, if at all, notwithstanding the homage paid to FC by their facilitators.

The other world is the newer, and infinitely more exciting, *FC world*, where a client can be—in the sentiments of one of the facilitators—released from the prison of his or her behaviors. In this world the client can suddenly "say" and "do" things that the dual diagnoses of autism and mental retardation have heretofore precluded. Clearly, this is a world in which FC reigns supreme—a world in which *every* form of communication, conventional or otherwise, is sacrificed to the facilitated message and a world in which facilitators, during times of discordance, appear to honor the technique over the comfort level of their clients. What seems to have been lost, however, is the fact that these two worlds are mutually exclusive even as they are "inhabited" by the clients in this study!

The FC Climate

This pattern of disconnection whereby facilitated communication isolates itself from so many of the issues, circumstances, and events that surround it permeated all aspects of this study and very much reflected the esteem in which FC was held by facilitators. Specifically, commitment to facilitated communication was marked by a wholesale endorsement of the methodology. In incident after incident in which I observed discordance, the well-nigh invincibility of this technique was reflected in the facilitators overriding virtually every piece of information that was either incongruous with or directly contradictory to FC. All issues of incongruity and incompatibility were inevitably resolved in favor of facilitated communication—a practice made simple by the facilitators' paucity of knowledge with respect to the syndrome of autism.

Despite their lack of knowledge about this complex, enigmatic disorder, facilitators were nonetheless quite willing to express their opinions about autism. Echoing what may arguably be defined as a significant element in FC's "party line," facilitators called for a reconceptualization of the autistic disorder. One has to question the wisdom (arrogance?) of a person or group calling for a reconceptualization of a complex, multifaceted disorder in the absence of a clear understanding on their part of its nature and symptomatology. I also feel compelled to question the extent to which this call for a redefinition of autism may be a reflection of the need to shape the syndrome to the contours of what is known about facilitated communication, since absent a reconceptualization of the disorder, facilitators are clearly at a loss to reconcile the inconsistencies and incompatibilities that inevitably abound.

It should be obvious that facilitators' intense commitment to FC and their all-encompassing belief in their clients' overall competence created a fertile soil for the seeds of unconscious facilitator influence to take root. Add to this a weak knowledge base regarding autism and its major symptomatology and a lack of knowledge regarding the complexities involved in language and communication. Finally, augment this blend of circumstances and assumptions with expectations not only for success but also for a specific type of stylized FC output and all of the ingredients necessary are present for suggestibility and ideomotor action to exert their influence on unsuspecting facilitators. This was the climate in which I found myself as I sought to unravel the awesome complexities of facilitated communication in order to better understand the method behind the mystique. It is also the atmosphere that defined the facilitated communication experience for each of the clients and facilitators in this study.

The Roots of Influence

What, then, can one conclude from the findings of this investigation? First and foremost, despite the clear indications of facilitator influence that occurred across all dyads, none of the influence was judged to be conscious in the sense of the facilitators *intending* to convey their own thoughts. Further, the facilitators in this study believed strongly in the efficacy of the technique of facilitated communication; they honestly believed that FC was in the best interests of their clients. They were guileless in rendering their opinions. Simply stated, believing in their "craft," they felt no need to obfuscate or to deceive. How, then, did they fall prey to facilitator influence?

In many respects influence is actually built into the process of facilitated communication. The facilitators' disregard for their clients' obvious verbal and nonverbal behavior denies clients the opportunity to protest, repair, modify, comment, or otherwise express the pragmatic functions of communication outside of the confines of facilitated communication. Such behavior on the part of the facilitator, intended only to further the cause of facilitated communication, by its very nature exerts a profound influence on the outcome of the message. In addition, the myriad decisions that facilitators make regarding when to pull the client's hand back or when to delete, coupled with their subjective interpretation of messages, provide additional fertile ground for facilitator influence to flourish.

Undoubtedly, the most dangerous and insidious form of facilitator influence is that which occurs below the level of consciousness. The atmosphere created by facilitators' inexorable commitment to FC, in concert with glaring weaknesses in their overall knowledge base and their unwavering belief in their clients' ability to generate messages (even in the face of significant evidence to the contrary), undoubtedly sets the perfect stage for suggestibility to take hold. My own interactions with two of the clients in this study underscore the power of the unconscious to insulate one from what is versus what appears to be. In such a subjective and emotionally charged atmosphere, seeing is believing, even if inexplicable. The question that really needs to be asked, however, is whether it was the facilitators' passion to believe that actually created the "image" that they saw.

In the Final Analysis

This study has raised several questions that need further elaboration both from a qualitative and from a quantitative research perspective. The areas of suggestibility and ideomotor action as they may relate to unconscious facilitator influence and the crucial issue of authorship need to be thoroughly investigated. Suggestibility and ideomotor action are not merely esoteric constructs on which to wax philosophical. They are elements deeply imbedded in human interactions, below the level of consciousness. Knowledge of these elements may provide valuable insights into the nature of unconscious facilitator influence. Moreover, techniques to investigate both phenomena have been available since long before facilitated communication made its debut on the disability scene.

Consequently, all possible avenues of facilitator influence ought to be explored, since it appears that the passion to believe in FC, and the proscriptions against all other forms of verbal and nonverbal behavior that may accompany it, create built-in artifacts that actually *support* some types of facilitator influence and *prevent discovery* of more insidious forms.

The results of this study also clearly demonstrate the need to investigate the effect that the use of facilitated communication may have on clients' verbal communication. Do the directions to ignore "interfering" verbal and nonverbal behavior actually *extinguish* or significantly reduce valid communication? Do they cause the client undue stress and anxiety? By disparaging some of their verbal output as stereotyped language (Biklen 1993), do proponents of facilitated communication deprive individuals with autism of the comfortable "Rainman speech" that some may resort to as a way of reducing anxiety when pressure mounts? In addition, given that there is a rich literature base that demonstrates its functionality as a communication strategy (Prizant and Duchan 1981; Prizant and Rydell 1984; Rydell and Prizant 1995), is the continual disparagement of and simplistic approach to echolalia detrimental to the overall development of oral language? Finally, serious consideration should be given to the possibility of changing the term facilitated *communication* to that of facilitated *language* in order to bring it more into line with what appears to be occurring in facilitation. Specifically, unless changes are made in the concept of facilitated communication to accommodate the verbal and nonverbal behavior that is an *intrinsic* part of an individual's communication system, *facilitated communication* as a construct is, without question, not only clearly misleading but a grave misnomer.

If we set aside such suppositious arguments as channeling and mind reading, unconscious facilitator influence has been demonstrated to be an unfortunate accompaniment of many FC experiences. That being the case, there is an urgent need to set aside the rhetoric and to put action before reaction in the form of careful scientific scrutiny of this controversial technique. After carefully considering the efficacy of facilitated communication, the American Speech-Language-Hearing Association (August 1994) issued the following statement:

> Uncontrolled observations and personal accounts suggest that messages produced by this process reveal previously undetected literacy and communication skills in large numbers of people with autism, mental retardation, and other communication disabilities. When information available to facilitators is controlled and objective evaluation methods are used, peer-reviewed studies and clinical assessments find no evidence that facilitated messages can be reliably attributed to people with disabilities. Moreover, *facilitated communication can have negative consequences if it prevents people with disabilities from receiving effective and appropriate treatment, suppresses genuine communication, and/or leads to unsubstantiated or false accusations of abuse or mistreatment* [italics added].

ASHA is the foremost professional organization of the country's leading authorities in the field of speech, language, and communication; its statement is nothing short of chilling in its charting of the negative consequences that can accompany the use of facilitated communication. This statement is made in the knowledge that not only is there a lack of evidence *for* FC, there is an abundance of evidence *against* it. Finally, the findings of this study clearly demonstrate that genuine communication was indeed suppressed time and again in all three clients simply because some other person decided that the *form* of that communication was unacceptable. It is difficult to imagine a more arrogant judgment, or a more tragic one!

With All Due Diligence

Court cases examining charges of sexual and physical abuse made through facilitated communication are a reality; so is the distress and embarrassment of family members and other caregivers who have been falsely accused. Validity testing is no longer a matter of choice. It is a matter of the highest urgency. There simply cannot be one standard for the courts and another for the rest of society. Green (1994b) foreshadowed the statement of the American Speech-Language-Hearing Association when she stated:

> That issue—determining unambiguous answers to the question of who's communicating in FC is not a matter anymore, and never was really, of pet theories or politics or ideology. It's now a very important practical question for families, for parents, for law enforcement officials, for funding and regulatory agencies, for policy makers, and researchers, and professionals in a lot of disciplines.

Given the unfortunate possible side effects of this treatment technique, one should proceed with caution in using facilitated communication as an end in itself as opposed to as a teaching tool, that is, as a stepping stone by which to teach skills (e.g., finger isolation) that can be used independently in a wide variety of augmentative communication systems.

Ironically, Donnellan (1984), herself a staunch proponent of facilitated communication and a major contributor to the autism research literature regarding the interrelatedness of behavior and communication, makes the best case for proceeding with caution in her characterization of the criterion of the least dangerous assumption, a strategy that was originally applied to behavioral intervention techniques. In defining this concept she stated, "This criterion or standard asserts that in the absence of conclusive data, educational decisions should be based on assumptions which if incorrect, will have the least dangerous effect on the students" (p. 142). Gast and Wolery (1987) refer to this criterion as an "interim standard" to be employed temporarily while awaiting the data that will guide decisionmaking.

Applying the criterion of the least dangerous assumption to facilitated communication could prevent the needless sorrow caused by false accusations that result when facilitators unknowingly influence the generation of their clients' messages. At the very least, ethical considerations—if not the standards of good practice—would seem to mandate the application of this criterion as an interim strategy pending the receipt of scientific documentation of the validity and efficacy of this controversial technique.

Indeed, if the FC saga has taught us nothing else, it has surely demonstrated the folly of the childhood cliché "Sticks and stones may break my bones, but names will never hurt me." In countless cases, the words generated by facilitated communication have been nothing short of devastating. That being the case, perhaps facilitated communication should come equipped with a warning label similar to that seen on cigarette packages—*Caution: Use of this technique may be dangerous to the mental health and well-being of client and caregiver alike!*

11

Beyond the Hype
and Circumstance:
The FC Culture Unveiled

But "glory" doesn't mean "a nice knockdown argument," Alice objected. "When I use a word," Humpty Dumpty said, in rather a scornful tone, "it means just what I choose it to mean—neither more nor less." "The question is," said Alice, "whether you can make words mean so many different things." "The question is," said Humpty Dumpty, "which is to be master—that's all."

—Lewis Carroll

With a rapidity and force rarely seen in the disability field, FC has become a sociopolitical phenomenon in which unanimity of thought and philosophy has created a class of believers whose "sacred" mission it is not only to advance the cause of FC but also to disparage the opposition (i.e., the skeptics). Within this culture, the boundaries that separate opinion from fact do not blur but actually cease to exist. In their place one finds an impenetrable line of defense against opinions to the contrary, however reasoned or reasonable, and an insurmountable wall of belief in which every action and reaction, however *unreasoned* or *unreasonable*, is rendered in service to facilitated communication. There are many ominous side effects of such an attitude, not the least of which is insulation from critical feedback. Absent such feedback, reality checks are rendered impotent and "unnecessary." Within such a context, assumptions are easily made and acted upon, and empirical evidence, insofar as it is incompatible with the tenets of the FC culture, is considered irrelevant. So it is that the sacred mission comes to have its sacred cow—facilitated communication itself.

The Rites of Initiation

The prime movers of the FC culture no doubt took their lead from its premier spokesperson, Douglas Biklen. In his sweeping indictment of the autism research literature—and by implication, its collective body of researchers—Biklen has set both the tone and the "fee" for membership in the FC culture. In a nutshell, the price of membership is complete surrender to the methodology. Not only are members required to demonstrate absolute loyalty to facilitated communication by accepting the technique's validity on face value, they are also required to explain away *any* and *all* disparities, incompatibilities, and evidence to the contrary. Anything considered a barrier to facilitated communication is simply and summarily dismissed despite the sound research base that may support it. In fact, Biklen's disdain for the research literature in autism is clearly seen in his ignominious reference to its documented research findings as mere "traditional assumptions."

The following statements by Biklen (1993) may provide insight into the fabric of the FC culture:

> If we had assumed that many individuals with autism had receptive and/or processing problems, had specific or global cognitive deficits, and had difficulty analyzing language, then *there would have been no reason to believe that facilitated communication would be helpful to the majority of people so classified.* Similarly, if acquisition of language skills had been presumed to be related to an ability to play with toys and to engage in imaginative play, given that we had no evidence that either was possible, *we would have had to presume that facilitated communication would have little likelihood of success* [italics added]. (p. 41)

Biklen goes on to list what he refers to as additional assumptions about autism. A virtual compendium of classic autistic symptomatology, they include intolerance to change, improper use of pronouns and verb tense, tactile defensiveness, and reproduction of words in the absence of comprehension. The latter is better known in the autism literature as echolalia! Biklen (1993) concludes by saying, "*These assumptions pose a formidable barrier to facilitated or any other means of augmenting or supporting communication*" (italics added; p. 41). Substituting the term *research findings* for *assumptions* not only improves the accuracy of the foregoing statement, it also makes a salient, if not inexorable, point!

Through such statements Biklen goes well beyond simple disdain for the research literature in the field of autism; he also summarily disregards solid and, in some cases, seminal research across several other fields and subjects (e.g., psychology, play and social behavior, imagination, language and communication). Thus by repackaging as *mere assumptions* the scientifically based research findings of carefully crafted and, in many cases, replicated studies across several fields, Biklen creates a smoke screen behind which the FC culture can blithely insulate itself from any arguments that run contrary to its position. Logic and reason are no match for the impenetrable wall of beliefs that protects the FC culture from the reality of what is rather than what its members would like there to be. In FC's wonderland, as in Alice's, terms are freely translated to reflect culture views. Autism is redefined as a movement disorder, and empirical evidence is repackaged as mere *traditional assumptions*.

The insulation from reality is all but complete. After all, "all statements are true, if you are free to redefine their terms" (Sowell 1995, p. 102). Armed with the "truth," one no longer needs to become involved in such plebeian enterprises as testing for validity. Nor does one need to be constrained by the disparities and incompatibilities that inevitably plague FC. And so it is that Biklen manages to debunk the entire concept of autism *without ever truly addressing the accompanying research on which it is based* and *without offering the slightest shred of scientific evidence for his position*. In its place one finds the following subjective and self-serving, justificatory statements:

> With facilitation, it becomes obvious that the students *do* understand and process language and that absence of usable spoken language does not justify an assumption of intellectual deficit, noninterest in social contact, absence of normal emotionals, or lack of other typical affective and intellectual abilities. We could not assume that students were incompetent in language, thinking, or feeling simply because they appeared to be so. Obviously, if students could respond to abstract questions and have conversations by typing, they must surely possess internal language. (Biklen 1993, p. 42)

The only missing link between Biklen's dismissal of the autism symptomatology he lists and his acceptance of the facilitated message as proof of its nonexistence is whether facilitated communication has actual scientific validity. Given the flimsiness of Biklen's own unsubstantiated assumptions and the volume of studies that have failed to demonstrate FC's validity, it would seem that the answer to that question could hardly be considered tangential to the issue!

Ironically, Biklen (1993) goes on to address the dangers inherent in confusing assumptions with facts: "It is not unusual to forget or ignore the fact that many assumptions about disabilities are merely that, assumptions. Too often assumptions are treated as facts" (p. 193). In his advancement of the myriad assumptions on which facilitated communication is based, Biklen would do well to heed his own good advice!

Redefining Reality

Casey Miller and Kate Swift said, "Language screens reality as a filter on a camera lens screens light waves." A cursory examination of the rhetoric that marks the FC culture clearly illustrates the veracity of their observation. Complex constructs such as hyperlexia and apraxia are either dismissed, as is the former, or glossed over, as is the latter. A closer look may serve to illustrate both observations.

Despite the growing body of research that characterizes hyperlexia as a precocious ability to decode words that is also associated with compromises in reading comprehension and with disordered language (Silberberg and Silberberg 1967; Whitehouse and Harris 1984), Biklen not only redefines the concept of hyperlexia but also disparages those who adhere to it: "Labeling such skills as 'decoding' and 'word calling' seems little more than an elaborate and not so subtle way of denying the students' competence, saying in effect: They are not reading" (Biklen 1993, p. 59). Further, unmindful of his own attack on the pitfalls of making assumptions, Biklen goes on to *assume* the opposite of what specific research findings have in fact *demonstrated*. Thus, in criticizing the work of Whitehouse and Harris (1984) with respect to hyperlexia, Biklen concludes:

> *Presumably*, [italics added] had these students been introduced to facilitated communication, the researchers for whom they were subjects would be able to see that their *so-called* decoding skills were in fact reading skills and that they were not hermetic or isolated; rather, the children simply lacked an effective means of expression [italics added]. (pp. 58–59)

In one sentence Biklen manages not only to discount the essence of what hyperlexia by definition is but also manages to unceremoniously reshape it to the contours of facilitated communication. Here again, one sees further evidence that in the context of the FC culture, reality is nothing more than a function of the terms used to define it. Anything can be "true" if the language used to define it can be changed to accommodate the new view. When reality becomes optional, however, the checks and balances with respect to it are omitted as well.

Before we look at the concept of apraxia, it is worthwhile to consider the following elementary principle governing one's belief system: A half truth can be far more damaging than an outright lie, perhaps because the obfuscatory presence of even a *shred* of truth tends to lend legitimacy even to a significant falsehood. Similarly, facilitators' pseudoscientific use of such complex terms as *apraxia* lend an air of credibility to arguments that might not be justified. A great gap lies between the superficiality of the knowledge base that accompanies those arguments and the complexity of the constructs they purport to address.

The FC culture's view of apraxia is simplistic at best and misleading at worst. Biklen (1993) describes people with autism as having a "global apraxia, affecting literally all aspects of voluntary physical activity" (pp. 79–80). He characterizes apraxia as a possible "physical analogue to echolalia," although he does not address the basis on which the analogy is made. Unfortunately, Biklen's discussion of apraxia is as global and lacking in documentation as is his pronouncement of how people with autism are allegedly affected by it. In addition, some of the examples of movement disturbances cited by Biklen (1993) in his discussion of apraxia are more aptly categorized under a different label (e.g., movement disturbances related to Parkinson's disease). This tendency to amalgamate movement and motor disturbances and to "globalize" them under the rubric of apraxia is an accoutrement of the FC culture that has been present since its beginnings. It has served the movement aptly. As the major raison d'être for the physical act of facilitation, apraxia has also conferred a degree of pseudoscientific respectability on the otherwise scientifically barren concept of facilitated communication.

The FC culture's characterization of apraxia as motorically rather than cognitively based—it often uses *apraxia* interchangeably with *neuromotor dysfunction*—overlooks a crucial aspect of praxis. Ayres (1985) defined *praxis* as the ability to deal adaptively with the physical world. She distinguished between *apraxia* and *dyspraxia*, using the former term to refer to motor planning ability that was once present but has been lost due to some injury to the brain, as in the case of a stroke or traumatic brain injury. The term *dyspraxia* is used to indicate that developmentally, this motor planning ability was never present. Both terms may apply in autism.

In describing the complexities inherent in the concept of praxis, Ayres makes two crucial points, both of which are overlooked by members of the FC culture. The first concerns the relationship of praxis to neuromotor function. According to Ayres (1985), "Praxis is not a strictly neuromotor function, but it uses the neuromotor system for execution of practic acts. Because it seldom occurs to people to consider all that goes into purposeful action, there is a common misconception that dyspraxia is only a motor disorder" (p. 2).

Ayres (1985) goes on to state that problems in praxis and neuromotor function may coexist; however, when they do, she cautions individuals "to report them as separate problems and treat them as separate problems" (p. 2). One can extrapolate from her comments that she would not take kindly to the FC practice of lumping together various types of motor and movement disturbances under the general heading of apraxia.

The second major point that Ayres makes concerns the ideational or conceptual aspect of praxis. And it is at this juncture that "the rubber hits the road," for not only are FC enthusiasts unmindful of this aspect of praxis, they have specifically argued against the presence of cognitive deficits in people with autism. According to Ayres (1985), "In treating dyspraxia, *the emphasis is on ideation (generating an idea), concept formation, and planning;* in treating a neuromotor problem, *the emphasis is on motor execution. Praxis and motor function are not synonymous*" (italics added; p. 2).

A Culture Apart

Ideologies, regardless of the subjects on which they are based, share several common features. The doctrine of beliefs on which a particular ideology rests provides both the framework and the guiding principles that govern its cause. Ideologies by their very nature are insular and self-contained; that is, they contain all of the elements needed for their own survival. These include, to one degree or another, a particular vision of reality, a style of rhetoric that is at once imposing and intimidating, and a class of believers who tenaciously proselytize and defend their views against any and all opinions to the contrary. Ideologies tend to rely on emotion and glittering generalities to captivate the imaginations of their supporters. Likewise, they tend to resist or derail arguments viewed as inimical to their positions and interests. Often, the people who hold such views are either disparaged or outright discredited as having opinions that are somehow inferior.

It should be obvious from this examination of the structure of the FC culture that its pattern of hype and circumstance is chillingly suggestive of an ideological crusade not unlike those that have polarized people throughout our history. In a brilliant treatise on the subject of the failed social policies of the past three decades, Thomas Sowell in *The Vision of the Anointed* hammers away at the ideologues whose rhetoric perpetuates the causes they support. The parallels to the FC movement are inescapable. According to Sowell (1995),

> One reason for the preservation and insulation of a vision is that it has become inextricably intertwined with the egos of those who believe it. Despite Hamlet's warning against self-flattery, the vision of the anointed is not simply a vision of the world and its functioning in a causal sense, but is also a vision of themselves and of their moral role in that world. *It is a vision of differential rectitude.* (p. 5)

In elaborating on the latter point, Sowell (1995) states, "What a vision may offer, . . . is a special state of grace for those who believe in it. Those who accept this vision are deemed to be not merely factually correct but morally on a higher plane" (pp. 2–3). One gets a glimpse of the FC culture's "morally higher plane" in Biklen's demeaning charge that the use of the descriptive term *decoding* is nothing more than a thinly veiled attempt to deny students' competence. This accusation is but one of many examples of judgments that "elevate" proponents of facilitated communication to a morally higher plane even as they relegate those who hold a different view—the so-called nonbelievers—to an inferior position.

A Hidden Agenda?

The phenomenon of facilitated communication may well go down in history as the ideological superstar of the disability movement. Not only is the movement itself enmeshed in its own self-perpetuating, ideological rhetoric, it has also served as a springboard for a larger cause: the inclusive education movement. That Douglas Biklen is also the inclusive education movement's most eloquent and vociferous proponent is a matter of either divine providence, remarkable coincidence, or brilliant strategic planning. Or perhaps it reflects something more wholesome and distinctly human—the desire to see things as they might be rather than as they are and an unconscious mind-set that brings about the preferred reality. Whatever the case, leaving nothing to speculation with respect to his philosophical perspective, Biklen (1993) challenges us "to shed the false dichotomy of 'ability' and 'disability'" (p. 177). He later elaborates:

> Treating people as capable learners reflects an ideology or belief that education should be fundamentally a process of interaction and support rather than one of testing and sorting. The latter creates a class system of schooling, with certain students, including those labeled "disabled," forced to the margins; the former, what we might term inclusive education, attempts to place traditionally marginalized students at the center of learning. Inclusive education assumes that students respond well to people who expect them to be able to communicate. . . . The opposite also holds: *Students generally do not communicate with people who are themselves not confident as facilitators or who doubt the students' abilities* [italics added]. (pp. 187–188)

So there it is—the message, loud and clear! In this one passage Biklen fuses the concepts of inclusive education and facilitated communication. That the party line of both movements is students' presumed competence should come as no surprise to anyone at this point. Neither should speculation regarding the possibility of a hidden agenda in the FC controversy.

In this regard, Biklen (1993) expresses his disappointment with those who view facilitated communication as "*merely a new teaching or communication technique*" (italics added; p. 187). Clearly, Biklen expects far more from facilitated communication. Could it be that the act of communicating is to be sacrificed to a *presumed* "greater good"—that is, the *use* to which the communicative message will be put? The short but colorful history of the FC movement speaks to the plausibility of this interpretation. So does Biklen (1993) himself:

> If facilitated communication is *just a technical innovation*, it can be provided wherever people are located, whether in institutions, sheltered workshops, special schools or regular schools, people's own homes, or regular workplaces; this view suggests that people's life circumstances need not necessarily change. But individuals using the method—that is, the communication users—suggest through their words and thoughts that *they want more from the discovery of facilitated communication than a communication method* [italics added]. (p. 185)

Clearly, Biklen considered facilitated communication to be a major weapon in the arsenal of disability rights advocates. As the purveyor of the inclusive education movement's most important message, FC had fulfilled its promise to be more than just a *mere* communication technique. Indeed, it had become an instrument of the new ideology—and an eloquent one at that!

The Voice of Reason

For too long now, the FC culture has granted sacred cow status to facilitated communication based on little more than assumptions regarding the detrimental effects of scientific scrutiny on the bond of trust between facilitator and client. Further, the hype and mystique surrounding this technique and the proscriptions that accompany it have built a wall of defenses around it that serve to preserve its sacrosanctity. For example, had I adhered to the directive to ignore the verbal and nonverbal behavior of clients while they are facilitating, I could not have reported their frustration or the attempt by one of them to repair and modify her messages. Consequently, an important part of the interaction would have been missed.

The time for logic and reason is long overdue. Without it, practices that under other circumstances would be considered questionable, if not inappropriate, are, in the case of facilitated communication, considered acceptable, if not good practice (e.g., ignoring verbal and nonverbal behavior, overinterpreting messages, accepting facilitated messages even when the clients' eyes and attention are obviously elsewhere or when the fingers make contact with several letters at the same time). In addition, by explaining away clearly contradictory information as *lying* or *mind reading* on the part of clients, proponents of FC actually rob the technique of the fail-safe devices that can help to reveal unconscious facilitator influence. Indeed, the use of such mystical arguments does little to improve the credibility of FC within the scientific community.

Clearly, facilitated communication is a seductive technique—one that se-
duces the imagination and anesthetizes the voice of reason. Somehow FC
and individuals with autism have gotten caught up in an ideological movement in which disability as a construct is being rethought and individuals
with autism are being *repackaged* as intelligent individuals trapped in bodies that don't work. At the same time they are being portrayed as victims of
a society that doesn't understand or respect them (Biklen 1993; Haskew
and Donnellan 1992).

Notwithstanding the well-meaning efforts of professionals to improve
the quality of life for people with disabilities, this view of individuals with
autism comes dangerously close to that prominent in the "infamous"
1940s, when autism was viewed as emotionally based and a result of poor
childrearing practices. According to Ciaranello (1988), during this time
"Kanner and other writers of that period painted a picture of near-genius,
beautiful children frozen into isolation by an unfeeling world. Unfortunately, they based their views on personal intuition rather than on scientifically based study" (p. 18). Despite the incorrectness of this view of autism,
it dominated thinking on autism for more than a generation and caused ir-
reparable harm to countless innocent people. Even today, its unfortunate
sequelae can still be found. Surely there is a lesson here for facilitated communication.

Like a Snowball Rolling Down a Hill

Neither before nor since FC's impressive debut as the undisputed darling of
media hype has a treatment technique for people with disabilities so captured the imagination of the American public. From the perspective of the
media, what could be more ideal than a treatment technique that could be
touted as a "miracle" or "an awakening"?—the very words used by Diane
Sawyer in her *Prime Time* piece on the subject. In these days of channel
surfing when sound bites have to be not only quick but titillating, what better way to attract the attention of an increasingly jaded public? Combine
the use of this fascinating new technique—replete with its audacious claims
of near instant success—with the perennially interesting and somewhat
mysterious disorder of autism and you have what is known in entertain-
ment circles as box office!

The media was not alone in deriving benefit from the FC-autism connection. This story had something in it for almost everybody. For disability
groups working tirelessly to break down barriers and banish stereotypes,
what could be more gratifying than seeing one of their own "party lines" in
the facilitated messages of the disabled (e.g., "I am not retarded")? And
what other forum could give those messages greater credence, not to mention greater visibility? For parents, FC was quite literally a dream come

true. Not only could they come to know their children's innermost thoughts and desires through the "miracle" of facilitated communication, they could also rekindle the hopes and dreams they had long since abandoned. And for treatment providers, especially those who worked with individuals considered less able, FC offered a quantum leap forward in a world where progress is usually measured in painstakingly slow, incremental steps.

Ironically, even though the application of facilitated communication to those with autism gave the technique some of its most shining moments, it also gave it some of its shabbiest. It was the poorness of the fit between autism and facilitated communication that caused the well-known polarization in the autism community. This created an FC counterculture whose members, rather than promoting solid research of their own, spent most of their time disparaging sound research across several fields when claims made for FC ran counter to it. Thus when the definition of autism didn't fit the contours of facilitated communication, the disability was simply and summarily reshaped (i.e., redefined). And when the terms *mental retardation* and *disability* became roadblocks on an otherwise yellow brick road, they too were set aside. Indeed, Biklen (1993) argued passionately in favor of "rethinking disability" in order to counteract what he called "the arbitrariness and wrongmindedness of the concepts of 'disability' and 'handicap'" (p. 174).

The Matter of Ethics and Responsibility

Hype, circumstance, and pomposity aside, what can one say about how facilitated communication was presented to a naive public? Should not respected news programs delve more deeply into controversial topics before they dazzle the public with special effects and emotionally charged rhetoric? Likewise, shouldn't professionals who hold positions of prominence adhere to a higher duty of care before they package opinions as facts and denigrate responsible criticism as reflective of baser motives? And wouldn't everyone have been better served by a standard that required important issues to be decided on the basis of solid research evidence rather than diaphanous, glittering generalities and emotionally charged testimonials? Finally, shouldn't sound theories be able to stand up to the rigors of scientific investigation? And if they cannot, should they not be discarded regardless of arguments about some amorphous greater good?

The dangers inherent in relegating scientific scrutiny to the scrap heap while elevating subjectivity and hype to the level of an art form may go undetected amid the evangelistic fervor of the moment. Such unrecognized dangers are nevertheless critical. *Saying* something is or is not so does not make it so. It is only through scientific investigation that one manages to get closer to what actually is. Vogt and Hyman (1979) speak eloquently to this issue:

To err is not only human for the scientist; it is the way he gains new information by which he can revise his map of "reality." But, for the believer, "truth" is already given; it is static. He "sees the light"; his only task is to convert the skeptic. Negative evidence does not lead him to revise his picture of "reality"; it only leads him to distrust and detest the scientist. For the adherent there are only two kinds of evidence. "Good evidence" is that which reinforces his belief; "bad evidence" is that which is at odds with his conviction. (p. 87)

The parallels to facilitated communication need no further elaboration here; nor should the case for responsible investigation of the technique.

The Bottom Line

There are many chapters yet to be written on the subject of facilitated communication. Those contained within the covers of this book represent my personal journey—my immersion, if you will—into the world of FC and the culture that it spawned. I do not present my findings as the final word on the subject of facilitated communication. But I do offer them as a red flag—an emblem of the need to determine, through reliable and responsible scientific methods, the validity of this controversial technique *before* making decisions based on it. Notwithstanding the reasonableness of this position, there are those who would argue that it really doesn't matter if the messages are coming from the client or the facilitator, citing overall improved behavior of the former as a direct result of improved treatment by the latter. The reason most often given for such improved behavior is twofold: the realization by the facilitator that he or she is dealing with a competent person who is merely trapped behind uncontrollable autistic symptomatology, and the facilitator's expectation for success. To those who hold this position I would ask: Is there not an implied arrogance in this argument that implicitly sanctions a double standard—one for *competent* individuals and a lesser duty of care for those whose *personhood,* but for FC, goes unrecognized? Stated differently, does one have to be competent and intelligent in order to be worthy of respect and dignity and to engender expectations for success? Are these issues what is really behind the rhetoric that seeks to "shed the false dichotomy between 'ability' and 'disability'"? The answers to these questions may not matter as much as that the questions need to be asked at all.

Clearly, authorship does matter, and so does the genuine verbal and nonverbal communication that FC all too often suppresses by its adherence to the alleged superiority of the typed word. Although I do not have a final word, I do have a bottom line: The ability to communicate thoughts, ideas, and intentions is humankind's most complex, multifaceted, and genuinely awesome achievement. Leaving the power of communication in the hands of the facilitator is *never* acceptable if there is *any* doubt regarding authorship, especially if the client is barred from using any communicative means *other than* FC to protest against words and thoughts that might not be his or her own.

And so it seems that we have come full circle, and as promised by T. S. Eliot in the quotation that commenced this journey, we have arrived at the place from which we started. It is my hope that we may now know that place a bit better than before.

If my possessions were taken from me with one exception, I would choose to keep the power of communication, for by it I would soon regain all the rest.

—Daniel Webster

Epilogue: The Reviews Continue to Come In

The May 1995 issue of *Exceptional Parent* was devoted to the topic of communication. Karen Levine and Robert Wharton, in an informative and thought-provoking article on the subject of facilitated communication, raised several critical issues related to the use and consequences of this controversial technique. Perhaps the most poignant, if not the most telling, aspect of their piece was their recital of the various position statements on FC by some of the professional and advocacy organizations that have taken stands on the issue. These statements, like the events that shaped them, bear witness to the consequences of a mind-set when it runs headlong into a passion to believe:

> Studies have repeatedly demonstrated that FC is not a scientifically valid technique for individuals with autism or mental retardation. In particular, information obtained via FC should not be used to confirm or deny allegations of abuse or to make diagnostic or treatment decisions. (American Academy of Child & Adolescent Psychiatry, October 1993; this position statement has also been endorsed by the American Academy of Pediatrics.)

> A substantial number of objective clinical evaluations and well-controlled studies indicate that FC has not been shown to result in valid messages from the person being facilitated.
>   . . . The Board of Directors of the American Association on Mental Retardation (AAMR) does not support the use of this technique as the basis for making any important decisions relevant to the individual being facilitated without clear, objective evidence as to the authorship of such messages. The AAMR strongly encourages the use and further development of valid augmentative and alternative communication techniques and approaches. (American Association on Mental Retardation, June 1994)

168

Specific activities contribute immediate threats to the individual civil and human rights of the person with autism or severe mental retardation. These include use of FC as a basis for:

a) actions related to nonverbal accusations of abuse and mistreatment . . . ;
b) actions related to nonverbal communications of personal preference, self-reports about health, test and classroom performance and family relations;
c) client response in psychological assessment . . . ; and
d) client-therapist communication in counseling or psychotherapy . . .

. . . Facilitated communication is a controversial and unproved communicative procedure with no scientifically demonstrated support for its efficacy. (American Psychiatric Association, August 1994)

When information available to facilitators is controlled and objective evaluation methods are used, peer reviewed studies and clinical assessments find no conclusive evidence that facilitated messages can be reliably attributed to people with disabilities. . . . Moreover, FC may have negative consequences if it precludes the use of effective and appropriate treatment, supplants other forms of communication, and/or leads to false or unsubstantiated allegations of abuse or mistreatment.

. . . Information obtained through or based on facilitated communication should not form the sole basis for making any diagnostic or treatment decisions.

ASHA strongly supports continued research and clinical efforts to develop scientifically valid methods for developing or enhancing the independent communication and literacy skills of people with disabilities. (American Speech-Language-Hearing Association (ASHA), October 1994)

The following statement was issued by The Association for Persons with Severe Handicaps (TASH). This organization is considered by many to be the foremost authority on matters related to disability rights, inclusive education, and related advocacy issues involving people with severe challenges. In stark contrast to the preceding cautionary statements that contain unequivocal language regarding the perils of FC, the TASH statement contains language noncommittal enough to qualify under the definition of a *hedge*: "to avoid commitment, especially by qualifying or evasive statements" (*Random House Webster's College Dictionary* 1991, p. 620). I leave further speculation to the reader.

TASH regards access to alternative means of expression [as] an individual right.

TASH encourages its membership to become informed about the complexities of FC training and practice and to stay informed of new research. . . . TASH encourages people who decide to become facilitators to seek training. . . . TASH encourages careful, reflective use of FC. TASH encourages facilitators to work in collaboration with individuals with severe disabilities to find ways of confirming communication competence when using facilitation. . . .

TASH urges that when allegations of abuse or other sensitive communication occur, facilitators and others seek clarification of the communication and work to ensure that users of facilitation are given the same access to legal and other systems that are available to persons without disabilities. It is important not to silence those who could prove their communication competence while using facilitation or any other method of expression. (TASH, October 1992)

Appendix

Of the many language use variables that could have been targeted for analysis, the two that were selected relate to the more controversial aspects of message generation in facilitated communication: function (i.e., pragmatics) and content (i.e., semantics). These dimensions are particularly controversial in FC users who have autism, since despite the constraints imposed by the disability, performance in FC often exceeds expectations.

The first two parts of the pragmatic analysis examine both the specific utterance function (SUF) and the broad pragmatic category (BPC) of facilitated messages in an attempt to tease apart the intentions behind communicative utterances. Interestingly, whereas the autism research literature cites as characteristic of language use in people with autism a predilection for the *instrumental* functions of language (i.e., the satisfaction of needs, as in requests) (Prizant and Schuler 1987), the pragmatic analysis of facilitated messages reveals far greater variety and flexibility in the use of other more *social* functions (e.g., informative, personal). In fact, an overview of the column devoted to broad pragmatic category in the Pragmatic/Content Analyses clearly demonstrates that the trend in these clients' facilitated messages is *away* from communication for instrumental purposes. This tendency is in direct contradiction to the autism research literature.

The third part of the pragmatic analysis focuses on the use of linguistic devices (LD) by clients. These devices help to regulate the ebb and flow of meaning between speaker and listener. Here too, as in the previous two cases of pragmatic usage, clients demonstrate greater sophistication in their use of linguistic devices both to introduce and to maintain topics—activities that are often problematic even in the most able, highly verbal people with autism.

Similarly, deixis, which has to do with the interpretation of information from the speaker's point of view (Owens 1991), is at a higher level of competence than one would expect given that perspective-taking difficulty is a well-known feature of autistic language behavior (Geller 1989). This is particularly noteworthy in the case of pronominal reversal (e.g., substituting the pronoun *you/I*), as there is a substantial literature that clearly documents this type of problem in people with autism (Fay 1980; Paul 1987; Ornitz 1987).

What is most remarkable about these findings is what they allegedly signify about the knowledge base of the FC language user. Specifically, competence in the use of linguistic devices implies a priori knowledge of the informational status and needs of the listener. This particular type of information is known as presuppositional knowledge. Competence in this domain enables speakers (in this case FC users) to tailor their language to the communicative partner's informational needs, based on an understanding of what the speaker already knows and what he or she needs to know. Unlike communicative intentions per se, linguistic devices such as deixis and presuppositions underlie the *whole* of conversational discourse (Owens 1991). As such, they are highly complex, as evidenced by the fact that their use continues to be problematic even at the highest levels of functioning in people with autism.

Finally, the content analysis of facilitated messages examines the use of abstract, relational terms; philosophical content; and the expression of thoughts and feelings. Although the results are more variable than those related to the pragmatic analysis, one does see greater facility in the use of more abstract concepts by the clients in this study than one would expect given what is known both about autism and about the backgrounds and documented functioning levels of these clients.

Pragmatic Analysis of Facilitated Messages

Unit of Analysis: The Speech Act

Rationale: According to Arwood (1984), "The basic unit of linguistic communication is not the sentence, word, or any symbol but the *production* [italics added] of a sentence in the *performance* of a speech act" (p. 25). *Note:* For the purposes of this study, the facilitated message unit will constitute the speech act for analysis. (e.g., "I want a drink.")

Specific Utterance Function (SUF): e.g., requesting
Broad Pragmatic Category (BPC): e.g., instrumental
Linguistic Device (LD): e.g., demonstration of correct pronoun usage (deixis)
Note: Overlap between and among categories is expected.

Specific Utterance Functions Codes

(based on the work of Twachtman 1990)

REQ	Requesting (action or object)
ACC	Accessing (e.g., obtaining attention, calling)
PRO	Protesting; Rejecting; Refusing
SEI	Seeking Information (e.g., requesting answer)
COM	Commenting (e.g., social indexing, establishing joint attention)
EXP	Expressing Feelings, Opinions, Emotional State
GRE	Greeting; Social Routine
OFF	Offering; Giving
ANS	Answering; Replying; Acknowledging (no new information given)
INF	Informing (new information supplied)
UNC	Uncodable Utterance (e.g., incomplete; unintelligible; source is unclear)
AMB	Ambiguous Utterance (i.e., not able to assign to a category without further information)
I	Initiation (i.e., utterance/topic is initiated by client)
R	Response

Broad Pragmatic Categories Codes

(Halliday 1975)
INS   Instrumental (i.e., satisfaction of needs/desires)
REG   Regulatory (i.e., regulation/control of other's behavior)
INT   Interactional (i.e., establishment of relationship; participatory)
PER   Personal (i.e., expression of feelings, opinions, individuality)
IMG   Imaginative (i.e., expression of imagination; "as if" thinking)
HEU   Heuristic (i.e., quest for information)
INF   Informative (i.e., provision of information)
AMB   Ambiguous Utterance (i.e., not able to assign a category without further information)
UNC   Uncodable Utterance

Linguistic Device Codes

Facilitated messages have been analyzed to determine the absence or presence and extent of use of the following (based on Owens 1988):
RP   Use of Repair Strategies (i.e., requests for clarification)
TI   Topic Introduction/Introduction of New Topic (Because of the cue-dependent nature of facilitated communication, topic introduction will also be extended to the client's response to, "Is there anything else you want to tell me?")
TM   Topic Maintenance (i.e., providing additional information on the subject; slightly altering the specific focus of the topic; requesting additional information)
DE   Deixis (i.e., the denotation of "places, times or participants in a conversation from the speaker's point of view" [Owens 1988, p. 296]). Analysis is limited to the following: here/there, this/that, and the personal pronouns.
NS   Non Sequitur
UNC   Uncodable Utterance
Note: Nonverbal behavior is examined and discussed within the narrative according to its perceived meaning. Judgments regarding the congruence between verbal and nonverbal behavior are based on the perceived synchrony regarding the message value of each. (E.g., hitting oneself while typing "I am happy" is judged as incongruent; hitting oneself while typing "I am angry" is judged as congruent.)

Content Analysis of Facilitated Messages

Codes Governing Main Areas of Focus

ABS   abstract, relational concepts (e.g., democracy), as defined and elucidated by Hubbell (1981): ". . . concepts that cannot be identified through perceptual attributes. They can be identified only in terms of relationships with other concepts" (p. 13).
PHL   philosophical content with respect to the nature of disabilities and society's attitudes toward persons with disabilities
ITR   expression of thoughts/feelings that evidence introspection and awareness

TABLE A.1   Pragmatic/Content Analysis of Preexistent Transcripts

Date: None Listed   *Dyad: F1/C1*

Utterances	Specific Utterance Function (SUF)	Broad Pragmatic Category (BPC)	Linguistic Device (LD)	Response (R) or Initiation (I)	Content
1	UNC	UNC	UNC	UNC	—
2	INF	INF	TI/DE	I	—
3	ANS/INF	INF	TM	R	—
4	ANS	INF	TM	R	—
5	REQ/INF	INS/INF	TI/DE	I	—
6	ANS	AMB	NS	R	—
7	ANS/INF	INF	TM/RP	R	—

PREEXISTENT TRANSCRIPT

Date: None Listed   *Dyad: F1/C1*

C1:	(1)	inUPP;
C1:	(2)	I WAS CLEANING JENNIFRS HOUSASE.
F1:		WHAT ROOM DID YOU CLEAN?
C1:	(3)	BATHROOM.
F1:		YOU ARE ALMOST INDEPENDENT IN SOME OF YOUR TYPING. I WOULD LIKE TO WORK ON THAT SOME MORE.
C1:	(4)	YES
C1:	(5)	IWANT SODA,
F1:		WHAT KIND OF SODA?
C1:	(6)	YES
C1:	**(7)**	**ORANGE**

TABLE A.2   Pragmatic/Content Analysis of Preexistent Transcripts

Date: 8/20/92   *Dyad: F1/C1*

Utterances	Specific Utterance Function (SUF)	Broad Pragmatic Category (BPC)	Linguistic Device (LD)	Response (R) or Initiation (I)	Content
1	ANS/INF	INF	TM	R	—
2	ANS	INF	TM/DE	R	ABS/ITR
3	ANS/INF	INF	NS/DE	R*	—
4	ANS/INF	INF	TM/DE	R*	—
5	ANS/AMB	INF/AMB	NS/DE	R*	—
6	ANS/INF/EXP	INF/PER/IMG	TM	R	ABS/ITR
7	ANS/INF/EXP	INF/PER/IMG	TM/DE	R	ABS/ITR
8	ANS	INF	TM	R	—
9	ANS	INF	TM/DE	R*	ABS/ITR
10	ANS/INF/EXP	INF/PER	TM	R	—
11	ANS/INF/EXP	INF/PER	TM/DE	R	—
12	ANS/EXP	INF/PER/IMG	TM/DE	R	ABS/ITR
13	ANS/INF/EXP	INF/PER	TM/DE	R	—
14	ANS	INF	TM	R	—
15	COM/EXP/INF	INF/PER	TM/DE	R	ITR
16	ANS/INF/EXP	INF/PER	TM/DE	R	ITR

*May indicate possible receptive language problem

PREEXISTENT TRANSCRIPT

Date: 8/20/92   *Dyad: F1/C1*

F1:	(1)	HOW DO YOU SPEND YOUR DAYS? MONDAY, WEDNESDAY AND THURSDAY?
C1:	(1)	JENNIFER'S HOUSE CLEANING HOUSE
F1:		DO YOU FEEL YOU HAVE A PRODUCTIVE DAYTIME THROUGH [Multi-Syllabic Name of Agency] DURING THE WEEK?
C1:	(2)	I THINK MUY DAYTIME IS PRODUCTIVE.
F1:		HOW DO YOU FEEL ABOUT THE WOMEN YOU WORK WITH?
C1:	(3)	WOMEN THAT WORK WITH ME CLEAN HOUSE.
F1:		DO YOU LIKE WORKING WITH THEM?
C1:	(4)	YES TILL I GO HOME.
F1:		WHAT ARE SOME GOALS FOR YOUR FUTURE? WHAT WOULD YOU LIKE TO ACCOMPLISH IN YOUR LIFE?
C1:	(5)	I AM [client's name spelled correctly].
C1:	(6)	BETTEER [client's name spelled correctly].
F1:		DO YOU HAVE ANY SPECIFIC IDEAS ABOUT BECOMING BETTER?
C1:	(7)	I AM BERTTER AIBLE TO GO TO WORK.

PREEXISTENT TRANSCRIPT *(continued)*

Date: 8/20/92		Dyad: F1/C1

F1:		WHEN WE TALK ABOUT THE FUTURE YOU MIGHT WANT TO WORD IT LIKE THIS: "I WANT TO BETTER BE ABLE TO GO TO WORK."
C1:	(8)	YES
F1:		DO YOU WANT TO LEARN JOB SKILLS?
C1:	(9)	YES I WANT TO PLEARN JOB SKILLS.
F1:		WHAT KIND OF JOB WOULD YOU LIKE TO HAVE SOME DAY?
C1:	(10)	GO OUT TO JOB [client's name spelled correctly].
F1:		WHAT WOULD THE JOB BE?
C1:	(11)	I WANT TO MAKE BOXES.
F1:		[client's name], COULD WE TALK ABOUT OTHER KINDS OF JOBS OVER THE NEXT FEW MONTHS. WE ARE GOING TO CREATE A LEARNING CENTER IN OUR NEW BUILDING. I HOPE TO HAVE INFORMATION ON DIFFERENT KINDS OF JOBS PEOPLE COULD DO. WOULD YOU BE WILLING TO EXPLORE NEW POSSIBILITIES?
C1:	(12)	I WOULD LIKE TO EXPLOTRE NEW POSSIBILITIES.
F1:		FOR THE TIME BEING WHAT WOULD YOU LIKE FOR YOUR DAY PROGRAM?
C1:	(13)	I WANT TO CLEAN BATHROOMS.
F1:		COULD WE MAKE EXPLORING NEW JOB POSSIBILITIES AN IPP GOAL?
C1:	(14)	YES
C1:	(15)	JOB GOOD FOR ME.
F1:		IS THERE ANYTHING ELSE YOU WANT TO SAY ABOUT WHAT YOU WANT TO DO WITH YOUR DAYS?
C1:	(16)	I WANT GOOD PATYING JOB.

TABLE A.3   Pragmatic/Content Analysis of Preexistent Transcripts

Date: 3/23/92					*Dyad: F2/C2*

Utter-ances	Specific Utterance Function (SUF)	Broad Pragmatic Category (BPC)	Linguistic Device (LD)	Response (R) or Initiation (I)	Content
1	UNC	UNC	UNC	I	—
2	ANS/EXP	INF/PER	TM/DE	R	ABS/ITR
3	COM/EXP/GRE	INF/PER/INT	TI/DE	I	ITR
4	COM/EXP/GRE	INF/PER/INT	TM/DE	I	ITR
5	COM/EXP/GRE	INF/PER/INT	TM/DE	I	—
6	COM/EXP/GRE	INF/PER/INT	TM/DE	I	ITR
7	ANS	INF	TM/DE	R	—
8	(AMB)COM/EXP	(AMB)/INT/PER	TI/DE	I	ABS/ITR
9	REQ	INS/REG	TI/DE	I	—
10	ANS/INF	INF	TM/DE	R	—
11	SEI	HEU	TM	I	—
12	ANS/INF	INF	TM/DE	R	ABS/ITR
13	SEI	HEU	TM	I	—
14	INF/EXP/COM	INF/PER/INT	TM/DE	I	ITR
15	ANS/INF	INF	TM/DE	R	—
16	ANS/INF/EXP	INF/PER	TM/DE	R	ITR
17	ANS/INF	INF	TM/DE	R	—
18	ANS	INF	TM	R	—
19	ANS/INF/EXP	INF/PER	TM/DE	R	ABS/ITR
20	ANS/INF	INF	TM/DE	R	ABS/ITR
21	ANS	INF	TM	R	—
22	ANS/INF	INF/REG/IMG	TM/DE	R	—
23	ANS/INF	INF/IMG	TM/DE	R	—
24	ANS	INF	TM	R	—
25	ANS/EXP	INF/PER	TM	R	—
26	ANS/INF	INF	TM/DE	R	—
27	ANS	INF	TM	R	—
28	ANS	INF	TM	R	—

PREEXISTENT TRANSCRIPT

Date: 3/23/92	*Dyad: F2/C2*

March 23

C2: (1) YESMMMMMMMMMMMMMMMMMM
MMMMMMMMMMMMMMMMMMMMMM

F2: YOU SEEM EXCITED ABOUT TYPING TODAY, SO WHY DON'T YOU START.

C2: (2) i am ex citred aboutc typing ttoday
(3) you look nice
(4) you look bdautiful
(5) i like your dress
(6) you look beutiful

Date: 3/23/92		Dyad: F2/C2

F2:   Well, you are full of compliments today. You're looking pretty good yourself. Did you get a haircut?

C2: (7)   yes i did

(8)   you are having some trouble at home

(9)   \\read to me cplease

F2:   We'll read in awhile. What makes you think that I'm having trouble at home?

C2: (10)   because you were talking to [name of person; 1st letter in lower case] about locks

(11)   doc you need some new locks

F2:   Yes I think I do need some more locks just to be safe.

C2: (12)   safe from who you feel unsafe ffrrom

(13)   who

F2:   I want them just as a precaution from anyone who might try to get into the house.

C2: (14)   you need to have [proper name of close personal friend of facilitator (initial letter lower case; one additional letter at end)] there with you

F2:   You have a solution for everything. Sounds real nice, but not possible right now.

F2:   I'm changing the subject now—what happened with [proper name] last Friday?

C2: (15)   i broked his glasses

F2:   why?

C2: (16)   because i wsas upset with him

F2:   why?

C2: (17)   he took my lunch

F2:   Is this the truth?

C2: (18)   no

F2:   What is the truth about this?

C2: (19)   he bugs me

F2:   In what ways does he bug you?

C2: (20)   he puts his nosde in what im doing

F2:   Does breaking his glasses help this?

C2: (21)   no

F2:   What would be a better way to handle this?

C2: (22)   *tell him to stop*

F2:   that is a better solution. What if he doesn't stop though. Then what could you do?

C2: (23)   i c ould tell jeff

F2:   Good idea.

F2:   Are you have a difficult time typing today?

C2: (24)   yes

F2:   why?

C2: (25)   typikng is harfd

PREEXISTENT TRANSCRIPT *(continued)*

Date: 3/23/92		Dyad: F2/C2
F2:		What's the hard part?
C2:	(26)	getting my finger to work
F2:		Do we need a short break?
C2:	(27)	yres
F2:		Is there anything else to type about today?
C2:	(28)	no

TABLE A.4   Pragmatic/Content Analysis of Preexistent Transcripts

Date: 8/8/91   Dyad: F3/C3

Utterances	Specific Utterance Function (SUF)	Broad Pragmatic Category (BPC)	Linguistic Device (LD)	Response (R) or Initiation (I)	Content
1	AMB	AMB	NS	AMB	—
2	ANS	INF	TM	R	—
3	ANS	INF	TM	R	—
4	UNC	UNC	UNC	UNC	—
5	ANS/INF	INF	TM	R	—
6	ANS	INF	TM	R	—
7	ANS/INF	INF	TM	R	—
8	ANS	INF	TM	R	—
9	INF/EXP	INF/PER	TI	I	—
10	ANS	INF	TM	R	—
11	REQ	INS/REQ	TI/NS	I	—
12	REQ/INF	INS/INF/REQ	TM	R	—

PREEXISTENT TRANSCRIPT

Client:	[C3]
Date:	8/8/91
Time:	10:00 A.M.

I wrote out instructions for [C3] to follow and it appeared as though he did not understand. He followed two instructions incorrectly in an attempt to receive a reward for complying. I brought his FC board and, in answer to my questions, [C3] spelled out the following:

F3:		[C3] do you know how to read?
C3:	(1)	DORITOS (A bag of DORITOS were sitting close by [client])
F3:		[C3] can you read?
C3:	(2)	YES
F3:		Do you understand what these directions mean?

PREEXISTENT TRANSCRIPT *(continued)*

Client:	*[C3]*	
Date:	*8/8/91*	
Time:	*10:00 A.M.*	

C3:	(3)	YES
C3:	(4)	MACARONI ing
F3:		What is the first thing we put in the pot?
C3:	(5)	WATER
F3:		[C3] do you want to have macaroni for lunch?
C3:	(6)	YES
F3:		Do you want to follow the instructions and make macaroni?
C3:	(7)	CAN
F3:		Do you mean that you can follow the instructions?
C3:	(8)	YES ... [pause] ...
C3:	(9)	BAD
F3:		Do you feel bad?
C3:	(10)	YES
F3:		Do you mean that you can read the instructions but you feel bad?
C3:	(11)	OPEN
F3:		Open what?
C3:	(12)	OPEN CAN OF MACARONI (repeated this sentence several) [transcript unclear]

TABLE A.5   Pragmatic/Content Analysis of Preexistent Transcripts

Date: 8/15/91					Dyad: F3/C3
Utterances	*Specific Utterance Function (SUF)*	*Broad Pragmatic Category (BPC)*	*Linguistic Device (LD)*	*Response (R) or Initiation (I)*	*Content*
1	ANS	INF	TM	R	—
2	ANS/INF/EXP	INF/PER	TM	R	ABS/ITR/PHL

PREEXISTENT TRANSCRIPT

Client:	[C3]
Date:	8/15/91
Time:	11:45 A.M.
Location:	Kitchen

F3:		[C3] does it bother you when I talk about you to other people in front of you?
C3:	(1)	Y
F3:		Why does it bother you? How does that make you feel?
C3:	(2)	AM DUMB

[C3] displayed numerous maladaptives for the rest of the day. When I would ask him what was bothering him on his FC board he would repeat the words "AM DUMB."

TABLE A.6   Pragmatic/Content Analysis of Preexistent Transcripts

Date: 8/16/91					Dyad: F3/C3
Utterances	Specific Utterance Function (SUF)	Broad Pragmatic Category (BPC)	Linguistic Device (LD)	Response (R) or Initiation (I)	Content
1	ANS/INF	INF	TM	R	ITR
2	ANS/INF/EXP	INF/PER	TM	R	ABS/ITR/PHL
3	ANS	INF	TM	R	—
4	ANS/INF/EXP	INF/PER	TM/DE	R	ITR/PHL

PREEXISTENT TRANSCRIPT

Client: [C3]
Date: 8/16/91
Time: 1:45 P.M.
Location: Park

F3:		[C3] Why are you upset? What is making you upset?
C3:	(1)	PEOPLE
F3:		What about people upsets you?
C3:	(2)	MEAN
F3:		Do you think that I am mean?
C3:	(3)	NO
F3:		What do people do that is mean?
C3:	(4)	LAUGH ME

[C3] seemed extremely depressed today. He would only get out of my car to eat and use the bathroom. Above is the conversation we had near the end of our day together.

TABLE A.7 Pragmatic/Content Analysis of Preexistent Transcripts

Date: 8/22/91   Dyad: F3/C3

Utterances	Specific Utterance Function (SUF)	Broad Pragmatic Category (BPC)	Linguistic Device (LD)	Response (R) or Initiation (I)	Content
1	ANS/INF	INF	TM	R	—
2	UNC	UNC	UNC	UNC	—
3	ANS/INF/EXP	INF/PER/IMG	TM	R	ABS/ITR
4*	ANS/PRO/EXP	INF/PER	TM	R	—
5	ANS/INF/EXP	INF/PER	NS/DE	R	ABS/ITR/PHL

*Nonverbal behavior but interpreted by facilitator as intentional. Therefore it was coded.

PREEXISTENT TRANSCRIPT

Client: [C3]
Date: 8/22/91
Time: 9:30 A.M.
Location: Park

F3:		What did you do with your dad yesterday?
C3:	(1)	DRIVE
F3:		What else did you do?
C3:	(2)	EA — ([C3] looked frustrated and started to walk away.)
F3:		[C3] why don't you like to type?
C3	(3)	DAM FACAED ([C3] spelled this twice. I wrote it down on a sheet of paper and asked [C3] if I had spelled it correctly. He nodded).
F3:		You think typing is a damn facade?
C3:	(4)	[C3] nodded. He then got angry and walked away.

11:00 A.M.

F3:		What makes you think that typing is a facade?
C3:	(5)	BECAUZ PEOPLE FEAR ME

TABLE A.8   Pragmatic/Content Analysis of Preexistent Messages

Date: 5/27/93   *Dyad: FC/C1*

Utterances	Specific Utterance Function (SUF)	Broad Pragmatic Category (BPC)	Linguistic Device (LD)	Response (R) or Initiation (I)	Content
1	ANS	INF	TM	R	—
2	REQ/INF	INS/INF	TI/DE	I	—
3	ANS	INF	TM	R	—
4	ANS/INF	INF	TM	R	—
5	ANS/INF	INF	TM	R	—
6	ANS	INF	TM	R	—
7	ANS	INF	TM	R	—

TRANSCRIPT OF OBSERVED SESSION

Date: 5/27/93   *Dyad: F1/C1*

(All utterances are attributed to C1.)

C1:   (1)   IWDIANE
C1:   (2)   I WANT COFFEE.
C1:   (3)   YES
C1:   (4)   [First four letters of the name of a town in client's state, accurately typed. Not included in the interests of confidentiality.]
C1:   (5)   [Proper name, perfectly spelled, of important person in client's life.]
C1:   (6)   RING
C1:   (7)   [Proper name of facilitator, perfectly spelled.]

TRANSCRIPT OF OBSERVED SESSION

Date: 5/12/93   *Dyad: F1/C1*

This transcript should be reviewed in conjunction with the narrative description of the session found in Chapter 4 of this report. This transcript does not lend itself to pragmatic analysis.

Word Association:

F1:		C1:	
F1:	car	C1: (1)	ride
F1:	glass	C1: (2)	drink
F1:	orange	C1: (3)	juice
F1:	tobogan	C1: (4)	dancing
F1:	good	C1: (5)	church
F1:	notorious	C1: (6)	bad
F1:	ancient	C1: (7)	old
F1:	impoverished	C1: (8)	old poor [F1 typed this]

TRANSCRIPT OF OBSERVED SESSION *(continued)*

F1:	regular (Initially typed her mother's name. [F1] said "normal" verbally.)	C1: (9)	normal	
F1:	summer	C1: (10)	swimming	
F1:	work	C1: (11)	money	

TABLE A.9   Pragmatic/Content Analysis of Facilitated Messages

Date: 12/9/92   *Dyad: F1/C1*

Utterances	Specific Utterance Function (SUF)	Broad Pragmatic Category (BPC)	Linguistic Device (LD)	Response (R) or Initiation (I)	Content
1	ANS	INF	TM	R	—
2	UNC	UNC	UNC	UNC	—
3	ANS	INF	TM	R	—
4	REQ/INF	INS/INF	NS/DE	I	—
5	REQ/INF	INS/INF	TM/DE	R	—
6	ANS	INF	TM	R	—
7	UNC	UNC	UNC	UNC	—
8	ANS	INF	TM	R	—
9	ANS	INF	TM/DE	R	—
10	ANS/INF	INF	TM/DE	R	ABS
11	ANS/INF	INF	TM/DE	R	—
12	ANS/PRO	INF	TM	R	—
13	UNC	UNC	UNC/DE	UNC	—
14	UNC	UNC	UNC/DE	UNC	—
15	ANS/INF	INF	TM/DE	R	—
16	ANS	INF	TM	R	—
17	ANS/INF	INF	TM	R	—
18	ANS	INF	NS	R	—
19	(AMB)ANS/INF	(AMB)INF	TM	R	—
20	ANS	INF	TM	R	—
21	ANS/INF/EXP	INF/PER	NS*	R	—
22	ANS/INF/EXP	INF/PER	TM/DE	R	ABS/ITR
23	(AMB)ANS	(AMB)INF	TM/DE	R	—
24	ANS/INF/EXP	INF/PER	TM/DE	R	—
25	ANS	INF	TM	R	—
26	REQ	INS	TI/DE	I	—
27	REQ/INF	INF/INS	TM/DE	R	—
28	ANS	INF	TM	R	—
29	UNC	UNC	UNC	UNC	—
30	AMB	AMB	NS	I	—

*Client may have misinterpreted question based on pause in sentence.

TRANSCRIPT OF OBSERVED SESSION

Date: 12/9/92   *Dyad: F1/C1*

This transcript should be reviewed in conjunction with the narrative description of the session found in Chapter 4.

F1:		"I'm going to be very glad when we get partitions in this room because we will be able to get more people in here."
C1:	(1)	"Yes" [said no immediately following].
F1:		[Repeated several times] "Yes what?"
C1:		Said "people" [was directed by F1 to type it].
(2)		"Pia." [said "no, no" and hit the delete key].
F1:		"Let's go to something else. Let's type your name."
C1:	(3)	[Typed name perfectly, all in lowercase. Much prompting needed.]
F1:		"You want to type your mother's name, go ahead."
C1:	(4)	"I want tomorrow." [Said "tomorrow," then "go home tomorrow".]
C1:	(5)	"I want to ["to" typed by F1] go home tomorrow."
Investigator:		"Can you tell me how you learned to read?"
C1:	(6)	[Said yes, then directed by F1 to type it] "Yes."
F1:		"I learned to read . . ." [both typed and verbalized].
C1:	(7)	[Said "word" or "workbook."] Typed "boo" and said no and deleted it.
F1:		Did someone teach you to read?
C1:	(8)	"No" [both typed and verbalized].
F1:		"Did you learn to read on your own?"
C1:	(9)	[Verbalized yes, then was directed by F1 to type her answer.] "Yes I taughy"
F1:		"Let's make a sentence. I what?"
C1:	(10)	"Yes, I taught myself." [In deleting "y," C1 used her left hand to press down on her right index finger over the delete key.]
F1:		"I learned to read from what?"
C1:	(11)	"I learned to read from world book"
F1:		"Do you mean encyclopedia?"
C1:	(12)	[verbally "No. no," agitated, then typed] "No."
F1:		"Type what you want to say."
C1:	(13)	"I reaser" [verbally said "no more [F1]" x 3]
F1:		"How did you learn to read? Tell us more about how you learned to read."
C1:	(14)	"You loojoo."
F1:		"I think we're getting stuck here. Start with 'I,' type, 'I.'"
C1:	(15)	"I learned to read world book." [First time F1 asked her if she had intended to type "learned" she said no. The second time she said yes.]
F1:		"Is it true? Yes or No?"
C1:	(16)	"Yes" [said verbally and typed].
F1:		"Was that at the State hospital?"

TRANSCRIPT OF OBSERVED SESSION *(continued)*

Date: 12/9/92		*Dyad: F1/C1*

C1: (17) [Said yes and typed] "hos — hospital [read "hospital"].

F1: "How old were you when you went to the State hospital?" [repeated]

C1: (18) [Said yes, and was instructed to type it. Said, "teeth out," then typed] "yes."

(19) 3; 39. [Her finger was over the "3." F1 took her arm at the mid-forearm level and she typed] "7."

F1: "Could you read words before you went to the State hospital?"

C1: (20) "Yes."

Investigator: "What do you like best [pause] about facilitated communication?"

C1: (21) [Said "eating [or] skiing," then "go out" after my pause then typed] "going out."

F1: "What do you like best about typing?"

C1: (22) "I like to say nice thoughts" [verbally said no regarding the word "thoughts"].

C1: (23) "I like to say nice good lot now."

F1: "I'm a little confused." [typed and said, "I'd like to say . . ." in response to C1 saying what sounded like "mother."]

C1: [Verbally] "Okay, okay. No. More please, more please, more please, more please" [client bolted].

C1: (24) [F1 rephrases question. C1 says, "Finished" x 2] "I like to type very good words."

F1: "Don't you want to finish now?"

C1: (25) "No."

C1: (26) "I want"

F1: "Let's put the word 'to' in."

C1: (27) "I want to go to stort" (F1 deleted the 't'].

C1: [Verbally, kept saying mother's name.]

F1: [typed out as fill-in] "She's your _____."

C1: (28) "Nother." [It appears from the video that she also typed in her mother's name.]

C1: (29) "j n"

F1: "There's a letter that comes first."

C1: (30) "Jan" [important person in client's life]

TABLE A.10   Pragmatic/Content Analysis of Facilitated Messages

Date: 5/27/93   Dyad: F2/C2

Utterances	Specific Utterance Function (SUF)	Broad Pragmatic Category (BPC)	Linguistic Device (LD)	Response (R) or Initiation (I)	Content
1	GRE	(ritualized) INT	TM	R	—
2	GRE	(ritualized) INT	TM/DE	I	—
3	ANS	INF	TM	R	—
4	REQ	INS	TI/DE	I	—
5	AMB	AMB	DE	UNC	—
6	ANS	INF	TM	R	—
7	ANS	INF	TM/DE	R	—
8	COM/EXP	INT/PER	TM/DE	I	—
9	COM/EXP	INT/PER	TM/DE	I	—
10	ANS	INF	TM	R	—
11	REQ	INS	TM/DE	R	—
12	OFF/INF	INF/INT	TM/DE	R	—
13	COM/EXP	INT/PER	TI/DE	I	—
14	UNC	UNC	UNC	UNC	—
15	UNC	UNC	UNC	UNC	—
16	UNC	UNC	UNC	UNC	—
17	UNC	UNC	UNC	UNC	—
18	UNC	UNC	UNC	UNC	—
19	UNC	UNC	UNC	UNC	—
20	UNC	UNC	UNC	UNC	—
21	UNC	UNC	UNC	UNC	—
22	UNC	UNC	UNC	UNC	—
23	UNC	UNC	UNC	UNC	—
24	REQ	INS	TI	I	—
25	ANS	INF	TM	R	—
26	SEI	HEU	TM/DE	R	ABS
27	SEI	HEU	TM/DE	I	ABS/ITR
28	COM/EXP	PER/IMG	TM/DE	I	ABS/ITR
29	REQ	INS	TI	I	—
30	ANS	INF	AMB	AMB	—
31	ANS/INF	INF	TM	R	—
32	UNC	UNC	UNC	UNC	—
33	UNC	UNC	UNC	UNC	—
34	COM/INF	INF	TM/DE	R	—
35	ANS/INF	INF	TM/DE	R	—
36	COM/INF	INF	TM/DE	R	—
37	ANS/INF	INF	TM	R	—
38	ANS/INF	INF	TM	R	—
39	SEI	HEU	TI/DE	I	—
40	COM/EXP	INT/PER	TM/DE	R	—
41	COM	INT	TI/DE	I	ABS/ITR
42	COM/EXP	INT/PER	TM/DE	I	ABS/ITR
43	EXP/INF	PER/INF	TM/DE	R	ITR
44	UNC	UNC	UNC	UNC	—

TABLE A.10 *(continued)*   Pragmatic/Content Analysis of Facilitated Messages

Date: 5/27/93   *Dyad: F2/C2*

Utterances	Specific Utterance Function (SUF)	Broad Pragmatic Category (BPC)	Linguistic Device (LD)	Response (R) or Initiation (I)	Content
45	ANS	INF	TM	R	—
46	AMB	AMB	TM/DE	AMB	ABS
47	COM/EXP/INF	INF/PER/IMG	TI/DE	I	ABS/ITR
48	ANS/INF	INF/PER	TM/DE	R	ABS/ITR
49	ANS/INF	INF	TM/DE	R	—
50	ANS/EXP	PER/INF	TM/DE	R	ABS/ITR
51	INF/EXP	INF/PER	TM/DE	I	ABS/ITR
52	ANS/INF/EXP	INF/PER	TM	R	ABS/ITR
53	ANS	INF	TM	R	—
54	COM/ANS	INF	TM/DE	R	—
55	REQ	REG	TI/DE	I	—
56	ANS/INF	INF/REG	TM	R	—
57	ANS/INF	INF	TM	R	—
58	ANS	INF	TM	R	—

TRANSCRIPT OF OBSERVED SESSION

Date: 5/27/93   *Dyad: F2/C2*

This transcript should be reviewed in conjunction with the narrative description of the session found in Chapter 5.

F2:		Good morning
C2:	(1)	good morening
C2:	(2)	how are you [facilitator's name in lowercase letters]
F2:		I'm ok today. Do you want to type about what just happened?
C2:	(3)	no
C2:	(4)	pleqse read to me
C2:	(5)	please purple to me
F2:		I'd like to type for a bit first. I have some things to tell you.
C2:	(6)	ok
F2:		Do you remember Diane, the lady who came to see you last winter?
C2:	(7)	yes i rememb er her
C2:	(8)	i like her
C2:	(9)	she is nice
F2:		Is there anything that you would like to ask or say to Diane?
C2:	(10)	yes
C2:	(11)	please 5type with me
C2:	(12)	i open the open door to typing withme
C2:	(13)	you my friend [facilitator's name in lowercase letters]
[Investigator's attempt to facilitate with client. Refer to narrative, Chapter 5]		
	(14)	yew\

TRANSCRIPT OF OBSERVED SESSION *(continued)*

Date: 5/27/93   *Dyad: F2/C2*

	(15)	l;.uy
	(16)	.y y y the brady mh bj bunch i buc h them nobnm nob ody
	(17)	.//yhgjk
	(18)	kkk ikljn
	(19)	ll, m klllnjhb
	(20)	kdny kenyrkn
	(21)	lofftfv
	(22)	carnl y
	(23)	lknb n n m7uuu omn,,mnk jnnnn
	(24)	go to worlk
		y
F2:		Diane wanted to know if you had a question for her?
C2:	(25)	yes
C2:	(26)	uis she marrieeed
C2:	(27)	\are you happy in life
C2:	(28)	yo7 klook happy
C2:	(29)	bacvkn to woriok
C2:	(30)	yeesyes
F2:		How is work?
C2:	(31)	i5t is gooed
C2:	(32)	8i ol8 like st3eve
C2:	(33)	iolk l8ikee you
C2:	(34)	i like to work]
F2:		We all like to work. What do you like best about work?
C2:	(35)	i like tyh3e fl0wers
C2:	(36)	8io8i 8i likw to work
F2:		What flowers are in bloom at the cemetery right now?
C2:	(37)	purple ohes rewe e red ones and pinikk onesa \\
F2:		Do you know the names of these flowers?
C2:	(38)	lilacs red cARHNATIONS PEACY BLOSS9IMS
C2:	(39)	how iss your purple dress\]1
F2:		Just fine. It's just hanging out in my closet!
C2:	(40)	you looik good in thAt dress
F2:		Thank you. I'm glad you like it.
C2:	(41)	6you like me
C2:	(42)	y6ou make m3e feel good\\
F2:		I do like you, [C2]. That's why it troubles me to see you hurt your-self like you did this morning.
C2:	(43)	ii did not swant to go wirth you
C2:	(44)	8i m qw mqake you wait
F2:		But you did go with me. Did you want to go then?
C2:	(45)	yyes
C2:	(46)	you wsait

TRANSCRIPT OF OBSERVED SESSION *(continued)*

Date: *5/27/93*   Dyad: *F2/C2*

F2:		I didn't mind waiting and would have waited until you were ready. You didn't have to hit yourself to get me to wait.
C2:	(47)	i red in the face
F2:		What does that mean?
C2:	(48)	i am wsa]\ sorry
F2:		Sorry for who?
C2:	(49)	youy
F2:		What about you?
C2:	(50)	i ajm hnot skorry for me
C2:	(51)	i was mqad
F2:		That was obvious, but why hurt yourself?
C2:	(52)	becqaus4e it feelsz tyt too tgood
F2:		How does hurting yourself make you feel good?
C2:	(53)	b3ecause it does
C2:	(54)	i like it
C2:	(55)	please tqke me t0 work
F2:		What should we do?
C2:	(56)	go fine st4ve
F2:		Where might he be with the others?
C2:	(57)	at the ljibrary storew 0puerop the b owling alley the dshop yea
F2:		Is there anything else that you want to type today?

TABLE A.11   Pragmatic/Content Analysis of Facilitated Messages

Date: 3/18/93   *Dyad: F3/C3*

Utterances	Specific Utterance Function (SUF)	Broad Pragmatic Category (BPC)	Linguistic Device (LD)	Response (R) or Initiation (I)	Content
1	ANS/INF/EXP	INF/PER	TM	R	ABS/ITR
2	INF/EXP	INF/PER	TI	I	ABS/ITR
3	ANS	INF	TM	R	ABS/ITR
4	ANS	INF	TM	R	ABS/ITR
5*	UNC	UNC	UNC	UNC	—
6	UNC	UNC	UNC	UNC	—
7	AMB	AMB	AMB	AMB	—
8**	UNC	UNC	UNC	UNC	—
9	ANS	INF	TM	R	—

*Meaningless string of letters interpreted by facilitator as the word *mad*.
**Meaningless string of letters interpreted by facilitator as the word *bad*.

TRANSCRIPT OF OBSERVED SESSION

Date: 3/18/93   *Dyad: F3/C3*

Note: This dyad facilitated through the use of an alphabet board that also contained key words (e.g., yes, no). Because there was no transcript produced, the following represents this investigator's record of the session, corroborated via videotaped analysis. All utterances attributed to F3 were rendered verbally; those attributed to C3 were facilitated manually with intensive support extending to the index finger.

This transcript should be reviewed in conjunction with the narrative description of the session found in Chapter 6.

F3: [Reading from a list] "How have you been feeling lately? Are you *angry, depressed, anxious, excited, stressed?* How have you been feeling? [She turned the page and continued reading.] *mad, relaxed, sad, o.k., tired, sick?*"

C3: [Facilitating with high-level support, facilitator called out the letters to which F3 pointed] A – B – B

F3: "Keep your finger out." [Pause] "Keep your finger out."
     Client hiccuped and got up and walked away. F3 told him that he didn't have to look at her list, she just wanted to know how he was doing.

C3: A – B – A – B – A [Facilitator looked up at C3 and noticed that he wasn't looking at the board. She directed his attention back to the board and said, "What comes after A?"]

C3: [continued] D – O – N – E – D

F3: "Abandoned."

Investigator's note at time of observation: When F3 is unaware that C3 is not looking at the board, letter selection continues. When she is aware that he is not look-

TRANSCRIPT OF OBSERVED SESSION *(continued)*

Date: 3/18/93   *Dyad: F3/C3*

ing, she treats the lack of visual attention as though it is very important and always directs his attention back to the board.

C3:   B – Y

Investigator's note: Support was more at the palm as opposed to the wrist. Index-finger isolation was virtually nonexistent, and there was no attempt to provide it. Consequently, letter selection was extremely unclear.

F3:   "What's next?"

Investigator's note: C3 hit the board twice. No letters were called out.

F3:   "What's the next word?"

C3:   D – D [Pause]

F3:   "What comes after *D?*"

C3:   A

F3:   "What's next?"

C3:   A – A

F3:   "What comes after A?"

Investigator's note: C3 pointed to the next letter in what was eventually interpreted as facilitator's name, hitting it three times. He also pointed to another letter in the middle of the board that the facilitator did not read. C3 tried to put his arm around F3's neck, and then he touched his nose to her nose. F3 said, "I know, it's really good to see you." She eventually redirected his attention back to the board. He then hit the last letter in facilitator's name, twice. This narrative has been rendered in the interests of preserving confidentiality regarding the facilitator's name.

F3: (1)   "Abandoned by [F3]." [considered utterance 1] "I know you've said that before, but I keep coming to see you. I come to your house."

F3:   "I know, you're just a sweetie" [in response to client's nonverbal behavior].

C3:   B – B – A – [unclear] – D – D [Client was not looking at board for several letters.]

F3:   "Bad."

C3:   C

F3:   "What's next?"

C3:   A

F3:   "Can."

C3:   C – D – A – D [Client not looking at board for several letters.]

F3:   "Bad."

C3:   C – A [Client not looking at board.]

C3:   C – A – N – D – A – D

F3:   "Dad"

C3:   B – A – D – D – A – D

F3: (2)   "It looks like you're typing Dad's bad or dad bad." [considered utterance 2]

F3:   "Why would you say that. Could you explain that one?"

C3: (3)   A – B – A – D – O – N – E – D [abandoned]

F3:   "abandoned." [Client smiled.]

TRANSCRIPT OF OBSERVED SESSION *(continued)*

Date: 3/18/93	*Dyad: F3/C3*

F3:   "Do you want to stop talking about that?"

C3:   K – [unclear string of letters] – Z

F3:   "Okay, let's talk about something else."

Investigator's note: Client got up and walked away, precipitously, as F3 was talking to him. He went over to the corner of the room and sat down on the floor. All attempts to redirect him back to the table were futile.

F3:   "I know it's hard to talk about. You feel abandoned by a lot of people. [Directing her attention to me] Dad comes to see him every week even though it's far away and was in the process of getting him to move closer to him [directing her attention back to client] so he can see you more. So, I don't think that he'll abandon you. He cares very much for you."

Investigator's note: Facilitator tried to cajole client into continuing, promising frequent breaks; however, she eventually brought the board over to him and asked him to type that he was done.

C3: (4)   A – B – A – D – O – N – E – D [abandoned]

F3:   "Abandoned. How does that make you feel?"

C3: (5)   M – A – D – F – A – C – C – E – A – B – A – D

F3:   "Mad."

C3: (6)   B – B – A – C – D [unclear string of letters]

F3:   "I know this is frustrating especially when I can't figure out what you're typing."

C3: (7)   A – B – A – D [Facilitator stopped him.]

F3:   "Bad." [considered utterance 7]

C3: (8)   C – A – B – A – B [unclear, after this], then B – A – D

Investigator's note: Review of the videotaped footage revealed that facilitator said the last letter "D" a split second before client selected it on the board.

F3:   "Bad because what? Can you finish the sentence? I feel bad because what? [Client engaged in various maladaptive behaviors.]

F3:   "I'm not sure what you're typing. I'm not sure what this word means." [Client engaged in self-injurious behavior.]

F3:   "It's tough. It's not as easy as talking, is it?" [Client continued to engage in self-injurious behavior.]

F3:   "Do you want a break?"

Investigator's note: Client stopped biting his arm. Facilitator put the board in front of him, took his right hand to facilitate, and he again began to bite his arm, moaning what appeared to be a no.

F3:   "You know what to do if you're getting upset. You can type that you're done. It's as easy as that, but you have to type it."

C3:   [He typed three letters in a row, but I could not determine what they were.]

F3: (9)   "Okay, that's great. That's good that you could type that 'No.'" [considered utterance 9]

References

American Speech-Language-Hearing Association. (August 1994). *Technical report on facilitated communication*. Draft no. 7. Rockville, MD: ASHA Ad Hoc Committee on Facilitated Communication.

Arin, D. M., Bauman, M. L., and Kemper, T. L. (1991). The distribution of Purkinje cell loss in the cerebellum in autism. *Neurology, 41* (Suppl), 307.

Arwood, E. L. (December 1983). *Pragmaticism: Treatment for language disorders*. National Student Speech Language Hearing Association, Serial no. 8.

Attwood, T. (1993). *Do people with autism have limited range of activities?* [Cassette Recording]. Ontario: Audio Archives, International.

Ayres, A. J. (1979). *Sensory integration and the child*. Los Angeles: Western Psychological Services.

Ayres, A. J. (1985). *Developmental dyspraxia and adult-onset apraxia*. Torrance, CA: Sensory Integration International.

Baron-Cohen, S. (1993). From attention-goal psychology to belief-desire psychology: The development of a theory of mind, and its dysfunction. In S. Baron-Cohen, H. Tager-Flusberg, and D. J. Cohen (Eds.), *Understanding other minds* (pp. 59–82). New York: Oxford University Press.

Baron-Cohen, S. (1995). *Mindblindness: An essay on autism and theory of mind*. Cambridge, MA: MIT Press.

Bartak, L., Rutter, M., and Cox, A. (1975). Comparative study of infantile autism and specific developmental receptive language disorder: I. The Children. *British Journal of Psychiatry, 126,* 127–145.

Bates, E. (1979). Intentions, conventions, and symbols. In E. Bates, T. Benigni, I. Bretherton, L. Camaioni, and V. Volterra (Eds.), *The emergence of symbols: Cognition and communication in infancy*. New York: Academic Press.

Bettelheim, B. (1967). *The empty fortress: Infantile autism and the birth of self*. New York: Free Press.

Biklen, D. (1990). Communication unbound: Autism and praxis. *Harvard Educational Review, 60,* 291–314.

Biklen, D. (1992). Typing to talk: Facilitated communication. *American Journal of Speech-Language Pathology, 1*(2), 15–17.

Biklen, D. (1993). *Communication unbound*. New York: Teachers College, Columbia University.

Biklen, D., and Shubert, A. (1991). New words: The communication of students with autism. *Remedial and Special Education, 12*(6), 46–57.

Biklen, D., Morton, M. W., Gold, D., Berrigan, C., and Swaminathan, S. (1992). Facilitated communication: Implications for individuals with autism. *Topics in Language Disorders, 12*(4), 1–28.

Biklen, D., Morton, M. W., Saha, S. D., Duncan, J., Gold, D., Hardardottir, M., Karna, E., O'Connor, S., and Rao, S. (1991). "I AMN NOT A UTISTIVC OH THJE TYP" (I am not autistic on the typewriter). *Disability, Handicap & Society*, 6, 161–180.

Bogdan, R. C., and Biklen, S. K. (1982). *Qualitative research for education: An introduction to theory and methods.* Boston: Allyn and Bacon.

Brazelton, T. B., and Cramer, B. G. (1990). *The earliest relationship.* Reading, MA: Addison-Wesley.

Bruner, J. (1990). *Acts of meaning.* Cambridge, MA: Harvard University Press.

Cairns, R. B. (1986). *Social development: Recent theoretical trends and relevance for autism.* In E. Schopler and G. B. Mesibov (Eds.), *Social behavior in autism* (pp. 15–33). New York: Plenum.

Calculator, S. (1992). Communication support for children with severe disabilities in regular classrooms: Life after facilitated communication. *Clinical Connection*, 6, 1–4.

Calculator, S., and Singer, K. (1992). Letter to the editor: Preliminary validation of facilitated communication. *Topics in Language Disorders*, 13, ix–xvi.

Candland, D. K. (1993). *Feral children & clever animals: Reflections on human nature.* New York: Oxford University Press.

Cantwell, D., Baker, L., and Rutter, M. (1978). A comparative study of infantile autism and specific developmental receptive language disorder. IV: Analysis of syntax and language function. *Journal of Child Psychology and Psychiatry*, 19, 351–362.

Caparulo, B., and Cohen, D. (1977). Cognitive structure, language, and emerging social competence in autistic and aphasic children. *Journal of the American Academy of Child Psychiatry*, 16, 620–645.

Carr, E. G. (1982). Sign language acquisition: Clinical and theoretical aspects. In R. L. Koegel, A. Ricover, and A. L. Egel (Eds.), *Educating and understanding autistic children.* New York: College Hill.

Carr, E. G., and Kologinsky, E. (1983). Acquisition of sign language by autistic children. II: Spontaneity and generalization effects. *Journal of Applied Behavior Analysis*, 16, 297–314.

Ciaranello, R. D. (Summer 1988). Autism: The prison of self. *Stanford Magazine*, pp. 17–22.

Courchesne, E. (1991). *A new model of brain and behavior development in infantile autism* [Cassette Recording]. Silver Spring, MD: Autism Society of America.

Courchesne, E., Yeung-Courchesne, R., Press, G. A., Hesselink, J. R., and Jernigan, T. L. (1988). Hypoplasia of cerebellar vermal lobules VI and VII in infantile autism. *New England Journal of Medicine*, 318, 1349–1354.

Crossley, R. (1994). *Facilitated communication training.* New York: Teachers College, Columbia University.

Crossley, R., and Remington-Gurney, J. (1992). Getting the words out: Facilitated communication training. *Topics in Language Disorders*, 12(4), 29–45.

Curcio, F. (1978). Sensorimotor functioning and communication in mute autistic children. *Journal of Autism and Childhood Schizophrenia*, 8, 281–292.

Dawson, G. (1989). Preface. In G. Dawson (Ed.), *Autism: Nature, diagnosis and treatment* (pp. xv–xx). New York: Plenum.

Dawson, G. and Galpert, L. (1986). A developmental model for facilitating the social behavior of autistic children. In E. Schopler and G. B. Mesibov (Eds.), *Social behavior in autism* (pp. 237–261). New York: Plenum.

Dawson, G., and Lewy, A. (1989). Arousal, attention, and the socioemotional impairments of individuals with autism. In G. Dawson (Ed.), *Autism: Nature, diagnosis and treatment* (pp. 49–74). New York: Guilford Press.

Definition of autism. (January-February 1994). *Advocate, 26*(1), 3.

Donnellan, A. M. (1984). The criterion of the least dangerous assumption. *Behavior Disorders, 9,* 141–150.

Donnellan, A. M., and Leary, M. R. (1995). *Movement differences and diversity in autism/mental retardation.* Madison, WI: DRI.

Donnellan, A. M., Mirenda, P. L., Mesaros, R. A., and Fassbender, L. L. (1984). Analyzing the communicative function of aberrant behavior. *Journal of the Association for Persons with Severe Handicaps, 9,* 201–212.

Duchan, J., and Higginbotham, J. (1992). Panel discussion on facilitated communication. American Speech-Language-Hearing Association National Conference, San Antonio.

Dunn, M. (1994). Neurophysiologic observations in autism and implications for neurologic dysfunction. In M. L. Bauman and T. L. Kemper (Eds.), *The neurobiology of autism* (pp. 45–65). Baltimore, MD: Johns Hopkins University Press.

Durand, V. M., Berotti, D., and Weiner, J. (1993). Functional communication training: Factors affecting effectiveness, generalization and maintenance. In J. Reichle and D. P. Wacker (Eds.), *Communicative alternatives to challenging behavior: Integrating functional assessment and intervention strategies* (pp. 317–340). Baltimore, MD: Paul H. Brookes.

Fay, W. H. (1980). Aspects of language. In W. Fay and A. Schuler, *Emerging language in autistic children.* Baltimore, MD: University Park.

Fay, W. H., and Schuler, A. L. (1980). *Emerging language in autistic children.* Baltimore, MD: University Park.

Fein, D., Pennington, B., Markowitz, P., Braverman, M., and Waterhouse, L. (1986). Toward a neuropsychological model of infantile autism: Are the social deficits primary? *Journal of the American Academy of Child Psychiatry, 25*(2), 198–212.

Fox, S. (April 6, 1992). Facilitating the communication of autistic individuals. *Advance, 2*(7), 8–9.

Frith, U. (1989). *Autism: Explaining the enigma.* Cambridge, MA: Blackwell.

Frith, U. (June 1993). Autism. *Scientific American,* pp. 108–114.

Gast, D. L., and Wolery, M. (1987). Severe maladaptive behaviors (3rd ed.). In M. E. Snell (Ed.), *Systematic instruction of persons with severe handicaps.* Columbus, OH: Merrill.

Geller, E. (1989). The assessment of perspective-taking skills. *Seminars in Speech and Language, 10*(1), 28–41.

Green, G. (October 1992). *Facilitated communication: Scientific and ethical issues.* Paper presented in the E. K. Shriver Center UAP Research Colloquium Series, Waltham, MA.

Green, G. (1994a). The quality of the evidence. In H. Shane (Ed.), *Facilitated communication: The clinical and social phenomenon* (pp. 157–225). San Diego: Singular.

Green, G. (1994b). *Toward informed decision-making about facilitated communication* [Cassette Recording, Tape 1]. Houston: Ears.

Halliday, M.A.K. (1975). *Learning how to mean: Exploration in the development of language*. New York: Elsevier North Holland.

Haskew, P., and Donnellan, A. M. (1992). *Emotional maturity and well-being: Psychological lessons of facilitated communication*. Moving on beyond facilitated communication series. Danbury, CT: DRI.

Heinrichs, P. (February 16, 1992a). State 'tortured' family. *Sunday Age*, p. 1.

Heinrichs, P. (February 16, 1992b). Suffering at the hands of the protectors. *Sunday Age*, p. 9.

Hill, D. A., and Leary, M. R. (1993). *Movement disturbance: A clue to hidden competencies in persons diagnosed with autism and other developmental disabilities*. Madison, WI: DRI.

Hobson, R. P. (1989). Beyond cognition: A theory of autism. In G. Dawson (Ed.), *Autism: Nature, diagnosis and treatment* (pp. 22–48). New York: Plenum.

Hubbell, R. D. (1981). *Children's language disorders: An integrated approach*. Englewood Cliffs, NJ: Prentice-Hall.

Jacobson, J. W., Mulick, J. A., and Schwartz, A. A. (1995). A history of facilitated communication: Science, pseudo-science, and antiscience. *American Psychologist, 50*, 750–765.

Kanner, L. (1943). Autistic disturbances of affective contact. *Nervous Child, 2*, 217–250.

Kaye, K. (1982). *The mental and social life of babies*. Chicago: University of Chicago Press.

Kliewer, C., and Currin, Z. (1992). Facilitated communication. Unpublished manuscript.

Layton, T. L. (1987). Manual communication. In T. L. Layton (Ed.), *Language and treatment of autistic and developmentally disordered children* (pp. 189–213). Springfield, IL: Charles C. Thomas.

Levine, K., and Wharton, R. (May 1995). Facilitated communication: What parents should know. *Exceptional Parent, 25*, 40, 42–44, 49, 51–53.

Meltzoff, A., and Gopnik, A. (1993). The role of imitation in understanding persons and developing a theory of mind. In S. Baron-Cohen, H. Tager-Flusberg, and D. J. Cohen (Eds.), *Understanding other minds* (pp. 335–366). New York: Oxford University Press.

Miles, M. B., and Huberman, A. M. (1984). *Qualitative data analysis: A Sourcebook of new methods*. Newbury Park, CA: Sage.

Miller, L. (1990). The roles of language and learning in the development of literacy. *Topics in Language Disorders, 10*(2), 1–24.

Mulick, J. A., Jacobson, J. W., and Kobe, F. H. (1993). Anguished silence and helping hands: Autism and facilitated communication. *Skeptical Inquirer, 17*(3), 270–280.

Mundy, P., and Sigman, M. (1989). Specifying the nature of the social impairment in autism. In G. Dawson (Ed.), *Autism: Nature, diagnosis and treatment* (pp. 3–21). New York: Guilford Press.

Mundy, P., Sigman, M., Ungerer, J., and Sherman, T. (1986). Defining the social deficits of autism: The contribution of non-verbal communication measures. *Journal of Child Psychology and Psychiatry, 27*, 657–669.

National Institutes of Health (NIH). (July 1995). *Preliminary report of the autism working group* (pp. 1–30). Bethesda, MD: NIH Inter-Institute Autism Coordinating Committee.

Nicholich, L. M. (1977). Beyond sensorimotor intelligence: Assessment of symbolic maturity through analysis of pretend play. *Merrill-Palmer Quarterly, 23*, 89–99.

Ornitz, E. M. (1985). Neurophysiology of infantile autism. *Journal of the American Academy of Child Psychiatry, 24*, 251–262.

Ornitz, E. M. (1987). Neurophysiologic studies in infantile autism. In D. J. Cohen, A. M. Donnellan, and R. Paul (Eds.), *Handbook of autism and pervasive developmental disorders* (pp. 148–165). New York: John Wiley.

Ornitz, E. M. (1989). Autism at the interface between sensory and information processing. In G. Dawson (Ed.), *Autism: Nature, diagnosis and treatment* (pp. 174–207). New York: Guilford Press.

Owens, R. E. (1988). *Language development: An introduction* (2nd ed.). Columbus, OH: Merrill.

Owens, R. E., Jr. (1991). *Language disorders: A functional approach to assessment and intervention.* Columbus, OH: Macmillan.

Ozonoff, S. (1995). Executive functions in autism. In E. Schopler and G. B. Mesibov (Eds.), *Learning and Cognition in Autism* (pp. 199–215). New York: Plenum.

Palfreman, J. (1994). The Australian origins of facilitated communication. In H. Shane (Ed.), *Facilitated communication: The clinical and social phenomenon* (pp. 33–56). San Diego: Singular.

Patton, M. Q. (1980). *Qualitative evaluation methods.* Beverly Hills: Sage.

Paul, R. (1987). Communication. In D. J. Cohen, A. M. Donnellan, and R. Paul (Eds.), *Handbook of autism and pervasive developmental disorders* (pp. 61–84). New York: John Wiley.

Piaget, J. (1962). *Play, dreams, and imitations.* New York: W. W. Norton.

Piaget, J. (1967). *Play, dreams, and imitation in childhood.* London: Routledge & Kegan Paul.

Prizant, B. M. (1983). Language acquisition and communicative behavior in autism: Toward an understanding of the "whole" of it. *Journal of Speech and Hearing Disorders, 48*, 296–307.

Prizant, B. M., and Duchan, J. F. (1981). The functions of immediate echolalia in autistic children. *Journal of Speech and Hearing Disorders, 46*, 241–249.

Prizant, B., and Rydell, P. (1984). An analysis of the functions of delayed echolalia in autistic children. *Journal of Speech and Hearing Disorders, 27*, 183–192.

Prizant, B. M., and Schuler, A. L. (1987). Facilitating communication: Theoretical foundations. In D. J. Cohen, A. M. Donnellan, and R. Paul (Eds.), *Handbook of autism and pervasive developmental disorders* (pp. 289–300). New York: John Wiley.

Prizant, B. M., and Wetherby, A. M. (1988). Providing services to children with autism (ages 0 to 2 years) and their families. *Topics in Language Disorders, 9*(1), 1–23.

Random House Webster's College Dictionary. (1991). New York: Random House.

Ricks, D. M., and Wing, L. (1975). Language, communication and the use of symbols in normal and autistic children. *Journal of Autism and Childhood Schizophrenia, 5*, 191–221.

Rimland, B. (1964). *Infantile autism.* New York: Appleton-Century-Crofts.

Rimland, B. (1992). Facilitated communication: Now the bad news [Editorial]. *Autism Research Review International, 6*(7), 3.

Rogers, S. (1992). *Studies of executive function in preschoolers and older children with autism* [Cassette Recording, ASA]. Houston: Ears.

Rydell, P. J., and Prizant, B. M. (1995). Assessment and intervention strategies for children who use echolalia. In K. A. Quill (Ed.), *Teaching children with autism: Strategies to enhance communication and socialization* (pp. 105–132). Albany, NY: Delmar.

Sachs, J. (1984). Children's play and communicative development. In R. L. Schiefelbusch and J. Pickar (Eds.), *The acquisition of communicative competence* (pp. 109–140). Baltimore, MD: University Park.

Sacks, O. (1995). *An anthropologist on Mars*. New York: Random House.

Sawyer, D. (January 1992). Facilitated communication. *Prime Time*. New York: American Broadcasting Company.

Schaffer, R. (1977). *Mothering*. Cambridge, MA: Harvard University Press.

Schuler, A. L., and Prizant, B. M. (1987). Facilitating communication: Prelanguage approaches. In D. J. Cohen, A. M. Donnellan, and R. Paul (Eds.), *Handbook of autism and pervasive developmental disorders* (pp. 301–315). New York: John Wiley.

Seibert, J. M., and Hogan, A. E. (1982). A model for assessing social and object skills and planning intervention. In D. P. McClowry, A. M. Guilford, and S. O. Richardson (Eds.), *Infant communication: Development, assessment and intervention* (pp. 21–53). New York: Grune & Stratton.

Shane, H. (1994). Facilitated communication: Factual, fictional, or factitious. In H. Shane (Ed.), *Facilitated communication: The clinical and social phenomenon* (pp. 1–31). San Diego: Singular.

Sheehan, M. R. (1994). *Facilitated communication: The continuing controversy—unconscious facilitator cueing* [Cassette Recording]. Houston: Ears.

Sigman, M. (1989). *Bridges between psychology and medical research* [Cassette Recording]. Silver Spring, MD: Autism Society of America.

Sigman, M., Ungerer, J. A., Mundy, P., and Sherman, T. (1987). Cognition in autistic children. In D. J. Cohen, A. M. Donnellan, and R. Paul (Eds.), *Handbook of autism and pervasive developmental disorders* (pp. 103–120). New York: John Wiley.

Silberberg, N., and Silberberg, M. (1967). Hyperlexia: Specific word recognition skills in young children. *Exceptional Children, 34*, 41–42.

Silliman, E. R. (1992). Three perspectives of facilitated communication: Unexpected literacy, Clever Hans or enigma? *Topics in Language Disorders, 12*(4), 60–68.

Smith, M. D., and Belcher, R. G. (1993). Facilitated communication with adults with autism. *Journal of Autism and Developmental Disorders, 23*(1), 175–183.

Sodian, B., and Frith, U. (1992). Deception and sabotage in autistic, retarded and normal children. *Journal of Child Psychology and Psychiatry, 33*, 591–605.

Sodian, B., and Frith, U. (1993). The theory of mind deficit in autism: Evidence from deception. In S. Baron-Cohen, H. Tager-Flusberg, and D. J. Cohen (Eds.), *Understanding other minds* (pp. 158–177). New York: Oxford University Press.

Sowell, T. (1995). *The vision of the anointed: Self-congratulation as a basis for social policy*. New York: Basic Books.

Stern, D. (1977). *The first relationship: Mother and infant.* Cambridge, MA: Harvard University.

Tanguay, P. E. (November-December 1990). Early infantile autism: What have we learned in the past fifty years? *Brain Dysfunction, 3,* 197–207.

Tsai, L. Y. (1992). Diagnostic issues in high-functioning autism. In E. Schopler and G. B. Mesibov (Eds.), *High-functioning individuals with autism* (pp. 11–40). New York: Plenum.

Twachtman, D. D. (1990). Examples of 3 critical features of communication/language behavior. Unpublished manuscript.

Twachtman, D. D. (1995). Methods to enhance communication in verbal children. In K. A. Quill (Ed.), *Teaching children with autism: Strategies to enhance communication and socialization* (pp. 133–162). Albany, NY: Delmar.

Twachtman, J. L. (1996). Improving the human condition through communication training in autism. In J. R. Cautela and W. Ishaq (Eds.), *Contemporary issues in behavior therapy: Improving the human condition* (pp. 207–231). New York: Plenum.

Twachtman-Cullen, D. (in press). Language and communication in high-functioning autism and Asperger syndrome. In E. Schopler and G. B. Mesibov (Eds.), *Asperger syndrome and high-functioning autism.* New York: Plenum.

Vanderheiden, G. C., and Yoder, D. E. (1986). Overview. In S. W. Blackstone (Ed.), *Augmentative communication: An introduction* (pp. 1–28). Rockville, MD: ASHA.

Vogt, E. Z., and Hyman, R. (1979). *Water witching U.S.A.* (2nd ed.). Chicago: University of Chicago Press.

Watson, L. R. (1987). Pragmatic abilities and disabilities of autistic children. In T. L. Layton (Ed.), *Language and treatment of autistic and developmentally disordered children* (pp. 89–127). Springfield, IL: Charles C. Thomas.

Watzlawick, P., Beavin, J., and Jackson, D. (1967). *Pragmatics of human communication.* New York: W. W. Norton.

Wetherby, A. M. (1986). Ontogeny of communicative functions in autism. *Journal of Autism and Developmental Disorders, 16,* 295–316.

Wetherby, A., and Prizant, B. (1992). Facilitating language and communication development in autism: Assessment and intervention guidelines. In D. Berkell (Ed.), *Autism: Identification, education, and treatment.* Hillsdale, NY: Lawrence Erlbaum.

Wetherby, A., and Prutting, C. (1984). Profiles of communicative and cognitive-social abilities in autistic children. *Journal of Speech and Hearing Research, 27,* 364–377.

Wheeler, D. L., Jacobsen, J. W., Paglieri, R. A., and Schwartz, A. A. (1993). An experimental assessment of facilitated communication. *Mental Retardation, 31,* 49–60.

Whitehouse, D., and Harris, J. C. (1984). Hyperlexia in infantile autism. *Journal of Autism and Developmental Disorders, 14,* 281–289.

Wing, L. (1981). Language, social, and cognitive impairments in autism and severe mental retardation. *Journal of Autism and Developmental Disorders, 11,* 31–34.

Wing, L. (1992). Manifestations of social problems in high-functioning autistic people. In E. Schopler and G. B. Mesibov (Eds.), *High-functioning individuals with autism* (pp. 129–142). New York: Plenum.

About the Author

Diane Twachtman-Cullen is executive director of the Autism and Developmental Disabilities Consultation Center in Cromwell, Connecticut. She is a licensed speech-language pathologist and a communication disorders specialist.

Index

AIT. *See* Auditory integration training
American Academy of Child &
    Adolescent Psychiatry, 168
American Academy of Pediatrics, 168
American Association on Mental
    Retardation, 168
American Psychiatric Association, 169
American Speech-Language-Hearing
    Association, 143, 153–154, 169
Annie's Coming Out (Crossley and
    MacDonald), 2
Anxiety/stress
    during client-facilitator sessions,
        82–86, 90, 103–107, 113–114,
        153
    FC as aggravating, 153
Apraxia, 12, 93–94, 160–161
Arousal modulation, 7
Arwood, E. L., 130
Association for Persons with Severe
    Handicaps (TASH), 169–170
Attention
    joint, 118
    shifts, 7–8
Auditory integration training (AIT), 63
Augmentative communication, 132
Australia, 14
Autism
    and clients in research study, 50, 51,
        53, 55
    facilitated communication and
        redefining, xii, 11–14, 121, 151,
        165
    and facilitated communication
        controversy, 1, 3–4, 157–158
    facilitator knowledge about, 24–27,
        129, 140–141, 151
    history of theory on, 5–11, 164

symptomatology, 11, 62, 87, 88, 96,
    116–118, 119–120
    See also Facilitated communication
Ayres, A. J., 160–161

Baron-Cohen, S., 8
Bates, E., 117
Beavin, J., 130
Behavioral regulation, 118
Belcher, R. G., 15, 132
Bettelheim, B., 6
Biklen, Douglas
    and inclusive education movement,
        162–163
    influence in United States, xii, 3–4,
        145
    on research and redefining autism,
        12–13, 121, 126, 139, 144,
        157–158, 159, 160, 165
    on validation studies for FC, 144
Blondlot, M., 13
BPC. *See* Broad pragmatic category
Bracketing, 22
Broad pragmatic category (BPC), 74, 79

Cairns, R. B., 9
Calculator, S., 15–16
Candland, D. K., 135
Carpenter, William B., 146
Cerebral palsy, 51
    athetoid, 2
Chadwick, Marilyn, xii–xiii
Channeling, 130, 148
Chesterton, 73
Ciaranello, R. D., 164
Clever Hans, 134–135
Clients, research study
    histories/diagnoses, 49–65, 127–128